Wilderness Waterways

SPORTS, GAMES, AND PASTIMES INFORMATION GUIDE SERIES

Series Editor: Ronald M. Ziegler, Humanities Reference Librarian, Washington State University Library, Pullman, Washington

Also in this series:

BICYCLING—*Edited by Mark P. Schultz and Barbara A. Schultz**

CAMPING AND BACKPACKING—*Edited by Cecil Clotfelter and Mary L. Clotfelter**

GAMBLING—*Edited by Jack I. Gardner**

GARDENING AND HOME LANDSCAPING—*Edited by Michel Michelsen**

GOLF—*Edited by Janet Seagle and Joseph S.F. Murdoch**

HORSEMANSHIP—*Edited by Ellen B. Wells**

MOTORSPORTS—*Edited by Susan Ebershoff-Coles and Charla Ann Leibenguth**

PRIVATE AVIATION—*Edited by Floyd Nester Reister**

RACKET AND PADDLE GAMES—*Edited by David Peele**

WINTER SPORTS—*Edited by Diane C. Balodis**

WOMEN IN SPORTS—*Edited by Mary L. Remley**

*in preparation

The above series is part of the
GALE INFORMATION GUIDE LIBRARY

The Library consists of a number of separate series of guides covering major areas in the social sciences, humanities, and current affairs.

General Editor: Paul Wasserman, Professor and former Dean, School of Library and Information Services, University of Maryland

Managing Editor: Denise Allard Adzigian, Gale Research Company

Wilderness Waterways

A GUIDE TO INFORMATION SOURCES

*Volume 1 in the Sports, Games, and Pastimes
Information Guide Series*

Ronald M. Ziegler

*Humanities Reference Librarian
Washington State University Library
Pullman*

Gale Research Company
Book Tower, Detroit, Michigan 48226

Library of Congress Cataloging in Publication Data

Ziegler, Ronald M
    Wilderness waterways.

    (Sports, games, and pastimes information guide
series ; v. 1)
    Includes indexes.
    1. Canoes and canoeing—United States—Bibliography.
2. Canoes and canoeing—Canada—Bibliography. 3. Raft-
ing (Sports)—United States—Bibliography. 4. Rafting
(Sports)—Canada—Bibliography. 5. Wilderness areas—
United States—Bibliography. 6. Wilderness areas—
Canada—Bibliography. I. Title. II. Series.
Z7514.C3Z53   [GV776.A2]   016.7971   78-10410
ISBN 0-8103-1434-7

Copyright © 1979 by
Ronald M. Ziegler

To Elli

VITA

Ronald M. Ziegler is a member of the library faculty at Washington State University where he serves as supervisor of the Humanities Area Library reference unit. He received his A.B. from the University of Miami and his M.S. from Florida State University. Ziegler is subject specialist and collection developer in the general areas of sports and recreation, with a particular interest in outdoor recreation. He is series editor for the Sports, Games, and Pastimes Information Guide Series of the Gale Research Information Guide Library.

CONTENTS

Contents

PREFACE

This book is the first in the Sports, Games, and Pastimes Information Guide Series. The series embraces a diversity of literature on leisure activities. It may be axiomatic that when an individual is attracted to a sport or pastime, he or she longs to learn more about it, making a fertile spawning bed for specialized publications on the subject. Such publication possibilities do not languish unnoticed for long.

As a result, an announcement that there is a proliferation of sports and recreation literature hardly qualifies as news. However, to those not associated with recreation research, subject-area collection building, and the publication of reference works in the field, it may be less obvious that there has not been a concurrent development in sports and recreation bibliography to accurately record this growth. This series of information guides represents an acknowledgment of the need for bibliographic control, and an attempt to impose that control through the identification of books and other information sources within a wide range of sports, games, and pastimes. Volumes in this series will attempt to provide librarians, researchers, practitioners, and others with selective annotated lists of books and other pertinent information.

It has been my intention in this volume to determine the nature and extent of the literature on wilderness waterways, and to see and annotate as much of it as possible. For the most part, I have been successful. This is largely due to the understanding and cooperation of scores of publishers, organizations, and individuals in the world of outdoor recreation in general, and canoeing, kayaking, and rafting in particular.

Much of my research was done with the aid of bibliographical resources and interlibrary-loan facilities at Washington State University Library. Whatever qualities this book may have would be diminished without my having made on-site use of the unique resources at the Library of Congress. Work at the Library of Congress was supported in part by means of a grant provided by the E.O. Holland Scholarship and Research Funds. Finally, my colleagues in the Humanities Library deserve thanks for amiably assuming the burden of added labor while I was absent on sabbatical leave assembling parts of this book.

Ronald M. Ziegler

Part 1

BOOKS

INTRODUCTION

By paddling a canoe, kayak, or raft, one is able to pass through natural areas for extended periods of time without leaving signs of that passing. The sport provides serenity as well as excitement. It may be enjoyed by young and old, the indolent or energetic. It has obvious commercial possibilities as evidenced by the large numbers of equipment manufacturers, retail outlets, guide and outfitter services, liveries, and other entrepreneurs. Little wonder, then, that waterways touring continues to experience steady growth, and that a considerable literature (most of it relatively recent) has arisen to satisfy related information needs.

Chapter 1 lists specialized reference works providing specific information on paddling, and general reference works having appropriate subject relevance. The sports encyclopedias cited in the final section of chapter 1 contain information under the headings, "canoeing," "kayaking," or "rafting." When using the sports dictionaries, one should use specific terminology, for example, "Eskimo roll," "eddy turn," or "draw stroke."

The great majority of canoeing, kayaking, and rafting books published in North America during the last ten years are listed in chapters 2, 4, 8, and 9. Chapter 5 lists selected historical works, included both for their suitability to an information guide on wilderness waterways and for the perspective across several centuries that their reading affords. Provided in chapter 6 is a very selective listing of the many books about waterways environment. The books cited have been chosen for inclusion largely because they furnish an indication of the diversity of information in this field. Books about camping skills and first aid (cited in chapter 3) include those written for the paddler, in particular, as well as a selection of others having universal application to all wilderness travelers.

It is anticipated that the descriptive annotations will provide the reader with an understanding of the contents of a work, thereby furnishing a basis on which to make qualitative judgments where necessary. Books which could not be actually secured, read, and judged have been omitted, with the exception of those cited in the addendum. (The addendum contains, for the most part, recent publications which could not be obtained for review prior to the publication deadline for WILDERNESS WATERWAYS. The addendum information was taken from secondary sources.) Since virtually all nonreference works are illustrated, this information is not included in the citations. In the rare instance of an unillustrated work, mention of this fact is made in the annotation.

Chapter 1

REFERENCE WORKS

BIBLIOGRAPHIES ON CANOEING, KAYAKING, AND RAFTING

Bodin, Arthur Michael. "Bibliography of Canoeing." New York: By the author, 1954. 64 p. Mimeographed.

> The bibliography represents an attempt to list all canoeing books published in the United States since 1900. Periodical articles, motion pictures, and pamphlets are also listed. Many foreign materials are cited--predominantly those of Great Britain, Holland, Germany, France, and Italy. The annotations tend to be brief. Two main sections present general canoe literature and guidebooks to canoe tours.

THE GRUMMAN BOOK RACK FOR CANOEISTS. Marathon, N.Y.: Grumman Boats, n.d. 8 p. Paperbound.

> This list contains about seventy citations for books on canoe technique and camping as well as trip guidebooks. Citations include author, title, publisher's address, and price. Approximately half of the citations have brief descriptive annotations.

Saskatchewan Provincial Library. Bibliographic Services Division. CANOEING: A BIBLIOGRAPHY. Regina, Saskatchewan: 1973. 17 p. Paperbound.

> The information in this list largely duplicates that in the library's 1972 publication, CANOES AND CANOEING: A BIBLIOGRAPHY (see below). However, it does differ in three respects: (1) the books cited are available in Saskatchewan libraries, (2) no periodical articles are cited, and (3) a title index is provided.

_____. CANOES AND CANOEING: A BIBLIOGRAPHY. Regina, Saskatchewan: 1972. 44 p. Paperbound.

> Because of their meager number, there is a tendency to welcome

almost any addition to canoeing bibliography for no reason beyond that of publication. This bibliography, however, falls far
short of what one would expect of a library bibliographic under-
taking. The citations are incomplete: many do not list an author's first name and all are without place of publication. The
annotations are extremely brief. A further annoyance is the
rather advanced age of some of the nonhistorical materials cited.
An unannotated list of about 130 periodical articles completes
the bibliography. It is potentially the most useful portion, as
it gathers together articles indexed (if at all) in several sources.

U.S. Department of the Interior. Bureau of Outdoor Recreation, Mid-continent
Region. A SELECTED BIBLIOGRAPHY OF CANOEING INFORMATION FOR
THE MID-CONTINENT UNITED STATES. Denver: 1976. ii, 22 p. Paper-
bound.

The states comprising the Mid-continent Region are: Colorado,
Iowa, Kansas, Missouri, Montana, Nebraska, North Dakota,
South Dakota, Utah, and Wyoming. There are eight pages containing citations to guidebooks and general information on canoeing, kayaking, and rafting. The remainder of the booklet lists
state agencies and the materials they offer, boating clubs, and
other organizations.

U.S. Department of the Interior. Bureau of Outdoor Recreation. Southeast
Region. A BIBLIOGRAPHY OF CANOEING INFORMATION FOR THE SOUTH-
EASTERN UNITED STATES. Atlanta: 1975. 12 p. Paperbound.

The seven states in the Southeast Region are: Alabama, Florida,
Georgia, Kentucky, Mississippi, North Carolina, and Tennessee.
The bibliography organizes information into federal, state, local,
and private categories. Included are lists of clubs and canoe-
raft races and sponsors.

Wright, Eleanor L. "An Annotated Bibliography of Books and Articles on Canoeing from 1939 through 1951." Master's thesis, University of Maryland,
n.d. 115 p. Mimeographed.

This bibliography may have value to those interested in older
works on canoeing. There are 106 citations on the subject, divided between periodical articles and books. The canoeing section is but a portion of the total bibliography. The remaining
sections list books and articles on swimming, diving, boating,
seamanship, paddleboards, and sailing.

OUTDOOR BIBLIOGRAPHIES WITH WILDERNESS
WATERWAYS RELEVANCE

Horkheimer, Foley A., ed. EDUCATOR'S GUIDE TO FREE HPER MATERIALS.
Randolph, Wis.: Educator's Progress Service, 1968-- . Annual. Paperbound.

Sources for free films, filmstrips, slides, transparencies, tapes, scripts, transcriptions, and printed materials in the areas of health, physical education, and recreation are listed in this multimedia guide. Each guide has more than 500 pages, with some 2,500 individual listings. The paddler may be most attracted to the "Outdoor Activities" category under each media type. Indexing is by title and subject. There are also "availability indexes" for Canada and the United States.

"River Recreation Management and Research Symposium Literature Cited." In PROCEEDINGS: SYMPOSIUM ON RIVER RECREATION MANAGEMENT AND RESEARCH, edited by North Central Forest Experiment Station, pp. 422-36. St. Paul, Minn.: 1977. Paperbound.

In addition to citations of the fifty-five papers and nine workshop summaries associated with the symposium, this bibliography lists references to unpublished manuscripts, theses, and personal communications on river recreation. The unannotated bibliography totals more than 180 citations. An annotated bibliography is in preparation by the station's River Recreation Research Work Unit.

Schipf, Robert G. OUTDOOR RECREATION. Spare Time Guides, no. 9. Littleton, Colo.: Libraries Unlimited, 1976. 278 p. Preface.

More than 700 books about enjoying the outdoors have been included in this annotated bibliography and information guide. The annotations are evaluative. Citations are grouped within the following categories: camping and hiking, foods and cooking, identifying and collecting, vehicle, winter, water, aerial, country living, and animal-related activities. The category on water activities lists seventeen books on canoeing, kayaking, and rafting. In addition to the bibliography, there are listings of outdoor magazines, organizations and associations, and publishers in the field.

U.S. Department of the Interior. Bureau of Outdoor Recreation. A CATALOG OF GUIDES TO OUTDOOR RECREATION AREAS AND FACILITIES. Washington, D.C.: 1973. 79 p.

The sources for published information on canoeing and hiking are listed in this unannotated bibliography under national, regional, and state headings. Cross references are by recreational activity.

PERIODICAL INDEXES WHICH REGULARLY CITE CANOE, KAYAK, AND RAFT ARTICLES

CANADIAN PERIODICAL INDEX. Ottawa, Ontario: Canadian Library Association, 1948-- . Monthly.

This index to both general and specialized magazines is arranged by author and subject. Cumulations are annual. For the first sixteen volumes, the index was called the CANADIAN INDEX TO PERIODICALS AND DOCUMENTARY FILMS. Beginning in 1964, the indexing of documentary films was taken over by the National Library of Canada. Subject headings are in English with French cross-references. Articles about paddle sports are cited under: "Canoe Trips," "Canoes and Canoeing," and "River Trips."

READERS' GUIDE TO PERIODICAL LITERATURE. New York: H.W. Wilson Co., 1900-- . Semimonthly.

Commonly called READERS' GUIDE, this index analyzes periodicals of a popular nature in all important subject fields. Entries are listed under author, subject, and title (when necessary). There are annual and biennial cumulations. Subject headings are descriptive rather than of the catchword type. Articles on paddling are cited under: "Canoe Trips," "Canoes and Canoeing," "Kayak Racing," "Kayaks and Kayaking," "Rafts," and "Running Rivers."

SPORTS INDEX. Austin, Tex.: George T. Harris and Michael Thomas, forthcoming. Quarterly.

This author-subject index to more than 200 sports and recreation periodicals is to begin publication in 1978. Thrice-yearly issues of this index are planned for April, July, and October, with an annual cumulation in January. It will provide access to the following magazines of specific interest to the paddler: AMERICAN WHITEWATER, CANOE, DOWN RIVER, MARIAH, and WILDERNESS CAMPING.

DIRECTORIES AND GUIDES TO CONSERVATION, INSTRUCTION, MANUFACTURERS, AND RECREATION

CONSERVATION DIRECTORY, 1976: A LIST OF ORGANIZATIONS, AGENCIES, AND OFFICIALS CONCERNED WITH NATURAL RESOURCE USE AND MANAGEMENT. 21st ed. Washington, D.C.: National Wildlife Federation, 1976. xi, 235 p. Paperbound.

This directory brings into one reference source an extraordinary amount of conservation information. It contains lists of names, addresses, and telephone numbers of Canadian and U.S. organizations and individuals involved in widely varied conservation activities, and includes listings of university courses taught, fish and game officials, and periodicals and directories.

Hale, Alan N., ed. DIRECTORY: PROGRAMS IN OUTDOOR ADVENTURE ACTIVITIES. Mankato, Minn.: Outdoor Experiences, 1975. iv, 74 p.

An attempt to bring together a complete listing of North American outdoor experiential education programs has been made by the editor of this directory. The majority of the approximately two hundred groups listed are affiliated with colleges and universities. About fifty of the groups offer canoe, kayak, or raft programs. The directory is an outgrowth of the Conference on Outdoor Pursuits in Higher Education held at Appalachian State University, Boone, North Carolina, in February 1974.

Illinois Paddling Council. MIDWEST CANOE LIVERY GUIDE. 3d ed. Evanston, Ill.: 1975. 66 p. Paperbound.

This directory lists more than 175 places within an eight-state region where canoes may be rented. The listings cover Indiana, Iowa, Kentucky, Minnesota, Michigan, Missouri, Ohio, and Wisconsin. Typical information given for each includes: name, address, phone, number of canoes available, cost, pick-up service, life jackets, and deposit required (if any). A state index map shows livery locations.

LEARN-TO-CANOE DIRECTORY. Marathon, N.Y.: Grumman Boats, 1975. 13 p. Paperbound.

More than 250 canoe clubs, safety groups, and commercial teaching establishments are presented in this directory. Some offer basic canoe training; others, whitewater and racing skills. No details are given on the precise type of courses taught.

"1977 Canoe/Kayak Buyer's Guide." CANOE 4 (1976): 29-60.

This canoe selection directory has become a yearly feature of the magazine. The fall issue usually includes the guide, which is also made available as a separate publication. More than 115 builders and 900 models of canoes, kayaks, inflatables, rafts, folding boats, rowing shells, and kits are listed. Information is organized into columns giving: model name, material, basic use, length, width, depth, weight, capacity, keel, and suggested retail price. Some of the models described are photographically illustrated. There is a special section explaining the various modern construction materials and methods.

Perrin, Alwyn T., ed. THE EXPLORERS LTD. SOURCE BOOK. 2d ed. New York: Harper and Row, Publishers, 1977. 413 p. Paperbound.

The Explorers Ltd. is an adventure-oriented group which acts as a clearinghouse and publications center for information on outdoor equipment, techniques, and facilities. Over twenty areas of activity have been defined as "exploring." Information given is divided into organizations dealing with the activity, books and periodicals, instruction and equipment sources, places to go,

and expedition outfitters and guides. Of specific interest to
"explorers" of wilderness waterways may be the chapter on river-
touring sources. Other applicable chapters by expert correspon-
dents list sources for wilderness living, survival, first aid, pathfinding, and photography.

RENT-A-CANOE DIRECTORY. Marathon, N.Y.: Grumman Boats, 1975.
23 p. Paperbound.

> Approximately five hundred canoe liveries in the United States
> are listed within state groupings in this directory. There are
> also minimal Canadian listings. A short bibliography of canoe-
> ing information is appended.

THE SPORTING GOODS DIRECTORY: CLASSIFIED INDEX OF PRODUCTS
MADE BY SPORTING GOODS MANUFACTURERS. 65th ed. St. Louis, Mo.:
Sporting Goods Dealer, 1976. 388 p. Paperbound.

> "Baseball," "Boating," and "Camping" are typical of the general
> subject headings used in this classified directory. Within each
> category, the products for the sport are listed alphabetically.
> There are several indexes, including one by product. The pub-
> lisher maintains a "Buyer's Service Department" which promises
> to supply information on merchandise not listed—as well as the
> source of any branded or trademarked line of sporting goods.

U.S. Department of the Interior. Bureau of Sport Fisheries and Wildlife.
DIRECTORY OF NATIONAL WILDLIFE REFUGES. Washington, D.C.: 1972.
16 p. Paperbound.

> The National Wildlife Refuge System is comprised of about thirty
> million acres (including wetlands) and extends through virtually
> every state. The directory lists the refuges by state and county,
> date established, acreage, and primary species of wildlife. There
> is a map of locations and an index by refuge.

DIRECTORIES OF PROFESSIONAL OUTFITTERS AND GUIDES

Automobile Club of Southern California. "Riverboat Trips." Travel Services
Bulletin, no. 12. Rev. ed. Los Angeles: 1976. 27 p. Mimeographed.

> This is a loose-leaf directory of western river outfitters. An in-
> formative introduction gives general descriptions of river-running
> and the most popular rivers. There is relatively complete data
> on all the listed trips, including place, price, type of craft,
> dates, and reservation requirements. The directory is intended
> for the use of ACSC members only.

Dickerman, Pat. ADVENTURE TRAVEL U.S.A. 3d ed. New York: Adventure Guides, 1976. 224 p. Paperbound.

> Trips of every variety are cataloged in this guide to information sources for moving about on foot, horseback, wheels, water, snow, and in the air. Paddling enthusiasts will perhaps be most interested in the forty-two pages of the chapter "On or in Water." This chapter presents outfitters, liveries, and guides for canoe, kayak, and float trips. The information provided in all listings is fairly standard and includes: name, address, phone, area of operation, group size, duration of trip, cost, and a few sentences describing the service. A listing of river runs by state and outfitter may assist the reader in accessing the scope of trip opportunities. Most of these listings are for western rivers. Camping, fishing, hunting, and downhill skiing services are omitted. Previous editions of this book were titled ADVENTURE TRIP GUIDE.

FIELD AND STREAM. New York: C.B.S. Publications, 1895-- . Monthly.

> The "Where to Go" section is a monthly grouping of advertisements by various guide and outfitting services.

Idaho Outfitters and Guides Association. CATALOG. Boise, Idaho: 1976. 64 p. Paperbound.

> Approximately 150 guides and outfitters either advertise in or are otherwise cited in this directory. However, those licensed for one or more Idaho rivers are indicated by a special symbol. The majority of the listings are for hunting and fishing guides. Many of the "wilderness" provinces and states have directories similar to this one. Their existence may usually be verified and addresses obtained through the appropriate governmental agency.

1978 INTERNATIONAL ADVENTURE TRAVELGUIDE. Forest Grove, Oreg.: Timber Press, 1977. 500 p. Paperbound.

> More than 2,000 adventure trips worldwide are listed in this directory. Every trip listed is open to public participation. Entries are divided into four major sections: (1) Land Adventures, (2) Sea Adventures, (3) Air Adventures, and (4) Underwater Adventures. Subjects in the Sea Adventures section may be of the most interest to the paddler: wilderness canoeing, kayaking, sailing, river rafting, windjamming, houseboating, and river touring. The directory is indexed by category and country.

Oregon Guides and Packers. HUNTING AND FISHING IN OREGON. Sublimity, Oreg.: 1977. 37 p. Paperbound.

> The title may be somewhat misleading, as there are many float-

trip rivermen included in this directory. The listings are alphabetical by town within three coastal and three inland regions,
which are designated on an index map. This directory typifies
those listing outfitters and guides in most "wilderness" provinces
and states. The existence of such directories may usually be
verified and addresses obtained through the appropriate governmental agency.

OUTDOOR LIFE. New York: Times-Mirror Magazines, 1898-- . Monthly.

The monthly "Where to Go" section is an advertising directory
of camps, lodges, guides, outfitters, resorts, fly-in services, and
more. The volume of advertisements swells in late winter and
early spring.

SIERRA CLUB BULLETIN. San Francisco: Sierra Club, 1915-- . Monthly.

An annual "Outing Issue" which cites Sierra Club trips is published in January. A "Water Trips" section includes information
such as location, dates, length, and leader. The type of craft
varies widely from kayak to leisure boat. The 1977 issue listed
forty-six water trips.

SPORTS AFIELD WITH ROD AND GUN. New York: Hearst, 1888-- . Monthly.

There is a monthly classified advertising section which identifies
guides, packers, outfitters, and other services.

Western River Guides Association. PROFESSIONAL OUTFITTERS. Salt Lake
City: 1977. 11 p. Paperbound.

This directory lists seventy-two outfitters which operate trips on
western rivers. The list is alphabetical; addresses and telephone
numbers are given. A descriptive paragraph on the rivers which
are run and the type of trip which may be anticipated completes
the information.

GENERAL SPORTS ENCYCLOPEDIAS AND DICTIONARIES

Anderson, Bob, ed. SPORTSOURCE. Mountain View, Calif.: World Publications, 1975. 430 p.

Arlott, John, ed. THE OXFORD COMPANION TO WORLD SPORTS AND
GAMES. London: Oxford University Press, 1975. viii, 1,143 p. Preface.

Burton, Bill, ed. THE SPORTSMAN'S ENCYCLOPEDIA. New York: Grosset
and Dunlap, 1971. 638 p.

Diagram Group. RULES OF THE GAME. New York and London: Paddington Press, 1974. 320 p.

McWhirter, Norris D., and McWhirter, A. Ross, eds. 1974-1975 GUINNESS SPORTS RECORD BOOK. Rev. ed. New York: Sterling Publishing Co., 1974. 191 p.

Menke, Frank G., and Treat, Suzanne, eds. THE ENCYCLOPEDIA OF SPORTS. 5th rev. ed. South Brunswick, N.J. and New York: A.S. Barnes and Co., 1975. 1,125 p.

Sparano, Vin T. COMPLETE OUTDOORS ENCYCLOPEDIA. An Outdoor Life Book. New York: Outdoor Life, Harper and Row, 1972. xi, 622 p. Preface.

WEBSTER'S SPORTS DICTIONARY. Springfield, Mass.: G. and C. Merriam Co., 1976. viii, 503 p. Preface.

Chapter 2

TECHNIQUE AND INSTRUCTION

American National Red Cross. BASIC CANOEING. Washington, D.C.: 1963. 67 p. Paperbound.

This booklet is a condensation of the American National Red Cross textbook CANOEING (see below) and is primarily for use by students in basic canoeing courses. The contents include chapters on canoe history, selection, technique, safety, and repair. More than one hundred illustrations provide visual representations of the various techniques explained in the text.

_____. CANOEING. Garden City, N.Y.: Doubleday and Co., 1956. ix, 445 p. Preface. Paperbound.

Since the 1940s, the Red Cross has included canoeing instruction in its water-safety programs and small-craft schools. This canoeing textbook was prepared to support these programs at both introductory and instructor levels. It is a cautious and exhaustive book on the recreational aspects of the sport. Some of the material is dated, such as that on canoe camping. There are chapters on conducting racing and novelty events. As of 1974, the book was in its sixth printing. A revised edition was published in 1977, and is cited below. There is also an inexpensive condensed version, entitled BASIC CANOEING (see above).

_____. CANOEING. 2d ed. Garden City, N.Y.: Doubleday and Co., 1977. 452 p. Paperbound.

All information required for the Red Cross canoeing programs, basic through instructor level, is contained in this revision of the ANRC standard work (see above). There are hundreds of two-color sketches illustrating specific activities--a change from the 1956 edition's almost exclusive use of photographs. The book attempts to cover all areas of paddle sports including kayaks and rafts. Mention of the latter two crafts, however, is of a very limited nature: kayaking occupies a chapter and rafting, a paragraph (with the explanation that most of the safety information in the text has raft application). The instructions on canoe poling strokes, carrying, rescue, repair, camping, competition, and sailing are very detailed. Safety is stressed throughout.

Angier, Bradford, and Taylor, Zack. INTRODUCTION TO CANOEING. Harrisburg, Pa.: Stackpole Books, 1973. 191 p. Paperbound.

Angier and Taylor take the position that the canoe is foremost a wilderness vehicle. As the title implies, the book is weighted toward technique. However, the authors carry you much farther--into the woods, in fact--with chapters on cruising, camping, river-running, portaging, and a selection of favorite canoe trips.

Beletz, Al, et al. CANOE POLING. St. Louis, Mo.: A.C. Mackenzie Press, 1974. 147 p. Paperbound.

The authors, noted for their proficiency in the specialized art of poling canoes, are poling chairmen for the American Canoe Association. Poling can be competitive or the technique can be used to provide access to remote areas surrounding the upper reaches of rivers and small streams. Basic and advanced strokes, pole shoes and spikes, double poling, competition, acquiring standing position stability, and small-stream travel are six of the topics covered in the twenty-two chapters. The book is illustrated with more than 180 photographs and drawings.

Blandford, Percy William. TACKLE CANOEING THIS WAY. New ed. London: S. Paul and Co., 1969. U.S. distributor is New Rochelle, N.Y.: Sportshelf. 128 p.

Blandford is one of England's best-known canoeists. He is also a professional small-boat designer. Readers should always remember that in Great Britain canoes are what we in North America understand to be kayaks. Only the most basic techniques are discussed; there is no mention of the Eskimo roll, for example. The photographs are less than effective as teaching aids; however, the other illustrations and narrative provide adequate explanation of method.

Boy Scouts of America. CANOEING. Merit Badge Library, no. 3308. North Brunswick, N.J.: 1968. 56 p. Paperbound.

The fundamentals of canoe-paddling technique are presented in this inexpensive manual. Preparing for a canoe trip, lifesaving with a canoe, canoe repair, racing and sailing, and lining and poling are short, additional chapters supplementing the section on the basics.

Byars, Julie, and Byars, Rick. "The American Whitewater School Whitewater Rafting Manual." 2d ed. Oakland, Calif.: American River Touring Association, 1976. 12 p. Preface. Mimeographed.

> This manual is used in conjunction with a rafting course offered by the American Whitewater School and sponsored by the American River Touring Association. The descriptions of paddling, rowing, and recovery technique are brief. Emphasis is on actual on-the-river skills of seeing and reacting. The illustrations, taken from William McGinnis's WHITEWATER RAFTING, are visually descriptive.

Byde, Alan. BEGINNER'S GUIDE TO CANOEING. London: Pelham Books, 1974. U.S. distributor is Levittown, N.Y.: Transatlantic Arts. 184 p.

> Coach instructing pupil on a one-to-one basis is the method of teaching skills employed in this introductory work on canoeing (kayaking). The description of paddling procedure is presented in outline form. In addition to the instruction chapters are several, very basic chapters on canoe history, equipment, construction, and rescue methods.

_____. LIVING CANOEING. 2d ed. London: Adam and Charles Black, 1973. U.S. distributor is Levittown, N.Y.: Transatlantic Arts. 266 p.

> Byde, a professional instructor, takes the beginning canoeist in precise step-by-step progression through the techniques of canoeing (kayaking) while encountering an infinite variety of water conditions. He describes swimming pool-instruction technique as well as that of slalom and heavy surf paddling. Caution and safety are stressed. Paddling instruction dominates, but there are chapters on selecting, building, and transporting canoes. Other chapters contain seldom-seen information on an instructor's responsibilities to his pupils and on organizing training groups and clubs. The book is illustrated with twenty-five racing action photographs and one hundred diagrams.

Davis, Dennis J. THE BOOK OF CANOEING. London: Arthur Barker, 1969. 111 p.

> Numerous large photographs are the outstanding feature of this introductory book on canoeing (kayaking) techniques. Considerable attention is given to canoe and accessory construction methods. Further chapters address more advanced skills, maintenance and repairs, knot tying, and safety.

Dwyer, Ann. HAVE A HAPPY DAY CANOEING. Kentfield, Calif.: G.B.H. Press, 1975. 32 p. Paperbound.

> This booklet provides information for the beginning canoeist on technique, safety, and general river-running knowledge. William

Ribar's cartoons may prove to be effective teaching tools for the younger canoeist using this book.

Elvedt, Ruth. CANOEING A-Z. Minneapolis, Minn.: Burgess Publishing Co., 1964. vii, 71 p. Preface. Paperbound.

This book is primarily intended for instructors who teach canoeing to groups. The author is an authority on the methodology of teaching the sport. Sections for teachers include stroke analysis, pointers on instruction, and course analysis. The book may also be effective in presenting information directly to beginning canoeists. Description of safety skills, launching, docking, strokes, and equipment is presented in a compact format and is further aided by illustrations. Safety is emphasized; the chapter dealing with safety has been placed first. In another section, the author presents the principles and laws of physics which govern a canoe.

Evans, Robert Jay. FUNDAMENTALS OF KAYAKING. Hanover, N.H.: Ledyard Canoe Club of Dartmouth College, 1974. 69 p. Paperbound.

This manual, written by a former U.S. Olympic Whitewater coach, begins with a discussion of the advantages of building versus buying a kayak. This section is followed by an explanation of basic kayaking techniques. Evans has expanded the material in this book and has incorporated it into a more recent work entitled KAYAKING: THE NEW WHITEWATER SPORT FOR EVERYBODY (see below).

_____. WHITEWATER COACHING MANUAL. Hanover, N.H.: Ledyard Canoe Club of Dartmouth College, 1973. 56 p. Paperbound.

The serious slalom whitewater competitor and coach are the intended audience for this book. There are sections on physical and mental preparation, pool training, equipment, technique, and conducting a training camp.

Evans, Robert Jay, and Anderson, Robert R. KAYAKING: THE NEW WHITE-WATER SPORT FOR EVERYBODY. An Environmental Sports Book. Brattleboro, Vt.: Stephen Greene Press, 1975. 192 p. Paperbound.

This is an often-cited manual about kayaking and closed-deck canoeing. It replaces Evans's earlier book entitled FUNDA-MENTALS OF KAYAKING (see above). The beginning and intermediate paddler comprise the intended audience for the book; however, the information and illustrative material is of a quality which can make profitable reading for kayakists of any proficiency. The step-by-step instructions for the Eskimo roll are exhaustive. The book has more than one hundred photographs and drawings to illustrate chapters on types of craft, equipment, touring, whitewater and racing technique, reading the river, training, race organization, and finding a suitable river.

Farmer, Charles J. THE DIGEST BOOK OF CANOES, KAYAKS, AND RAFTS. Digest Books. Chicago: Follett Publishing Co., 1977. 192 p. Paperbound.

Farmer's book makes the attempt to be all things to all paddlers. Advice on the use of canoes, kayaks, and inflatable boats is offered to the beginner and intermediate. This information includes a description of the craft, how to choose and equip it, and tips on camping, paddling, and safety. A general introductory section offers brief coverage of a host of paddling concerns: maps and guidebooks, legal rights, river ratings, hunting and fishing, food, first aid, and proper clothing. There are scores of black and white photographs and drawings illustrating techniques, water conditions, and equipment. A special feature section entitled "Ask the Experts" gives answers to a set of questions posed to eleven well-known practitioners of the paddling sports.

Ferguson, Stuart. CANOEING FOR BEGINNERS. Reed Beginners Series. Sydney, Australia.: A.H. and A.W. Reed, 1976. U.S. distributor is Rutland, Vt.: Charles E. Tuttle Co. 111 p. Paperbound.

This book on introductory canoe technique (Canadian-style canoe and kayak) relies heavily on demonstration photographs as an instructional device. The illustrations are clear and none is smaller than a quarter-page in size. Nine chapters describe canoe history, selection, style, technique, paddles, safety, rolls, camping, and first aid. The appendix includes a list of Australian Canoe Federation and New Zealand Canoe Association state affiliate addresses.

Fillingham, Paul. THE COMPLETE BOOK OF CANOEING AND KAYAKING. New York: Drake Publishers, 1974. viii, 175 p.

This book has been organized for self-instruction by the beginner. There are many illustrations depicting technique; some of these, however, are located in an appendix rather than with the text. Chapters are presented on history, slalom and straight racing, cruising and camping, maintenance, and construction. There is a comprehensive glossary of canoeing terms marred somewhat by a page containing incorrect alphabetization.

Franks, C.E.S. THE CANOE AND WHITE WATER: FROM ESSENTIAL TO SPORT. Toronto: University of Toronto Press, 1977. iv, 237 p.

This introductory work on paddling whitewater approaches its subject from the diverse contexts of Canada's rich canoeing tradition as well as a practical understanding of fluid dynamics. This duality of the historical and technical is interwoven throughout the work. The illustrations include a combination of modern photographs, drawings, and historical paintings and photographs. The seven chapters comprising the book instruct the reader in the canoe and its history, strokes, whitewater tactics, river judgment, trip planning, Canadian rivers, and legal rights and ecological problems of rivers. An appendix contains a bibliography and chapter notes.

Hartline, Bev, and Hartline, Fred. A SKETCHY INTRODUCTION TO WHITE-WATER AND KAYAKING. 2d ed. Seattle, Wash.: Bev and Fred Hartline, 1975. 24 p. Paperbound.

One should not be misled by the title of this booklet. "Sketchy" refers to the many drawings used to illustrate whitewater technique, not to the material, which is thorough. The drawings evolved from those done for a slide presentation at the University of Washington Canoe Club. Although there is an emphasis on kayaking skills, the safety rules and the section on handling whitewater also apply to other methods of running a river.

Huser, Verne. RIVER RUNNING. Chicago: Henry Regnery Co., 1975. x, 294 p. Preface.

While hard-hull paddlers should find some useful information in this book, it is primarily intended for those who run whitewater in an inflatable raft. This book and William McGinnis's WHITE-WATER RAFTING (see below) are the two best general information sources for the rafter (for whom there continues to be a very small body of specific literature). Huser presents river-running as the attractive wilderness adventure it should be. He stresses caution and respect for the power of whitewater. His many years of experience as a professional guide on western rivers show in the practicality of his advice on preparations, regulations, equipment, reading a river, and safety and camp routine. There is a selective listing of runnable rivers in the United States and Canada.

Hutchinson, Derek C. SEA CANOEING. London: Adam and Charles Black, 1976. U.S. distributor is Levittown, N.Y.: Transatlantic Arts. 204 p.

This may be the only book published that is entirely devoted to ocean canoeing (kayaking). It deals with K-1s (single seat kayak) only. Ocean kayaking is unique in that one's skill and endurance are tested against heavy wave hydraulics as well as the frequent added element of wind. The book begins with a discussion of equipment and fundamental kayak technique. Hutchinson then explains the various rolls and advanced surfing technique. There are in-depth analyses of wind, weather, waves, sea rescue, tides, and navigation. Much of this information is seldom found in sufficient detail in the usual books describing kayak technique.

Jagger, Basil. CANOEING. An Arco Mayflower Handybook. London: Mayflower Books, 1969. 143 p.

> CANOEING (kayaking) is an introductory-level book. There is a natural progression of chapters, beginning with the selection of a kayak and continuing through to slalom racing. The inclusion of a chapter on home construction may seem outside the scope of a work aimed at beginners, but one should remember that the British consider the building of a craft as a fundamental part of the sport. There are fewer illustrations than the norm for a beginner's book. North American readers must also contend with British usages, such as "dead spot" for "eddy."

Leachman, Mark. THE RIVER RAFTER'S MANUAL. Denver: Colorado Outward Bound School, 1972. 34 p. Paperbound.

> The Colorado Outward Bound School uses this booklet as a teaching tool for its instructors. The arrangement is by outline. Instructors are presented sequenced information on food organizing, raft inflation, boat maintenance, role of the river staff, equipment, and emergency procedure. A brief history and geological interpretation of the Green River is included.

McGinnis, William W. WHITEWATER RAFTING. Toronto: Fitzhenry and Whiteside; New York: Quadrangle/The New York Times Book Co., 1975. 379 p. Preface.

> The enjoyment McGinnis has for his work as a professional boatman is reflected in the way he writes about whitewater rivers and how to guide a raft down them with finesse and safety. Part 1, with seventy-six drawings, is the "how to" section with chapters on equipment, technique, emergencies, first aid, meals, and camping. Part 2 tells "where to," in a guide to thirty-four runs in all regions of the United States. The author manages to convey much of the life-to-the-fullest feeling combining anticipation and satisfaction that is at the heart of running big rivers. Appendixes list rafting-equipment supply houses, raft-trip photography, conservation organizations, rafting outfitters, and more.

McNair, Robert E. BASIC RIVER CANOEING. 3d ed. Martinsville, Ind.: American Camping Association, 1972. 103 p. Paperbound.

> This is one of the relatively few books which specialize in describing whitewater canoe technique. The author is exceptionally well qualified by being a slalom competition canoeist of long experience and an engineer with a knowledge of hydraulics. He recommends learning skills through continual on-the-river

group practice. Chapters are presented on equipment, strokes, river reading, maneuvering tactics, safety, rescue, and overall strategy. Descriptions and diagrams presenting concepts are included. Chapter 9 is a preliminary guide for instructors, with an outline covering preschool assigned readings, ten hours of class instruction on the river, and five hours of lecture and discussion.

Malo, John W. CANOEING. An All-Star Sports Book. Introduction by Gert R. Grigoleit. Chicago: Follett Publishing Co., 1969. 127 p.

Malo's book is strictly for the beginning canoeist. His explanations of paddling technique are precise, and the photographs with superimposed blade positions are visually effective. Chapters on safety, canoe description, camping, and canoe history are included. The introduction is by the coach of the U.S. Olympic Canoeing Team.

Michaelson, Mike, and Ray, Keith. CANOEING. An Outdoor Encounter Resource Book. Chicago: Henry Regnery Co., 1975. iv, 154 p. Paperbound.

CANOEING is an introductory book on the sport. It is intended as a teaching tool on technique and safety in an open canoe, although some material applies to kayaks. The authors are past editors of CANOE: MAGAZINE OF THE AMERICAN CANOE ASSOCIATION (see chapter 11). Considerable space is devoted to the presentation of practical advice on the best equipment for different kinds of canoeing. "Canoeing with the Kids" and "Getting in Shape for Canoeing" are two chapters presenting information not often seen elsewhere. Ten regional trips are suggested.

Monk, Carl, and Knap, Jerome. A COMPLETE GUIDE TO CANOEING: A MANUAL ON TECHNIQUE AND EQUIPMENT AND THE BEST CANOEING ROUTES IN NORTH AMERICA. Toronto: Pagurian Press, 1976. 192 p.

A brief history of the canoe begins this introductory book on all phases of the sport. The experience of the authors in the areas of conservation, biology, and photography are evident in the treatment of the chapters on technique, safety, and canoe hunting and fishing. The section on route information for trips in Canada and the United States lacks sufficient detail. More specific references to a wide selection of North American canoe trips may be found in such works as Rainer Esslen's BACK TO NATURE IN CANOES and CANOE CANADA by Nick Nickels (see chapter 8).

Norman, Dean, ed. ALL-PURPOSE GUIDE TO PADDLING. Matteson, Ill.: Great Lakes Living Press, 1976. vi, 218 p. Paperbound.

Fourteen paddlers, each an expert in his or her particular skill, have contributed to this book which attempts to address all aspects of paddle sport. Canoe, kayak, and raft technique; sailing; surfing; poling; whitewater; racing; construction; and the origin and history of paddle-powered boats comprise separate chapters. The breadth of subject matter does not afford massive detail, but there is a formidable gathering of information here, however brief.

Perry, Ronald H. CANOEING FOR BEGINNERS. Rev. ed. New York: Association Press; Toronto: G.R. Welch Co., 1967. 126 p. Preface. Paperbound.

This manual is intended for the beginning paddler and the instructor. Chapters designed for instructors in particular present suggestions for teaching strokes, summaries of instruction material, canoeing standards at camps, and canoeing tests. The material is given in large type, with cartoon-like characters demonstrating the various strokes and safety precautions. The book is a revised edition of THE CANOE AND YOU (Toronto: Dent, 1952).

Pursell, John M. KAYAK PADDLING STROKES: TECHNIQUES AND EQUIPMENT. Utilitarian Series, no. 33. 1962. Reprint. Seattle, Wash.: Shorey Publications, 1974. ii, 25 p. Paperbound.

The ostensible purpose of this booklet is to illustrate twenty basic kayak strokes. This is done through a series of drawings and symbols presented in the reverse sequence. It is contended that this method allows the reader to "ride behind" the "instructor" without the usual mental reversal process needed to follow text, symbols, and figures.

Riviere, Bill. POLE, PADDLE, AND PORTAGE: A COMPLETE GUIDE TO CANOEING. Boston: Little, Brown and Co., 1969. ix, 259 p. Paperbound.

Riviere is a professional "northwoods" guide with decades of canoe experience to lend authority to his views. Seventeen chapters describe all the fundamentals of canoe technique and associated information. One of these chapters, "Canoe Country," is a state-by-state, province-by-province listing of places a canoeist may enjoy touring--most of them paddled by the author. Photographs and drawings illustrate the work. The book is a source of timeless, basic information; however, the appendix listing of recreational canoe companies and other information sources is too dated for reliability.

Ruck, Wolfgang E. CANOEING AND KAYAKING. Toronto: McGraw-Hill Ryerson; New York: McGraw-Hill Book Co., 1974. 95 p.

Basic and advanced canoe and kayak handling is described in precise terms in this book about racing and touring technique. Narrative is minimal and is carefully coordinated with sequential photographs and diagrams on the same or facing pages.

Rutstrum, Calvin. NORTH AMERICAN CANOE COUNTRY. New York: Macmillan Co., 1964. vi, 216 p.

Virtually all books for the beginner and intermediate teach the "J" stroke as the correct compensatory canoe stroke to offset veer. Rutstrum makes a strong plea for another steering stroke of his own invention, the "pitch." Diagrams are included in the chapter on technique. Other chapters deal with the history of the canoe, trips taken by the author and others, and outfitting and equipment. Planning, direction-finding, and survival are other outdoor skills discussed. Rutstrum writes as one who prefers to travel alone; the reader planning a solo trip may be able to profit from this bias. Illustrations are by nature artist Les Kouba.

Sanders, Geoffrey, ed. COACHING HANDBOOK. 3d ed. London: British Canoe Union, 1969. iv, 190 p. Paperbound.

The contributors to this handbook are British paddling authorities, each presenting a chapter on his or her specialty. The book is for kayaking coaches and is arranged in a numbered sequence for preparing and teaching classes. Supplementing the chapters on technique is information on organizing races and tours, safety and rescue, and British Canoe Union proficiency tests and awards.

Sandreuter, William O. WHITEWATER CANOEING. New York: Winchester Press, 1976. 221 p. Preface.

From the fundamental "J" stroke to competition with experts, this book addresses all phases of downriver canoeing. Technique and water conditions are demonstrated through the use of well-staged photographs. Material on map and compass reading, repairs, camping, and a section on canoeing camps, schools, and competitions are included. A noteworthy chapter on clothing is given, including a description of felt-soled shoe construction.

Skilling, Brian Craig, ed. CANOEING COMPLETE. 2d ed. London: Kaye and Ward, 1973. U.S. distributor is New Rochelle, N.Y.: Soccer Associates. 236 p.

Each chapter ("Basic Technique," "Coastal Touring," "Racing," "Design," and more) is written by a recognized British authority. The editor maintains that modern canoeing (kayaking) can no longer be adequately explained by a single author. Chapter 11 lists hard-to-find descriptions of canoe games and ideas on organizing novelty canoe events.

Strung, Norman; Curtis, Sam; and Perry, Earl. WHITEWATER! New York: Macmillan Co.; London: Collier Macmillan Publishers, 1976. viii, 184 p. Preface.

> As the title suggests, the focus of this book is on fast-water paddling. Rafting, canoeing, and kayaking in whitewater are discussed in both philosophical and practical terms by Strung, Curtis, and Perry respectively. Each man is an expert in the use of his chosen craft. The work is profusely illustrated by drawings and photographs. In addition to technique, each of the three major sections contains supplementary information on portaging, construction and repair, clothing, and more. A feature of the book is the coverage of river hydromechanics, illustrated by diagrams. A potentially complicated subject is presented in accurate, nontechnical terms.

Sutherland, Charles. MODERN CANOEING. London: Faber and Faber, 1964. U.S. distributor is Levittown, N.Y.: Transatlantic Arts. 272 p. Preface.

> The methodology of canoeing and an overview of the sport in Great Britain are the subjects of this book. Chapter 1 presents a short history of canoes and canoeing, emphasizing European developments. A further chapter discusses the handling of Canadian canoes and kayaks. Other chapters cover touring, camping, and various aspects of flat and whitewater racing. The syllabus of the British Canoe Union canoe and kayak proficiency test is included in the appendix.

Urban, John T. A WHITEWATER HANDBOOK FOR CANOE AND KAYAK. Boston: Appalachian Mountain Club, 1965. vii, 77 p. Preface. Paperbound.

> Now in its eighth printing after having sold 80,000 copies, this handbook has become the standard against which subsequent canoe and kayak fast-water books are measured. The contents are compact yet comprehensive, and include basic technique, running and crossing current, eddy identification, eddy entrance and exit, safety, slalom skills, and equipment. Sequential photographs are used as instructional aids.

Vaughan, Linda Kent, and Stratton, Richard Hale. CANOEING AND SAILING. Physical Education Activities Series. Dubuque, Iowa: William C. Brown Co., 1970. vii, 72 p. Preface. Paperbound.

> Theory and technique are presented for the beginning canoeist in the first half of this book. Each stroke is illustrated and described in precise terms. In the second section, Stratton describes small-boat sailing technique.

Whitney, Peter Dwight. WHITE WATER SPORT: RUNNING RAPIDS IN
KAYAK AND CANOE. New York: Ronald Press, 1960. vii, 120 p. Preface.

> This must be thought of as an early work in the genre of white-
> water paddling books; many changes in technique and equipment
> have taken place since 1960. However, the book does give
> perspective to the comparatively short history of the sport. De-
> scriptions are clear and the drawings and photographs are sup-
> portive. The material is intended for the intermediate and
> skilled paddler. Whitney is a professional writer who learned
> kayak skills in France. He was founding chairman of the Appa-
> lachian Mountain Club and the American Whitewater Affiliation.

Williams, Peter Fairney. CANOEING SKILLS AND CANOE EXPEDITION
TECHNIQUE FOR TEACHERS AND LEADERS. London: Pelham Books, 1967.
155 p.

> Williams's canoeing (kayaking) manual has a textbook quality.
> This is exemplified by the precise progression of the material
> from the simple to the difficult. A feature is the listing of cor-
> rect technique and possible student faults in parallel columns.
> Camping, organizing expeditions, and teaching methodology
> comprise further chapters.

Chapter 3

CAMPING SKILLS AND FIRST AID

American National Red Cross. ADVANCED FIRST AID AND EMERGENCY CARE. Garden City, N.Y.: Doubleday and Co., 1973. 318 p. Preface.

> This is the basic work used by the Red Cross as a textbook in the instruction of advanced first aid classes. The content was developed by the Division of Medical Sciences, National Academy of Sciences-National Research Council, and physicianmembers of the Ad Hoc Committee for Revision of the Red Cross First Aid Manual. The descriptions of first aid techniques are concise and uncomplicated. There are 353 color drawings illustrating various ailments and injuries and their treatment by first aid methods.

_____. LIFESAVING, RESCUE, AND WATER SAFETY. Garden City, N.Y.: Doubleday and Co., 1974. 240 p. Preface. Paperbound.

> Designed by the Red Cross for the purpose of teaching and disseminating the skills of lifesaving and water safety, this authoritative work has become the standard resource in its field. Illustrations are in color. Recovery of the victim, artificial respiration, and basic first aid are explained in detail.

_____. STANDARD FIRST AID AND PERSONAL SAFETY. Garden City, N.Y.: Doubleday and Co., 1973. 268 p. Paperbound.

> The fundamentals of first aid are described in this authoritative standard text. The procedures explained are for application in fairly civilized surroundings. For wilderness applications, one could supplement this work with a manual such as Dick Mitchell's MOUNTAINEERING FIRST AID (see below). The drawings are in color--a distinct advantage in any book on first aid.

Anderson, Luther A. A GUIDE TO CANOE CAMPING. Chicago: Reilly and Lee Co., 1969. ix, 150 p.

Anderson presents all the essential basics in this book on back-country canoeing. The drawings illustrating wilderness techniques are explicit and simple to follow. This book has somewhat better coverage of the subject than WILDERNESS CANOEING by John Malo (see below), but lacks the folksy readability of Bill Riviere's POLE, PADDLE, AND PORTAGE (see chapter 2).

Angier, Bradford. HOW TO STAY ALIVE IN THE WOODS. New York: Macmillan Co., Collier Books, 1962. 285 p. Paperbound.

Angier estimates that thousands of people get lost in the woods of North America each year. He attempts to show that the wilderness will furnish the necessities of food, warmth, shelter, and clothing. These needs are addressed in the first two parts of the book. Part 3 explains orientation methods, part 4 safety and first aid measures. The first aid information was contributed by a physician. Anecdotes from the author's Canadian wilderness trips are used to further illustrate the hundreds of briefly stated survival pointers. The book has remained in print for more than twenty years; the Collier Books edition is in its twentieth printing.

_____. WILDERNESS GEAR YOU CAN MAKE YOURSELF. Harrisburg, Pa.: Stackpole Books, 1973. x, 115 p.

This book shows the outdoorsperson how to save money, and perhaps his or her life, by constructing, both at home and on-site, a profusion of camping and survival equipment. Angier, veteran woodsman and author of more than twenty outdoors books, explains the making of clothing, shelter, cooking gear, tools, and transportation devices. Descriptions are brief; however, this is in keeping with the general concept of the book, which is idea- more than project-oriented.

Bacon, Thorn. WEATHER FOR SPORTSMEN: A NEW KIND OF BOOK FOR SAILORS AND ALL OUTDOORSMEN. New York: Motor Boating and Sailing Books, 1974. ix, 115 p. Preface.

This book contains nontechnical reading for the outdoorsperson on predicting the weather. Bacon's book distills into readily comprehensible terms otherwise complicated meteorological material on clouds, forecasting, storms, and nature's signs. The information could be useful for those paddlers planning trips which include mileage on large or squall-prone lakes. Color photographs of thirty cloud formations are provided, although the choice of placing them on the dust jacket makes them subject to possible loss.

Bearse, Ray. THE CANOE CAMPER'S HANDBOOK. New York: Winchester Press, 1974. 380 p. Preface.

The author of this book begins with the assumption that the reader knows little about canoe camping and voyaging. The contents are organized into five parts: "The Canoe," "The Camp," "Canoe Techniques," "Voyaging Techniques," and "Where to go Voyaging." Canoeists who find themselves portaging often may find the data on equipment weight useful. The relatively small size of the book makes it useful as a carry-along reference.

Berglund, Berndt, and Bolsby, Clare E. WILDERNESS COOKING: A UNIQUE ILLUSTRATED COOKBOOK AND GUIDE FOR OUTDOOR ENTHUSIASTS. New York: Charles Scribner's Sons, 1973. 192 p.

The reader who may wish to travel with a minimum of preliminary packing is shown how to cook what the wilderness provides. Centuries-old recipes used by Indians, trappers, and pioneers are presented, as well as butchering and curing techniques.

Biggs, Don. SURVIVAL AFLOAT. New York: David McKay Co., 1976. 281 p.

Although primarily intended as a manual for yachtsmen, this book contains information which may prove useful to anyone experiencing an accident on water. Chapters giving advice of potential interest to wilderness voyagers are those on personal floatation devices, floatation materials, emergency repairs, and the proper reaction to storms occurring on large bodies of water. Case histories are used to illustrate survival principles. Biggs stresses preparation as the essence of survival afloat.

Bunnelle, Hasse, and Thomas, Winnie. FOOD FOR KNAPSACKERS AND OTHER TRAIL TRAVELERS. A Sierra Club Totebook. San Francisco: Sierra Club Books, 1971. 144 p. Preface. Paperbound.

Since carrying weight is often important or critical, the authors used slide rules to calculate the amounts of food needed for summer meals for large groups (fifteen to twenty-five persons). The recipes are built around a master food list giving weight, volume, calories, and additional comments. All recipes were back-country tested over a period of years by a multitude of Sierra Club hikers. The book is pocket size and has a durable cover. In addition to the recipes are chapters on the principles of food planning and on preparation procedure and equipment.

Burch, Monte [Gregory, Mark]. THE GOOD EARTH ALMANAC SURVIVAL HANDBOOK. An Alligator Book. New York: Sheed and Ward, 1973. 94 p. Paperbound.

This writer-woodsman presents fundamental outdoor survival skills as a series of short descriptions with accompanying drawings in this inexpensive paperback. The contents include sections on finding water, wild foods, heat and shelter, orientation, first aid, and safety. The final chapter instructs in methods to successfully cope with urban emergencies.

Cheney, Theodore A. CAMPING BY BACKPACK AND CANOE. New York: Funk and Wagnalls, 1970. xi, 210 p.

This is quite possibly the only book presenting basic information on camping without using any drawings or photographs. In spite of this seeming lack, Cheney's book succeeds as a "how-to" tool on the strength of his obvious knowledge of the subject and considerable descriptive powers. Three-quarters of the book is devoted to canoeing and camping technique; the remaining portion deals with backpacking. The section on canoeing has chapters on equipment, loading, launching, landing, strokes, portaging, and open-water and stream travel.

Cunningham, Gerry, and Hansson, Margaret. LIGHTWEIGHT CAMPING EQUIPMENT AND HOW TO MAKE IT. Rev. ed. New York: Charles Scribner's Sons, 1976. ix, 150 p. Preface. Paperbound.

Sleeping bags, packs, tents, and clothing are four camping necessities which can be inexpensively made with the help of the drawings and instructions in this book. This is not a book to be used in conjunction with kit assembly. All projects are made from basic materials, and a list of materials sources is provided. The author is the designer of the "Gerry" line of backpacking equipment.

Dalrymple, Byron W. SURVIVAL IN THE OUTDOORS. An Outdoor Life Book. New York: E.P. Dutton and Co., 1972. vii, 309 p.

Preplanning is emphasized as the most effective way to avert a disaster in the outdoors. The pocket size of the book makes it practical as a carry-along reference. The essentials of providing water, food, shelter and warmth are addressed, as well as other survival needs, such as signaling for help, map and compass use, and wilderness travel. The wilderness travel section instructs in canoe repair and building a raft.

Davidson, James West, and Rugge, John. THE COMPLETE WILDERNESS PADDLER. New York: Alfred A. Knopf, 1976. 284 p.

A voyage down Labrador's Moisie River is the context within which this primer on wilderness canoeing is written. Experiences from the actual trip are used to illustrate the skills needed and the pitfalls to avoid. The result is a personalized book on canoe camping technique devoid of guile. A chapter on map reading is presented as a workbook exercise, complete with test questions. The five parts in which the book is divided represent conditions fairly typical of an extended trip: preparation, paddling on smooth water, downriver paddling, scouting and lining, and whitewater paddling. Included within these divisions are chapters on first aid, cooking, navigation, camping, portaging, and associated skills. The drawings, by Gordon Allen, have a photographic quality well-suited to showing detail in the map, navigation, and equipment illustrations.

Evans, G. Heberton III. CANOEING WILDERNESS WATERS. Cranbury, N.J.: A.S. Barnes and Co., 1975. 211 p.

The audience for this book is intended to be the beginning and intermediate canoe tourer. More than 150 photographs illustrate the technique and mechanics of most types of wilderness voyaging, including strokes, open-water and stream travel, and portaging. Additional information is included on choosing a canoe, weather, repair and maintenance, and planning trips. Evans is an experienced canoeist and leader of trips into the interior of Ontario and Quebec.

Fear, Daniel E., ed. SURVIVING THE UNEXPECTED: CURRICULUM GUIDE. Rev. ed. Tacoma, Wash.: Survival Education Association, 1974. iv, 91 p. Paperbound.

This guide is intended for group use in conjunction with SURVIVING THE UNEXPECTED WILDERNESS EMERGENCY by Gene Fear (see below). It presents, in outline form, classroom lesson plans and field exercises in the psychology and methodology of survival. The guide is divided into four phases: general survival priorities, wilderness survival, coping with natural disasters, and coping with man-made disasters. Supplementary information on assembling a personal survival kit is presented. There is a brief bibliography of books, tests, and films on survival.

Fear, Gene. SURVIVING THE UNEXPECTED WILDERNESS EMERGENCY. Rev. ed. Tacoma, Wash.: Survival Education Association, 1975. iv, 196 p. Paperbound.

The author defines survival as the art of keeping the body alive during an emergency. He advocates less emphasis on teaching safety techniques and more on why and how environmental stress effects the total body while away from modern technology. Survival is nearly 100 percent mental challenge. Planning and problem anticipation, analysis of the problem, physical and psychological stress, and survival in cold and heat are only a few of the many topics discussed. In a chapter on improvising during an emergency, Fear suggests that needs be classified into those of shelter, water, fire, clothing, and food; these needs should then be prioritized. For group instruction in survival,

the companion volume, SURVIVING THE UNEXPECTED: CUR-
RICULUM GUIDE by Daniel E. Fear, may be used (see above).

Fisher, Mark. THE QUETICO-SUPERIOR CANOEIST'S HANDBOOK. 3d ed.
Winton, Minn.: Packsack Press, 1975. v, 81 p. Paperbound.

> After suggesting the best time for paddling the Boundary Waters
> Canoe Area, the author presents information in detail on equip-
> ment, food, and clothing best-suited for use in this region. Of
> course, most of this information is generally applicable to any
> wilderness canoe trip. The intended audience is the novice
> camper or the person who has camped before, but not with a
> canoe.

Fletcher, Colin. THE NEW COMPLETE WALKER: THE JOYS AND TECH-
NIQUES OF HIKING AND BACKPACKING. 2d ed. New York: Alfred A.
Knopf, 1974. 502 p. Preface.

> This book is a revision of Fletcher's highly successful THE COM-
> PLETE WALKER (New York: Alfred A. Knopf, 1968), which
> earned the readership of many backpackers for its scope and
> practicality. The revision is largely the result of the dynamic
> development of the backpacking equipment and supply industry
> and of state-of-the-art changes in environment and ecology re-
> search. Much of the information in the book has application
> to all self-propelled wilderness travelers. Specific information
> is best located by using the index, since the table of contents
> has somewhat cryptic chapter headings. There are chapters on
> walking, packs, tents, clothing, food, pathfinding, and much
> more. Four appendixes are included, containing equipment
> checklists, a directory of retailers, a list of hiking organizations,
> and a selection of quotes for contemplative walkers.

Germain, Donald L. WHEN YOU GO CANOE CAMPING. Nashville:
United Methodist Church, 1968. vi, 69 p. Paperbound.

> This manual is intended as a practical reference for individuals
> and groups. It has a definite but not dominant religious tenor.
> The rudiments of canoe and camping technique are presented.
> The eight chapters address scheduling, organization, location,
> canoe camping, meals, equipment, safety, and trip evaluation.

Graves, Richard H. BUSHCRAFT: A SERIOUS GUIDE TO SURVIVAL AND
CAMPING. New York: Schocken Books, 1972. vi, 344 p. Paperbound.

> The only way to anchor a tent rope in the sand is to tie it to
> the middle of the stake and then bury the stake. If you see a
> steady column of black ants climb a tree and disappear into a
> hole in the crotch, it is highly probable that there will be a
> hidden reservoir of fresh water stored there. These are two sug-

gestions, in modified form, representative of the hundreds presented in this book. Virtually every one of the camping and
survival tips has an accompanying drawing. Graves was the
creator and leader of the Australian Jungle Rescue Detachment
assigned to the U.S. Air Force. He explains how to use natural
materials and to adapt the skills of primitive man. Chapter
titles include "Building Huts," "Campcraft," "Finding Food and
Water," "Hunting and Trapping," and "Making Fire."

GROUP CAMPING BY CANOE. Marathon, N.Y.: Grumman Boats, n.d.
10 p. Paperbound.

A canoe group having some experience in paddling but little in
extended canoe voyaging is the intended audience for the suggestions in this booklet. Originally prepared by Girl Scout
Mariner Troop 567, the builders of Grumman canoes have since
taken over publication. There are short chapters on route selection, organizing duties, safety and first aid, camping, food,
equipment, and launching loaded canoes.

Handel, Carle Walker. CANOE CAMPING: A GUIDE TO WILDERNESS
TRAVEL. New York: A.S. Barnes and Co.; Toronto: Copp Clark Co., 1953.
192 p. Preface.

Handel's book retains its usefulness and authority despite showing
some signs of age. Age is noticeable when he writes about
equipment or camp foods, but it ceases to matter when time-
tested skills are the subject. The book is intended for the beginning and intermediate canoeist. The information is given in
detail and is augmented by relevant experiences from the author's
years as a licensed guide in the Canadian wilderness. The book
begins with a chapter on trip planning. Other chapters discuss
the canoe, strokes, packing, portaging, camping, cooking, survival, navigation, hunting, and fishing.

Jacobson, Clifford L. WILDERNESS CANOEING AND CAMPING. A Sunrise
Book. New York: E.P. Dutton and Co.; Toronto: Clarke, Irwin and Co.,
1977. 248 p. Paperbound.

General information on canoeing and canoe camping techniques
is given in this book. What may elevate it above the ordinary
introductory work are the scores of tips and experiential vignettes
provided. This has the combined effect of holding the attention
and building the confidence of the reader. In addition to material on paddling and portaging, Jacobson tells how to choose
a canoe and equipment, where to get it, and how to repair and
care for it. One chapter tells how to canoe camp with children
and teenagers. Another chapter presents instructions for cus-
tomizing canoes, paddles, and equipment. Appendixes list map and
guidebook sources, equipment suppliers, and canoe and paddle manufacturers.

Keatinge, W.R.   SURVIVAL IN COLD WATER: THE PHYSIOLOGY AND
TREATMENT OF IMMERSION HYPOTHERMIA AND OF DROWNING. Oxford,
Engl.: Blackwell Scientific Publications, 1969. x, 131 p.   Preface.

> The problem of saving the life of a victim of cold-water im-
> mersion is rigorously addressed in this work by an Oxford physi-
> ology professor.   The nature and scope of hypothermia (severe
> loss of body heat) are set forth and recent experiments are sum-
> marized.   Although the book is clinical in tone, paddlers with-
> out medical training should have little difficulty understanding
> the bulk of the material.   Conclusions are based on actual cold-
> water immersion experiments with Royal Navy volunteers as well
> as on past studies reported in medical literature.

Kjellstrom, Bjorn.   BE EXPERT WITH MAP AND COMPASS: THE ORIENTEER-
ING HANDBOOK.   Rev. ed.   New York: Charles Scribner's Sons, 1975.
vii, 136 p.   Paperbound.

> This book is for the outdoorsperson in general and the orienteer-
> ing enthusiast in particular.   Orienteering is the sport of directing
> one's way through the wilderness by map and compass while in
> competition with other individuals or groups.   The book can be
> used as a primer on map and compass use through the clearly
> presented explanations and the many illustrations, maps, and
> practice tests.   An envelope containing a compass and protractor
> is included with the book.

Kodet, E. Russel, and Angier, Bradford.   BEING YOUR OWN WILDERNESS
DOCTOR: THE OUTDOORSMAN'S EMERGENCY MANUAL.   Harrisburg, Pa.:
Stackpole Books, 1968.   127 p.

> This book describes the way a physician would approach a back-
> woods illness or injury and, according to the first chapter,
> "could enable you to make a correct and possibly life-saving
> decision at a critical time."   Of course, information in the
> book may also prevent you from doing something potentially
> harmful to the victim.   The kinds and quantities of drugs most
> often useful or needed are suggested.   There is a detailed in-
> dex, "The Problem Treatment-Finder," located at the beginning
> of the book.

Langer, Richard W. THE JOY OF CAMPING: THE COMPLETE FOUR-SEASONS,
FIVE-SENSES GUIDE TO ENJOYING THE GREAT OUTDOORS (WITHOUT
DESTROYING IT). New York: Saturday Review Press, 1973. 334 p.

> Camping skills and wilderness travel are given popular treatment
> in this book for the intermediate camper.   Some information for
> the paddler is given, but the hiker is emphasized.   Two chap-
> ters are exclusively devoted to water travel.

Lathrop, Theodore G. HYPOTHERMIA: KILLER OF THE UNPREPARED. Rev. ed. Portland, Oreg.: The Mazamas, 1975. 29 p. Paperbound.

> Lathrop reports that more than twenty mountaineers and other outdoorspersons have died recently from noninjury-related exposure to the elements. Through discussion of hypothermia (severe loss of body heat) and the reporting of case histories, the author-- a physician and mountaineer--attempts to explain the phenomenon and methods of its prevention and treatment.

Malo, John W. MALO'S COMPLETE GUIDE TO CANOEING AND CANOE CAMPING. Rev. ed. New York: Quadrangle Press/New York Times Book Co., 1974. x, 222 p.

> This book is intended for the beginner who wishes to learn the basics of using a canoe as a vehicle for recreational camping. Four main parts comprise the book: (1) choosing a canoe and paddles, (2) basic technique, (3) canoe camping, and (4) sources of canoe information, including competitions and organizations.

_____. WILDERNESS CANOEING. New York: Macmillan Co., 1971. xi, 176 p.

> The canoeist new to wilderness touring is the person for whom this book is written. Malo has organized his material into six parts, beginning with the planning phase of a trip and continuing with food preparation, canoe travel, campsite projects, safety, and sources for maps and further information. Despite its lengthy page count, the book is deceptively brief due to the large type and many illustrations used. Consequently, even the touring newcomer may require more information, such as that available in Calvin Rutstrum's NORTH AMERICAN CANOE COUNTRY or in POLE, PADDLE, AND PORTAGE by Bill Riviere (see chapter 2).

Mead, Robert Douglas. THE CANOER'S BIBLE. Outdoor Bible Series. Garden City, N.Y.: Doubleday and Co., 1976. 176 p. Paperbound.

> This book takes a general approach to the art and science of canoeing and canoe touring. Aimed at the novice canoeist, the book includes chapters on canoes and paddles, technique, equipment, and trip planning. However, touring is the core around which the other chapters are built. Safety is emphasized throughout. The book includes a lengthy section on suggestions for trips. In this section, canoeable waters throughout North America are discussed and sources for more specific information are listed.

Mendenhall, Ruth Dyar. BACKPACK COOKERY. Rev. ed. Glendale, Calif.: La Siesta Press, 1974. 47 p. Paperbound.

Mendenhall's booklet offers suggestions on the planning, purchasing, packing, and preparation of foods suitable for camping. Recipes have been tested on the trail by the author, an experienced backpacker. The menus are simple and have been chosen for ease of preparation, portability, and nutrition. Children's special food requirements and wishes are considered as is the very real problem of safeguarding and preserving the relative freshness of food in the wilderness.

Merrill, William K. THE SURVIVAL HANDBOOK. New York: Winchester Press, 1972. 312 p.

The extremes of cold and hot weather and water catastrophe survival are considered in this book for backcountry travelers. There is information on the survival arts of orientation, routefinding, food, and shelter. The book is fully illustrated.

Mitchell, Dick. MOUNTAINEERING FIRST AID: A GUIDE TO ACCIDENT RESPONSE AND FIRST AID CARE. 2d ed. Seattle, Wash.: The Mountaineers, 1975. 24 p. Paperbound.

This publication is a result of the experience gained from The Mountaineers--Red Cross (Seattle) first aid training program. It stresses not only emergency first aid skills, but pretrip preparation. Although designed for hikers and climbers, the approach to basic backcountry medicine has application to all who travel in the wilderness.

Morris, Dan, and Morris, Inez. CAMPING BY BOAT: POWERBOAT, SAILBOAT, CANOE, RAFT. Indianapolis: Bobbs-Merrill Co., 1975. xi, 243 p. Paperbound.

"Float Camping" and "Canoe Camping" are the two chapters in this book which provide specific information on camping by means of paddle craft. The chapter about canoes is divided into two parts: a description of the author's recent Delaware River trip and a listing of paddling techniques, equipment, and general canoeing advice. The chapter on float camping, by Norman Strung, has information on craft for float camping, special boating gear, loading, float technique, and campsite choice. Other parts of the book cover general boat-camping methods having universal application, and federal and state boating and camping information sources.

Olsen, Larry Dean. OUTDOOR SURVIVAL SKILLS. 4th ed. Provo, Utah: Brigham Young University Press, 1973. 203 p.

Olsen is a practitioner and teacher of outdoor survival; he was technical advisor to the recent feature film JEREMIAH JOHNSON. His approach to survival is that of training to live off the land without using manufactured gear. More than 2,000 people have wilderness-tested his theories. The book is organized according to requirements for wilderness survival: shelter, fire, water, plants, animals, and special skills. The concentration is on survival in the western desert and mountains; however, the core philosophy and skills of survival have wide utility.

Riviere, Bill. BACKCOUNTRY CAMPING. Garden City, N.Y.: Doubleday and Co., Dolphin Books, 1972. 320 p. Preface. Paperbound.

Riviere's book offers information on the full spectrum of camping and associated activities--from sleeping under the stars to sleeping under the roof of a self-constructed cabin, and from poling a canoe to trail biking. Camping advice is backed by personal experience (such as recommending two supplies of wooden matches instead of maintaining that romantic notion of using flint and steel or bow and drill as a fall-back way to make fire). Basic information is given on type and quality of equipment for provision of food, shelter, and comfort in wilderness. There are suggestions on clothing, cold-weather camping, conservation, emergencies, pathfinding, and recognition of plants and animals.

Rutstrum, Calvin. THE NEW WAY OF THE WILDERNESS. Rev. ed. New York: Collier Books, 1973. viii, 280 p.

In this book, Rutstrum, a renowned outdoorsman, reveals the ways an individual may intelligently live in and from the backcountry. A description of canoe technique comprises a major part of the book, since the author views the canoe as a prime mode of wilderness transportation. Equipment, orientation, food, hunting, fishing, first aid, and survival are discussed thoroughly. The book is illustrated by nature artist Les Kouba.

_____. THE WILDERNESS ROUTE FINDER. New York: Macmillan Co., 1967. x, 214 p.

Judging by content and size, this book is intended as a traveling companion for groups and individuals making trips into unfamiliar territory. Rutstrum uses step-by-step nontechnical explanations of the various route-finding procedures. In chapter one, he corrects the layman's misconception that man has an innate sense of direction. (Research shows that blindfolded subjects always veer into a circular course.) Natural guides to direction, such as moss growing most heavily on the north sides of trees and a supposed tendency of trees to have their heaviest branch and leaf growth on the sunny side, are shown to be inaccurate. Rutstrum explains reliable methods of wilderness travel in his chapters on maps, compass use, position lines, "positive" natural route-finders, and celestial navigation. An appendix contains brief descriptions of other simplified route-finding methods. The drawings are by nature artist Les Kouba.

Thomas, Dian. ROUGHING IT EASY: A UNIQUE IDEABOOK FOR CAMPING AND COOKING. Provo, Utah: Brigham Young University Press, 1974. 215 p. Preface. Paperbound.

> Outdoor cookery from apples to zucchini is thoroughly discussed in this authoritative book by a home economics and nutrition professor. The recipes have been tested under camping conditions and are given with cooking timetables. Cooking and fire-making techniques, often by unique means, are given detailed treatment in the text and by photograph. The popularity of this book resulted in part from its being featured as a book of the month for Field and Stream Book Club. This Brigham Young edition is in its sixth printing. A less expensive edition, without the scuff-proof cover is available from Warner Books.

_____. ROUGHING IT EASY 2. New York: Warner Books, 1977. 223 p.. Preface. Paperbound.

> Thomas's first book (listed immediately above) has heavy emphasis on the cooking-eating aspects of camping. This second book has much more material on some of the other elements of camping in comfort--creative ideas for shelter, sleeping, and keeping clean. Therefore, while the titles are almost identical, the second book supplements rather than supersedes the first. A timely section on solar-heat cooking is featured. Another chapter discusses pretrip drying of foods. More than 200 drawings and photographs (some in color) illustrate the work. Many new recipes are provided.

Wheelock, Walt. ROPES, KNOTS, AND SLINGS FOR CLIMBERS. Rev. ed. Glendale, Calif.: La Siesta Press, 1967. 36 p. Preface. Paperbound.

> This booklet is intended for the climber, as the title indicates. However, all the ropes and knots one could use on a wilderness-waterways journey are presented by means of clear drawings and precise descriptions in an inexpensive format. There is also considerable information on the care, properties, and history of European and American ropes.

Wilkerson, James, ed. MEDICINE FOR MOUNTAINEERING. Seattle, Wash.: The Mountaineers, 1967. 329 p.

> This is a comprehensive handbook about wilderness medicine; it is not a first aid manual. Some of the material may be complex (but not incomprehensible) for the nonphysician. Treatment for virtually any accident or illness is described within the wilderness context. The 6 x 8 inch dimension of the book makes it a carry-along candidate for a backcountry trip of any kind.

Chapter 4

BUILDING AND REPAIR

Blandford, Percy William. CANOES AND CANOEING. London: Lutterworth Press; New York: Norton, 1968. 207 p.

Instructions for building five different kayaks and canoes are presented by one of England's most widely known small-boat builders. The boats are: Kittiwake, a two-seater fabric kayak; Griffin, a single-seat fabric kayak; Gannet, a single-seat, plywood-skin kayak; Puffin, a single-seat folding kayak; and Teal, a two-seater canoe. Concluding sections of the book give information on accessories and canoeing techniques.

_____. HANDBOOK OF PRACTICAL BOAT REPAIRS. Blue Ridge Summit, Pa.: Tab Books, 1975. 224 p.

This handbook describes the technique of repairing all types of watercraft constructed from a variety of materials. Of particular interest to paddlers may be the chapters addressing the repair of aluminum, fiberglass, and canvas. The author is a naval architect with years of practical boat-building and repair experience.

Blandford, Percy William, and Littledyke, K.H. CANOE BUILDING, PART 1: SOFT SKIN AND MOULDED VENEER CANOES. London: British Canoe Union, 1968. ii, 51 p. Preface. Paperbound.

This booklet and its companion, CANOE BUILDING, PART 2: GLASS FIBRE CANOES by W.L. Saunders (see below), are intended to introduce the reader to some of the more popular methods of construction. In reading this publication, one must remember that the British canoe is the American kayak. Part 1 covers the traditional fabric-over-wooden-frame construction as well as construction by forming veneer. It also covers the "Kayel" method (sewing together sheets of plywood already cut to shape). The design of kayaks is not discussed. Instructions are general, with some chapters having more specific "building hints." Drawings are presented in an appendix. The preface acknowledges that this work is but a notebook and is intended only as an introduction to construction technique.

Byde, Alan. CANOE BUILDING IN GLASS REINFORCED PLASTIC. London: Adam and Charles Black, 1974. U.S. distributor is Levittown, N.Y.: Transatlantic Arts. 188 p. Preface.

> This book presents exactly one hundred steps to constructing a glass-reinforced plastic canoe (kayak). More advanced builders are instructed in the preparation of molds and plugs (solid shapes from which molds may be taken). Instructions are also given for do-it-yourself accessories--helmets, spray skirts, car-top carriers, and kayak trailers.

_____. CANOE DESIGN AND CONSTRUCTION. London: Pelham Books, 1975. 176 p.

> Canoe (kayak) construction in glass-reinforced plastic is explained. All phases of building are discussed--conception, pattern design, mold construction, fiber lamination, and finish work. Byde is a senior coach with the British Canoe Union as well as a designer and builder of canoes. The book is illustrated with drawings and diagrams by the author. There is an extensive glossary giving a lengthy explanation of terms, such as "master section" and "meta center." The appendix lists nine construction and thirteen safety standards recommended by the British Canoe Manufacturers Association.

Fichter, George S. HOW TO BUILD AN INDIAN CANOE. New York: David McKay Co., 1977. vi, 90 p.

> Fichter adapted this book from THE BARK CANOES AND SKIN BOATS OF NORTH AMERICA by Edwin Tappan Adney and Howard I. Chapelle (see chapter 5). The intended audience is the younger reader; although the vocabulary is reduced and syntax simplified, there has been evident care taken not to patronize the reader. The book instructs in the older, Indian method of canoe construction, and describes and inventories the materials and hand tools used. The author has divided the types of canoes by region and tribe. The final chapter presents information on canoes used in the fur trade.

Hazen, David. THE STRIPPER'S GUIDE TO CANOE BUILDING. 3d ed. San Francisco: Tamal Vista Publications, 1976. 95 p. Paperbound.

> This new and comprehensive edition of Hazen's manual on how to build strip canoes is certainly one of the few addressing the subject. The author has been building strip canoes professionally for four years. The book instructs the prospective builder in the total construction process by means of description, photograph, and drawing. Strip kayak construction is also shown. Three take-out diagrams are provided. The diagrams measure 23 x 35 inches. There are also instructions for making car-top carriers, canoe paddles, and canoe covers.

HOW TO REPAIR FIBERGLASS BOATS. Nashville: Ferro Corp., Fiberglass Division, 1969. 36 p. Preface. Paperbound.

> This manual is intended for readers needing a basic reference book on the repair of gel-coated fiberglass products. It is organized in four sections: (1) background information on fiberglass materials and their manufacture, (2) repair of surface damage, (3) repair of fractures and punctures, and (4) refinishing repaired areas with polyester gel-coat and epoxy enamel. The step-by-step procedures are in outline form with correlated illustrations.

Moore, Charles W. "Construction Techniques for Wood Strip Canoes." Rev. ed. Winamac, Ind.: United States Canoe Association, 1976. i, 18 p. Preface. Mimeographed.

> The intended readership of this manual is the previously uninitiated strip and fiberglass canoe builder--one who has the tools, time, and manual dexterity. The illustrations are carefully drawn and the text is simple yet not pedantic. Materials lists are included. Full-scale plans for various canoe designs may be purchased from the United States Canoe Association.

Ritzenthaler, Robert Eugene. "The Building of a Chippewa Indian Birch-bark Canoe." BULLETIN OF THE PUBLIC MUSEUM OF THE CITY OF MILWAUKEE 19 (November 1950): 53-99.

> In 1947, the author visited the Lac du Flambeau reservation in northern Wisconsin to record the making of a birch-bark canoe by an Indian craftsman. The canoe construction, which took two men thirteen days to complete,was recorded on film. This article presents a day-by-day account of the construction process and includes thirty-three drawings and photographs.

Saunders, W.L. CANOE BUILDING, PART 2: GLASS FIBRE CANOES. Rev. ed. London: British Canoe Union, 1972. vi, 42 p. Preface. Paperbound.

> This booklet and its companion, CANOE BUILDING, PART 1: SOFT SKIN AND MOULDED VENEER CANOES by Percy W. Blandford and K.H. Littledyke (see above), are intended to introduce the reader to some of the more popular methods of construction. Since this is a British publication, one must remember to substitute the word kayak for canoe. Part 2 covers equipment, material, mold-making, lay-up, finishing, and repair of fiberglass kayaks. There are photographs of various construction processes. The designing of kayaks is not discussed; one is referred to other British Canoe Union booklets on this aspect. The preface acknowledges that this work is but a notebook and is intended only as an introduction to construction technique.

SPORTSMAN'S KAYAK. Easi-Build series, no. 317. Briarcliff Manor, N.Y.: Directions Simplified, 1968.

> The information and patterns needed to build a seventeen- to eighteen-foot kayak are provided on a set of four 24 X 38 inch sheets. The kayak is made of canvas over wood stringers. It may also be covered with fiberglass or versatex to suit individual needs. The patterns for the framing members are full-size. Step-by-step directions are presented on the first sheet as well as a complete materials list for the wood and hardware required. Subsequent sheets show frame patterns and some illustrations of various stages of completion.

Walbridge, Charles. BOATBUILDER'S MANUAL: HOW TO BUILD FIBERGLASS CANOES AND KAYAKS FOR WHITEWATER. 2d ed. Penllyn, Pa.: Wildwater Designs, 1974. iii, 70 p. Preface. Paperbound.

> Boat building can be tedious and the working conditions abominable, but there are rewards—not the least of which may be economic. The author estimates that approximately half the cost of a commercial boat can be saved through home construction. This manual presents comprehensive material on how to construct one-person kayaks and one- and two-person decked canoes. The building techniques and alternatives are presented as are the advantages and disadvantages of epoxy versus polyester resin systems. Wholesale and retail supply sources are listed. Numerous small marginal drawings illustrate the text.

Wynn, Peter. FOAM SANDWICH BOATBUILDING: A PRACTICAL GUIDE TO HOME CONSTRUCTION. Camden, Maine: International Marine Publishing Co., 1972. 128 p. Preface.

> Wynn's book is a detailed approach to foam-core fiberglass boat building. While the description of the process follows the actual building of a dingy and a forty-foot trimaran, the materials and technique have practical application in the building of strong, light paddle craft. Descriptions are illustrated by drawings and photographs. There is an accompanying list of recommended and alternate materials.

Chapter 5

HISTORY, BIOGRAPHY, AND TRIP ACCOUNTS

EXPLORATIONS AND ACCOUNTS OF WATERWAYS TRIPS PRIOR TO 1920

BY CANOE FROM TORONTO TO FORT EDMONTON IN 1872, AMONG THE IROQUOIS AND OJIBWAYS, WITH A CHAPTER ON WINTER IN CANADA. 18-?. Reprint. Toronto: Canadiana House, 1968. 74 p. Paperbound.

> "To shoot rapids in a canoe is a pleasure that comparatively few Englishmen have ever enjoyed. . ." begins chapter 2 of this book on the Canadian wilderness "by an anonymous traveler." The thirty wood engravings show poorly on the porous yellow paper chosen for this reprint edition.

Campbell, Marjorie Elliott. THE SAVAGE RIVER: SEVENTY-ONE DAYS WITH SIMON FRASER. Great Stories of Canada, no. 33. Toronto: Macmillan of Canada, 1968. 146 p.

> The remarkable journey of Simon Fraser in 1808, from Fort George to the Strait of Georgia down the river named for him, is recounted in this popular version by the well-known writer on Canada's history, Marjorie Campbell.

Daniells, Roy. ALEXANDER MACKENZIE AND THE NORTH WEST. Toronto: Oxford University Press, 1971. 219 p. Paperbound.

> In this book, Mackenzie's voyages of fur trading and exploration from Lake Athabasca north to the Arctic Ocean and west to the Pacific Ocean are described by a respected Canadian scholar.

Dellenbaugh, Frederick S. A CANYON VOYAGE: THE NARRATIVE OF THE SECOND POWELL EXPEDITION DOWN THE GREEN-COLORADO RIVER FROM WYOMING, AND THE EXPLORATIONS ON LAND IN THE YEARS 1871 AND 1872. New York: G.P. Putnam's Sons, 1908. 299 p. Preface.

> The full story of the second Powell expedition, condensed in Dellenbaugh's THE ROMANCE OF THE COLORADO RIVER (New

York and London: G.P. Putnam's Sons, 1902), is presented in
this narrative. The first expedition in 1869 was one of daring
and adventure in the unknown. The second trip down the river
was far more scientifically based, with volumes of data collected
and recorded systematically. The book was compiled from the
diaries of Professor Thompson, John F. Steward, and the author.
Fifty early photographs and color sketches are included.

Featherstonhaugh, George William. A CANOE VOYAGE UP THE MINNAY
SOTOR, WITH AN ACCOUNT OF THE LEAD AND COPPER DEPOSITS IN
WISCONSIN, OF THE GOLD REGION IN THE CHEROKEE COUNTRY, AND
SKETCHES OF POPULAR MANNERS. London: R. Bentley, 1847. 788 p.

The book opens with the author's proposal to "make a tour of
exploration to the Coteau de Prairie, at the sources of the Minnay Sotor, or St. Peter's River, a northwest tributary of the Mississippi." In chapter 26, 228 pages later, having traversed the
eastern half of the United States, Featherstonhaugh arrives at
the banks of the river. The account of his travels is transcribed
from his journals. The latter part of the book describes his travels in the "gold region in the Cherokee country."

Hanbury, David T. SPORT AND TRAVEL IN THE NORTHLAND OF CANADA.
London: Edward Arnold, 1904. 351 p. Preface.

Hanbury was one of the early travelers in the Canadian Barrens
region lying between the northwestern coast of Hudson Bay and
Great Slave and Great Bear lakes. At the time Hanbury was
canoeing, sledding, and walking through this vast area, there
were no Caucasian settlements. He attempted with varying success to live among the Eskimos and to adopt their methods of
living and traveling in the wilderness. There are more than sixty
illustrations, including many photographs, of the land and its inhabitants. Appendixes list the author's observations on the weather, flora, fauna, trade articles, and the Eskimo language.

Henry, Alexander. TRAVELS AND ADVENTURES IN CANADA AND THE IN-
DIAN TERRITORIES BETWEEN THE YEARS 1760 AND 1776. 1901. Reprint.
New York: Burt Franklin, 1969. 389 p. Preface.

There are three parts to Henry's journals: (1) the travels, (2)
geography and natural history, and (3) observations on the Indians of Canada. The narrative begins with the campaign of
1760 in which the British and colonial forces were fighting the
remaining portion of the French army. Earlier, Henry had become aware of the opportunities to be taken in the French-
developed fur trade should French control be swept away. His
adventures in the wilderness encompass the ensuing sixteen years.

Houston, C. Stuart, ed. TO THE ARCTIC BY CANOE, 1819-1821: THE JOUR-NAL AND PAINTINGS OF ROBERT HOOD, MIDSHIPMAN WITH FRANKLIN. Montreal: McGill-Queen's University Press, 1974. 250 p. Preface.

> Hood's journal, although less formal than Sir John Franklin's official journal, is recognized by historians as an invaluable record of the first Franklin expedition. The expedition was sponsored by the Lords Commissioners of the Admiralty to seek the Northwest Passage. During the two-year exploration, much of which was by canoe, Hood recorded with both pen and brush his impressions of the beauty and harshness of the area. The book contains twenty-four Hood paintings, sixteen of which are in color.

Kolb, Ellsworth L. THROUGH THE GRAND CANYON FROM WYOMING TO MEXICO. New York: Macmillan Co., 1914. 358 p.

> This is an account of the ninth recorded trip (in 1911) down the Colorado River and through the Grand Canyon. Indeed, Kolb continued on to the Gulf of California, a passage inhibited by present-day dams.

Lewis, Meriwether. HISTORY OF THE EXPEDITION UNDER COMMAND OF CAPTAINS LEWIS AND CLARKE TO THE SOURCES OF THE MISSOURI, THENCE ACROSS THE ROCKY MOUNTAINS AND DOWN THE RIVER COLUMBIA TO THE PACIFIC OCEAN, PERFORMED DURING THE YEARS 1804-5-6 BY ORDER OF THE GOVERNMENT OF THE UNITED STATES. 3 vols. 1922. Reprint. New York: AMS Press, 1973.

> This is a popular edition of the complete journals of Lewis and Clark. It covers their famous exploratory journey through the northwest comprising the lands of the Louisiana Purchase. There are many editions of the journals; one wishing a condensation may read Lewis's THE JOURNALS OF LEWIS AND CLARK, ed-ited by Bernard DeVoto (see below).

_____. THE JOURNALS OF LEWIS AND CLARK. Edited by Bernard DeVoto. Boston: Houghton Mifflin, 1953. 556 p.

> This condensation of the journals is based on the seven-volume ORIGINAL JOURNALS OF THE LEWIS AND CLARK EXPEDITION, 1804-1806 edited by Reuben Gold Thwaites (New York: Dodd, Mead and Co., 1904-5). DeVoto's edition contains about half the running daily log. The book is intended for nonspecialists; omissions from the original log are not indicated.

McDonald, Archibald. PEACE RIVER; A CANOE VOYAGE FROM HUDSON'S BAY TO PACIFIC, BY SIR GEORGE SIMPSON (GOVERNOR, HON. HUDSON BAY CO.) IN 1828: JOURNAL OF THE LATE CHIEF FACTOR, ARCHIBALD MC-DONALD (HON. HUDSON BAY CO.) WHO ACCOMPANIED HIM. Edited and introduction by Malcolm McLeod. New ed. Rutland, Vt.: Charles E. Tuttle Co., 1971. 144 p.

Governor Simpson, traveling without freight, canoed a distance of 3,200 miles from York Factory to Fort Langley on the Fraser River in a period of three months. The journal, only thirty-nine pages long, is supplemented by a lengthy introduction and copious appendixes by the editor.

Mackenzie, Alexander. VOYAGES FROM MONTREAL THROUGH THE CONTINENT OF NORTH AMERICA TO THE FROZEN AND PACIFIC OCEANS IN 1789 AND 1793, WITH AN ACCOUNT OF THE RISE AND STATE OF THE FUR TRADE. London: R. Noble, 1801. viii, 546 p. Preface.

At least to Mackenzie's own satisfaction, his explorations served to settle conjecture over the existence of a practical northwestern sea passage between the oceans. Concurrently, he proved the possibility of transcontinental passage utilizing light vessels on a vast network of inland waterways. The major portion of the book consists of the explorer's journals, written in the style of the adventurer-businessman rather than the scientist.

Powell, John Wesley. THE EXPLORATION OF THE COLORADO RIVER. Abridged ed. Chicago: University of Chicago Press, 1957. 159 p. Paperbound.

This abridgement is based on the text of part 1 of the first edition of 1875, which appeared under the title EXPLORATION OF THE COLORADO RIVER OF THE WEST AND ITS TRIBUTARIES (Washington, D.C.: Government Printing Office). The book contains Powell's account, as he transcribed it from his journal, of the 1869-70 first voyage. The illustrations, with minor exceptions, have been reproduced from the 1875 edition.

Sears, George Washington [Nessmuk]. THE ADIRONDACK LETTERS OF GEORGE WASHINGTON SEARS, WHOSE PEN NAME WAS "NESSMUK." Edited and brief biography by Dan Brenan. Blue Mountain Lake, N.Y.: Adirondack Museum, 1962. vii, 177 p.

There are an estimated two hundred and fifty thousand words in "Nessmuk's" letters to the magazine, FOREST AND STREAM. A portion of these letters, first published during his eight-year Adirondack voyage in a J. Henry Rushton canoe, have been gathered for this book. "Nessmuk," of course, was the author of the classic American book on the wilderness, WOODCRAFT (New York: Forest and Stream Publishing Co., 1884). He was a lifelong outdoorsman. This collection of his letters presents a picture of nineteenth-century canoeing, hunting, and fishing.

Stanton, Robert Brewster. DOWN THE COLORADO. Edited by Dwight L. Smith. The American Exploration and Travel Series, no. 45. Norman: University of Oklahoma Press, 1965. 262 p. Preface.

This book is based on the second volume of an unpublished manuscript of 1,038 pages in which Stanton describes his 1889-90 expedition to survey a feasible east-west rail route through the canyonlands. Three men were drowned in Marble Canyon on this ill-fated trip, causing Stanton to note: "I then realized fully what it meant to be without life preservers, in such work on such a river." Soon after, this phase of the survey was abandoned.

Thwaites, Reuben Gold. DOWN HISTORIC WATERWAYS: SIX HUNDRED MILES OF CANOEING UPON ILLINOIS AND WISCONSIN RIVERS. 3d ed. Chicago: McClurg and Co., 1910. 300 p. Preface.

In this book, Thwaites, one-time secretary of the State Historical Society of Wisconsin, describes a series of canoe trips undertaken in the summer of 1887. The Rock River of Illinois and the Wisconsin and Fox rivers of Wisconsin were the streams traveled. The narrative may provide a historical perspective for canoeists making latter-day trips on these rivers.

Tyrrell, James W. ACROSS THE SUB-ARCTICS OF CANADA: A JOURNEY OF 3,200 MILES BY CANOE AND SNOWSHOE THROUGH THE BARREN LANDS. Coles Canadiana Collection. 1898. Reprint. Toronto: Coles Publishing Co., 1973. vii, 280 p.

In the spring of 1893, the Tyrrell brothers began an exploration of the Barren Lands for the Canadian Geological Survey. The journey began at Athabasca Landing, continuing northeasterly to Baker Lake. In September, they turned their canoes south, down the shore of Hudson Bay, returning finally to West Selkirk in January. The book is a record of the expedition. Appendixes list plants collected and an Eskimo vocabulary.

Vail, Philip. THE MAGNIFICENT ADVENTURES OF ALEXANDER MACKENZIE. New York: Dodd, Mead, 1964. vi, 216 p.

Alexander Mackenzie's exploration of Canada's northwest wilderness is given a popular treatment in this book. A more scholarly handling of the subject is Roy Daniells's ALEXANDER MACKENZIE AND THE NORTHWEST (see above).

ACCOUNTS OF WATERWAYS TRIPS SINCE 1920

Berton, Pierre. DRIFTING HOME. Toronto: McClelland and Stewart, 1973. 174 p.

Berton describes, with numerous historical and personal asides, a twelve-day family float trip down the Yukon River from Lake Bennett, British Columbia, to Dawson, Yukon Territory. The route is that taken by Berton's father and thousands of other Klondike gold-seekers in the summer of 1898. The author spent his childhood in Dawson--hence the title. Although not having the detail of a river guide, this book does present the river and its history, flora, and fauna in a way which may be useful to one contemplating a Yukon float.

Bolz, John Arnold. PORTAGE INTO THE PAST: BY CANOE ALONG THE MINNESOTA-ONTARIO BOUNDARY WATERS. Minneapolis: University of Minnesota Press, 1960. vi, 181 p.

Of course, the Boundary Waters area was an integral part of the route of the fur traders. Bolz relates a contemporary trip through these waters to some of those trips reported in early travel diaries by quoting extensively from the diaries. The book may serve as a supplemental waterways guide to be used in conjunction with maps of the area. Its main intent seems to be the provision of entertaining historical reading. Tranquil drawings by Francis Lee Jaques and sketch maps of the author's route decorate the pages.

Browning, Peter. THE LAST WILDERNESS. San Francisco: Chronicle Books, 1975. 117 p. Paperbound.

Between Lake Athabasca and Great Slave Lake is a wilderness of woods and water seldom traversed by man. The author and a companion canoed 600 miles within this area. Their route began at Black Lake, proceeded up the Chipman and Dubawnt rivers, turned westerly down the Talston and Snowdrift rivers, and finally, to the eastern arm of Great Slave Lake. Fifty photographs illustrate the book. An inventory of food and equipment is included.

Cantin, Eugene. YUKON SUMMER. San Francisco: Chronicle Books, 1973. ix, 198 p. Paperbound.

This book is the account of a solo kayak journey down the Yukon River from still-frozen Lake Bennett to Tanana, Alaska. Some of the colorful history of the river is covered, but Cantin concentrates on relating the day's events--the fatigue, solitude, anxiety, and growing sense of accomplishment inherent in a wilderness journey of this magnitude. The book is illustrated with scores of photographs.

DeRoss, Rose Marie. ADVENTURES OF GEORGIE WHITE, TV'S WOMAN OF THE RIVERS. 3d ed. Costa Mesa, Calif.: Gardner Printing and Mailing Co., 1970. Also distributed by Las Vegas, Nev.: Georgie's Royal River Rats. iv, 123 p. Paperbound.

Georgie White's first venture on the Colorado River was in 1945 when she and a companion swam 185 miles of the lower portion.

She was the first guide to lash neoprene rafts together, cutting out the bottoms to make them self-bailing. Today, some twenty years later, she continues to guide large groups through the Grand Canyon. The major portion of the book contains a narrative of a predam voyage through Glen Canyon and a mile-by-mile description of the Colorado from Lees Ferry to Temple Bar. DeRoss is White's sister.

Fiennes, Ranulph. THE HEADLESS VALLEY. London: Hodder and Stoughton, 1973. 222 p.

The Headless Valley lies between the first and second canyons of the South Nahanni River in Canada's Northwest Territories. The valley is the starting point for a trans-British Columbia river expedition by a British army team which, in part, follows the route of the early explorations of Alexander Mackenzie and Simon Fraser. The story of the expedition is told in an understated narrative and is illustrated with photographs and maps.

Frost, Kent. MY CANYONLANDS: I HAD THE FREEDOM OF IT. London: Abelard-Schuman, 1971. 160 p.

Cataract-type boat trips and overland treks highlight this biography of the life of a professional boatman and high-desert guide in the Four Corners region of Utah.

Gillis, Sandra, ed. "Canada's Centenary Journey: In the Steps Of the Voyageurs; Their Story, Our Story." Toronto: Canadian Camping Association, 1971. iv, 147 p. Mimeographed.

The Centenary Journey was a 1967 trans-Canada canoe voyage undertaken by relays of young Canadians in observance of the country's one-hundredth birthday. The material is arranged in comparative segments. The first describes the history of a particular waterway ("Their Story"), while a succeeding segment is a log of the experiences of the Centenary paddlers along the same waterway ("Our Story"). Sketch maps of the route accompany the text.

Goldwater, Barry M. DELIGHTFUL JOURNEY DOWN THE GREEN AND COLORADO RIVERS. Tempe: Arizona Historical Foundation, 1970. x, 209 p.

Senator Goldwater is listed as among the first one hundred persons to have traversed the Grand Canyon on the Colorado River as far as the mouth of the Virgin River. This trip was taken during the summer of 1940 with a party of eight, headed by Norman Nevills. The trip took two months and covered 1,463 miles between Green River, Utah, and Hoover Dam, Nevada. Photographs by the author are positioned opposite the appropriate

portion of the text. The present book evolved from a limited-
edition pamphlet, published in 1940, to the current hardbound
edition honoring John Wesley Powell.

Hancock, Lyn. THE MIGHTY MACKENZIE: HIGHWAY TO THE ARCTIC
OCEAN. Saanichton, British Columbia: Hancock House, 1974. 95 p. Paperbound.

The length of the Mackenzie, 1,089 miles from Great Slave Lake
to the Arctic Ocean, is described in this log of a trip taken by
motorized raft. Looking at the hundreds of black and white photographs of the people and surroundings that illustrate almost
every page of the book is an activity suggestive of thumbing
through a vacation album. Mileage is noted on outside page
margins. One map of the river is given as an overview of the
entire trip. An appendix lists the ways to get people and boats
to the Mackenzie, settlements offering accommodations, and air
routes in the region.

Jaques, Florence Page. CANOE COUNTRY. Minneapolis: University of Minnesota Press, 1938. 83 p.

This informal diary of a three-week canoe trip through the Quetico-
Superior has become a near classic of the genre. The book is in
its seventh printing. There are scores of drawings by Francis
Lee Jaques. In her writing, Jaques's wife conveys the heighten-
ing of the senses and enjoyment of simple things which may come
to those fortunate enough to experience the wilderness.

Krustev, Dimitar. RIVER OF THE SACRED MONKEY. Charleston, S.C.: Wilderness Holidays Publications, 1970. iv, 92 p. Paperbound.

This is a book about a trip down portions of the Lacanja, Lacan-
tum, and Ucumacinta rivers of Mexico and Guatemala. These
are true wilderness rivers which wind through jungle, canyon,
and the area of ancient Mayan temple ruins. The book contains
thirty-two well-reproduced color photographs and paintings of the
natives, terrain, wildlife, and the wild rivers.

Leslie, Robert Franklin. READ THE WILD WATER: 780 MILES BY CANOE
DOWN THE GREEN RIVER. New York: E.P. Dutton and Co., 1966. 192 p.

This book is about four canoes and eight persons (four of whom
are only thirteen years old) and their bombardment by heavy
water as they successfully run the length of the Green River.
They are the first to ever do so in canoes.

Mead, Robert Douglas. ULTIMATE NORTH: CANOEING MACKENZIE'S
GREAT RIVER. Garden City, N.Y.: Doubleday, 1976. 312 p.

Alexander Mackenzie's canoe voyage of 1789, from Lake Athabasca to the Arctic Ocean, was retraced by the author and his son in 1974. This book is an account of their adventure. The information on the route down the Slave and Mackenzie rivers will be of possible help to one paddling all or sections of these rivers. While the rivers and the references to Mackenzie's journey are at the center of the narrative, Mead has also included much about the land, people, and natural history of the region.

Nickerson, Elinor B. KAYAKS TO THE ARCTIC. Berkeley, Calif.: Howell-North Books, 1967. 197 p.

The Mackenzie River is the scene for this story of a thousand-mile paddle from the western tip of Great Slave Lake to the delta on the Beaufort Sea by a family of avid kayakists.

Olson, Sigurd F. THE LONELY LAND. 1961. Reprint. New York: Alfred A. Knopf, 1972. x, 273 p.

This book is about a 500-mile voyage along the Churchill River in which Olson served as the Bourgeois, or leader, of a party of six. He followed the trail of the fur traders who used the Churchill as a major passage from Hudson Bay to the Mackenzie. The story conveys the essence of wilderness travel. Olson combines his descriptions of the beauties of the Canadian northwest with the history of the region--the Cree, Chipewyan, Yellow Knives, and Dog Rib Indians as well as explorers and traders like Simpson, Thompson, Henry, and Mackenzie. The illustrations are by Francis Lee Jaques.

_____. RUNES OF THE NORTH. New York: Knopf, 1963. 266 p.

Olson's books have been likened to peaceful hymns to wilderness life; this book is no different. In it, he recounts his life and the canoe trips he took through two regions--the Quetico-Superior and the Northwest Territories-Alaska area.

_____. THE SINGING WILDERNESS. 1956. Reprint. New York: Alfred A. Knopf, 1975. ix, 245 p.

The sights and sounds of the Quetico-Superior area are recreated in this book by the famous woodsman from Ely, Minnesota. Olson evokes the mood and natural events of the seasons as they succeed each other. At the same time, he is instructive in the ways of the canoe, fishing, wildlife, and camping. The illustrations are by Francis Lee Jaques.

Patterson, Raymond M. THE DANGEROUS RIVER. 2d ed. Sidney, British Columbia: Gray's Publishing, 1966. 272 p. Paperbound.

The author's adventures on the South Nahanni River are told in this book. The river is located in Canada's Northwest Territories. Patterson began his search for gold in the area in the summer of 1927. His search was a failure, but he admits success in finding a resourcefulness within himself achieved through the trials of wilderness living. The narrative is understated and spare--qualities well-suited to this work of outdoor literature.

_____. FINLAY'S RIVER. New York: W. Morrow, 1968. 329 p.

Stories of journeys down the Finlay River in British Columbia, including some trips made by the author, comprise what could be called a Finlay anthology.

Phillips, C.E. Lucas. COCKELSHELL HEROES. London: Heinnemann, 1956. ix, 252 p.

This story of the raid on Axis shipping in Bordeaux Harbor, carried out by a small party of Royal Marines paddling kayaks, is compiled from official documents, diaries, and the narratives of others concerned with the planning and execution of the assault in 1942.

Sevareid, A. Eric. CANOEING WITH THE CREE. 1935. Reprint, rev. Foreword by Russell W. Fridley. St. Paul: Minnesota Historical Society, 1968. 228 p.

Sevareid was seventeen when he and Walter Post paddled 2,250 miles from Minneapolis to Hudson Bay. It was an adventure which, as Sevareid later said, "very young men can do--once in their lives--but never again." The book is based on a diary kept on the 1930 trip and on a series of newspaper stories filed en route. The addition of the foreword by the director of the Minnesota Historical Society, as well as the endpaper maps and an index containing corrections of the 1935 book, make the present volume a revised edition rather than only a reprint, as stated on the title page.

Staveley, Gaylord. BROKEN WATERS SING: REDISCOVERING TWO GREAT RIVERS OF THE WEST. Boston: Little, Brown and Co., 1971. 300 p.

A trip down the Green and Colorado rivers is described from the perspective of the professional boatman. "Nevills"-type cataract boats were used for the trip. Close description of each significant rapid provides potentially worthwhile information.to the river-runner.

Stegner, Wallace Earle, ed. THIS IS DINOSAUR: ECHO PARK COUNTRY AND ITS MAGIC RIVERS. New York: Alfred A. Knopf, 1955. 97 p.

Contained within the Dinosaur National Monument's canyons carved by the Green and Yampa rivers is some of the West's best whitewater. Stories of the early runners of the rivers, and the history and geology of the region, are supplemented by more than forty photographs.

Tousley, Albert S. WHERE GOES THE RIVER. Iowa City: Tepee Press, 1928. 314 p.

The Mississippi, from its source at Hernando de Soto Lake to the Gulf of Mexico, is the scene for this story of a 1925 canoe trip. The author paddled the 2,500-mile length of the river. His photographs augment the descriptions of the physical features, history, legends, and people encountered.

Zwinger, Ann. RUN RIVER RUN: A NATURALIST'S JOURNEY DOWN ONE OF THE GREAT RIVERS OF THE WEST. New York: Harper and Row, Publishers, 1975. 330 p.

Zwinger describes by word and drawing her impressions of the Green River. In many respects, the book is a field manual to the geology, flora, and fauna found along the total length of the river. Much of the river's 730 miles was run by either raft or canoe, with the canoes being replaced by rafts at the entrance to Lodore Canyon. The rest of the river was scouted on foot or by air.

WATERWAYS—ASSOCIATED HISTORY, BIOGRAPHY, AND LEGEND

Allen, William. BUILDER OF BIRCH BARK CANOES. Grand Rapids, Minn.: Herald-Review, 1969. 24 p. Paperbound.

Bill Hafeman is one of the very few persons able to build birchbark canoes using materials and methods similar to those used by the Indians. This pamphlet tells about the life of Hafeman and something of the building of a 36 1/2-foot replica of a Montreal canoe for the Minnesota Historical Society. Full-color photographs record the steps of the building process from selection of the trees to final caulking of the joints.

Baker, Pearl Biddlecome. TRAIL ON THE WATER. Boulder, Colo.: Pruett Publishing Co., 1969. 134 p.

The professional river-runner Albert (Bert) Loper is the subject of this biography. It is based on his daily journals and provides some insights into early developments in whitewater rowing technique--including entering rapids stern-first.

_____. THE WILD BUNCH AT ROBBER'S ROOST. Rev. ed. New York: Abelard-Schuman, 1971. 224 p.

> As cattle rustlers, horse thieves, bank and train robbers, the Wild Bunch hid between exploits in the Robber's Roost area between the canyons of the Dirty Devil, Green, and Colorado rivers. The group included, at various times, Flat Nose George, Elzy Lay, Gunplay Maxwell, Peep O'Day, Silver Tip, Indian Ed, Butch Cassidy, and the Sundance Kid. Baker grew up with the legends of the gang--her father's ranch included Robber's Roost. Much of her material was developed from conversations with contemporaries of the outlaws and interviews with eyewitnesses to crimes.

Campbell, Marjorie Elliott. THE NORTH WEST COMPANY. New York: St. Martin's Press, 1957. 295 p.

> One of North America's great fur-trading companies is traced from its beginnings to its demise at the hands of its main competitor, the Hudson's Bay Company.

_____. THE NOR'WESTERS: THE FIGHT FOR THE FUR TRADE. Great Stories of Canada series. New York: St. Martin's Press, 1956. 176 p.

> This book presents a popular account of the North West Company and its fur empire, linked by canoe. For a more detailed version, read Campbell's THE NORTH WEST COMPANY (see above).

Cawley, James S., and Cawley, Margaret. ALONG THE DELAWARE AND RARITAN CANAL. Rutherford, N.J.: Fairleigh Dickinson University Press, 1970. 128 p.

> Seven canoe trips taken by the authors are very briefly discussed in a chapter on present recreational use of an area, which includes the lower Delaware Valley, the Millstone River and Valley, and the lower Raritan River and Valley. The primary focus of the book is on the history of the canal from its construction in 1830 until the present.

Davis, Edwin Adams, ed. THE RIVERS AND BAYOUS OF LOUISIANA. Baton Rouge: Louisiana Education Research Association, 1968. 215 p.

> The waterways of Louisiana have played a pivotal role in the state's development. This history gives emphasis to the importance of the rivers and bayous as avenues of commerce and communication since the day Hernando de Soto first saw the Mississippi. Thirteen historians each contribute a chapter on one of the state's major waterways.

Gibbon, John Murray. THE ROMANCE OF THE CANADIAN CANOE. Toronto: Ryerson Press, 1951. 159 p. Preface.

Gibbon's book of canoe lore is an eclectic overview of legend
and socioeconomic history of a region with a vast network of
waterways and a single, perfectly adapted vessel to utilize that
network. The book contains many short accounts of the journeys
of Canada's great explorers and fur traders. This information is
augmented by material not often encountered, including narratives
of canoe trips by lesser personalities, photographs and paintings
of historical significance, voyageur chansons, Indian life in which
the canoe was a dominant factor, and the canoe as seen by Canadian poets.

Irving, Washington. ASTORIA: OR ANECDOTES OF AN ENTERPRISE BEYOND
THE ROCKY MOUNTAINS. The Works of Washington Irving, vol. 2. 1889.
Reprint. New York: AMS Press, 1973. 698 p.

This classic work contains some accounts of early western river
fur-trading voyages between eastern trading centers and the ter-
minus at the mouth of the Columbia River--Astoria. Irving under-
took the book at the request of John Jacob Astor. It is based
on Astor's voluminous business documents.

Krutch, Joseph Wood. GRAND CANYON: TODAY AND ITS YESTERDAYS.
New York: William Sloane and Associates, 1958. 276 p.

The geology and history of the Grand Canyon is presented, for
the most part, as a tourist would encounter it from the rim. Here
is valuable information for any layman's understanding, but the
perspective is from above rather than from river level.

Lunt, Dudley Cammett. THE WOODS AND THE SEA: WILDERNESS AND
SEACOAST ADVENTURES IN THE STATE OF MAINE. New York: Alfred A.
Knopf, 1965. x, 305 p.

In this chronology, Lunt recalls sixty years of travel, much of
it by canoe, along Maine's waterways. The book contains the
history and numerous legends of the region.

McPhee, John. THE SURVIVAL OF THE BARK CANOE. New York: Farrar,
Straus and Giroux, 1975. 145 p.

Henri Vaillancourt of Greenville, New Hampshire, builds birch-
bark canoes. He is one of the few remaining individuals in the
world so occupied. He builds them alone, with hand tools, and
fastens them with split roots and pegs. The canoes are perfect
water vehicles and are for sale only to people who have gained
his trust. Vaillancourt is determined to preserve a dying art.
Included with the book are thirty-one pages of sketches and models of Edwin Tappan Adney canoes, most published for the first
time, which have served as prime inspiration for Vaillancourt's
work.

Manley, Atwood. RUSHTON AND HIS TIMES IN AMERICAN CANOEING. Syracuse, N.Y.: Syracuse University Press, 1968. 223 p.

> This biography of J. Henry Rushton is a scholarly account of the life of a master builder of canoes and cofounder of the American Canoe Association. As a boy in Canton, New York, Manley watched Rushton build his canoes. Numerous photographs, many of which are contemporary, illustrate the work. There are five appendixes: (1) Rushton's methods of hull construction for rowboats and canoes, (2) his son Harry's recollection of his father's craftsmanship, (3) line drawings and specifications of some Rushton boats, (4) an 1885 article by George W. Sears [Nessmuk], and (5) an account of the Rushton canoes still in existence.

Merrill, Daphne Winslow. LAKES OF MAINE: A COMPILATION OF FACT AND LEGEND. Rockland, Maine: Courier-Gazette, 1973. x, 263 p. Preface.

> The history, lore, and other data of Maine's lakes and ponds are assembled by region--such as Allagash, Rangeley, Moosehead, and Sebago. Many photographs are included which are contemporary to the time and personalities discussed. The detailed index is an aid in locating the description of particular lakes. Numbered but as yet unnamed wilderness lakes are not included.

Morse, Eric Wilton. CANOE ROUTES OF THE VOYAGEURS: THE GEOGRAPHY AND LOGISTICS OF THE CANADIAN FUR TRADE. Toronto: Quetico Foundation of Ontario; St. Paul: Minnesota Historical Society, 1962. i, 42 p. Paperbound.

> Morse is a historian and a canoeist. He has traveled most of the 3,000 miles of the route from Montreal to Fort Chipewyan. Despite its relative brevity, this is a very thorough account of the often-told story of the fur trade. The work first appeared as a series of three articles in the May, July, and August 1961 issues of the CANADIAN GEOGRAPHICAL JOURNAL, under the title "Voyageurs' Highway." Many photographs are by the author. Supplementing these are reproductions of paintings from Canadian archives.

_____. FUR TRADE CANOE ROUTES OF CANADA, THEN AND NOW. Ottawa: Queen's Printer, 1969. vii, 125 p.

> Canadian fur traders were working the Athabasca country thirty years before Americans had even a foothold west of the Mississippi. The trade routes from Montreal are retraced and described by Morse, who has also searched Canadian archives for early illustrations.

Nute, Grace Lee. THE VOYAGEUR. 1931. Reprint. St. Paul: Minnesota Historical Society, 1955. x, 289 p. Preface.

The eighteenth- and early nineteenth-century fur trade between the lower St. Lawrence River and the continental northwest was dependent on the French Canadian woodsman, canoeist, and load-bearer known as voyageur. This is a documented story of these men. Many of the songs for which the voyageurs are known are brought together in a lengthy chapter and supplementary section of notes. Chapter 3 describes the canoes used. Nute, an authority on the early French explorers, was also a member of the Minnesota Historical Society staff from 1921 to 1957. The reprint edition is now in its fourth printing.

_____. THE VOYAGEURS' HIGHWAY: MINNESOTA'S BORDER LAKE LAND. St. Paul: Minnesota Historical Society, 1941. 126 p. Paperbound.

The history of the Quetico-Superior region centers on its use as a highway for the canoes of the fur trade. Nute's book traces the history of the fur-trading companies and their voyageurs. However, the history of Minnesota's border lakes also encompasses many who came before and since: Sioux, Cree, and Chippewa Indians; explorers; miners; lumberjacks; guides; and trappers. The book selectively presents a general discussion of all these groups.

Thoreau, Henry David. THE ILLUSTRATED MAINE WOODS. Edited by Joseph J. Moldenhauer. Princeton, N.J.: Princeton University Press, 1974. xxiii p., 347 cols.

This is Thoreau's second posthumous volume (after EXCURSIONS [Boston: Ticknor and Fields, 1863]). It was first published in 1864, and is a composite of three accounts of Maine canoe trips: "Ktaadn," "Chesuncook," and "The Allegash and East Branch." The photographs in this edition are by the early twentieth-century photographer Herbert Wendell Gleason, and are chosen from a large selection he had assembled for a planned but never published pictorial encomium to Thoreau.

Veit, Richard F. THE OLD CANALS OF NEW JERSEY: A HISTORICAL GEOG-RAPHY. Little Falls: New Jersey Geographical Press, 1963. xi, 106 p.

The Morris and the Delaware and Raritan canals were principal arteries for early New Jersey commerce. The main focus of this book is on the mechanics and attendant difficulties of construction and operation of the two canals. Although little remains of these waterways, there is a portion of the Delaware and Raritan, near Lambertville, still able to be enjoyed by the canoeist. A field guide locating extant sites of locks, canal banks, homes of lock-tenders, and other canaliana is provided in an appendix.

HISTORIES OF SMALL WATERCRAFT

Adney, Edwin Tappan, and Chapelle, Howard I. THE BARK CANOES AND
SKIN BOATS OF NORTH AMERICA. U.S. National Museum, Bulletin no. 230.
Washington, D.C.: Smithsonian Institution, 1964. 256 p.

> Bark canoes and kayaks are two primitive craft which have re-
> mained basically unchanged through the centuries. Adney,
> through research and experience building his own canoes with
> the Indians, became virtually the only individual to document
> bark-canoe building. This documentation was gathered together
> by Chapelle and published posthumously as a unique source for
> information on the design and construction of canoes and kayaks
> by the original North Americans.

Arima, Eugene Y. A CONTEXTUAL STUDY OF THE CARIBOU ESKIMO KAYAK.
Canadian Ethnology Service Paper, no. 25. Ottawa: National Museums of
Canada, 1975. vi, 267 p. Paperbound.

> This study views the Caribou Eskimo kayak as a part of the total
> cultural system, and demonstrates that the context-conscious ap-
> proach is an effective means of bolstering the ethnological sig-
> nificance of material culture studies. Arima's material came
> from field research among the tribe at Baker Lake, Northwest
> Territories, between 1966 and 1969. The primary quality sought
> in a Caribou kayak was high speed. Caribou are strong, fast
> swimmers capable of swimming four miles per hour over a distance
> and six miles per hour in brief spurts. Consequently, the kayaks
> were narrow and long for quickness and minimal water resistance.
> Thorough coverage is given to the actual construction of a kayak.
> Diagrams and photographs are provided.

Blandford, Percy William. AN ILLUSTRATED HISTORY OF SMALL BOATS: A
HISTORY OF OARED, POLED, AND PADDLED CRAFT. Bourne End, Engl.:
Spurbooks, 1974. U.S. distributor is Levittown, N.Y.: Transatlantic Arts.
143 p.

> Blandford writes that some dug-out canoes in the South Pacific had
> open sterns, and that water was kept out by seating a woman at
> the end of the craft. His account of manpowered small boats
> from earliest to modern times is, like the above example, con-
> sistently readable. Numerous photographs illustrate the narrative;
> a glossary and index are provided.

Durham, Bill. CANOES AND KAYAKS OF WESTERN AMERICA. 1960. Reprint. Seattle, Wash.: Shorey Book Store, 1974. 104 p. Paperbound.

> Approximately one hundred of the principal types of aboriginal
> watercraft used in western America are cataloged. Early drawings
> and paintings are of the greatest value in establishing the ap-

pearance of these watercraft. There were five major categories
of boats in the coastal region: (1) Eskimo skin-covered craft,
(2) bark canoes, (3) dugouts, (4) balsas, and (5) plank-built
boats. The book chapters follow these categories; the chapter on
canoes is available separately. Pen drawings and reproductions
of early illustrations accompany the text. The latter are indis-
tinctly rendered in this reprint edition.

Nishimura, Shinji. SKIN BOATS. A Study of Ancient Ships of Japan, pt. 4.
Tokyo: Society of Naval Architects, 1931. 261 p. Preface.

Perhaps the title is misleading, for Nishimura includes considerable information on basket boats, turtle-shell boats, and the birch-
bark canoe. (His reasoning is that all such boats consist of some
framework or wickerwork covered with the skin of an animal or
plant.) The position which skin boats hold in the history of boat
building in Japan is documented in some of the oldest writings
of that country. Frequent reference is made to folk legends concerning boats and the sea, and to skin boat development throughout the world.

Nooter, Gert. OLD KAYAKS IN THE NETHERLANDS. Mededelingen van het
Rijksmuseum voor Volkenkunde, Leiden, no. 17. Leiden, Netherlands: E.J.
Brill, 1971. viii, 76 p. Paperbound.

As early as 1625 a Greenlander demonstrated the use of a kayak
in the Netherlands. There are eighteen old kayaks in Holland;
almost all are of East Greenland origin. Nooter provides photographs and a scholarly appraisal of ten kayaks, the earliest dating
from 1663.

Quirke, Terence T. CANOES THE WORLD OVER. Urbana: University of
Illinois Press, 1952. 137 p.

American bark and skin canoes are discussed as are other canoes
and rafts from around the world. Quirke describes dugouts of
America, Australia, and New Zealand; Egyptian reed canoes;
outriggers; and many more. There are drawings of the various
craft, but no plans or construction details are given.

Chapter 6

THE WATERWAYS ENVIRONMENT: DAMS, POLLUTION, AND WILDERNESS PRESERVATION

THE BIG WATER FIGHT: TRIALS AND TRIUMPHS IN CITIZEN ACTION ON PROBLEMS OF SUPPLY, POLLUTION, FLOODS, AND PLANNING ACROSS THE U.S.A. Brattleboro, Vt.: Stephen Greene Press, 1966, for the League of Women Voters Education Fund. ix, 246 p. Preface.

> The research on which this is based was financed by a grant from Resources for the Future. The purpose of the book is to broaden awareness and stimulate participation by an informed public. Few local or state water problems are unrelated to regional or national ones. The book includes accounts of the experiences and results of ten years of water problem-solving through planning and intelligent action.

Boyle, Robert H.; Graves, John; and Watkins, Tom. THE WATER HUSTLERS. San Francisco: Sierra Club, 1971. 253 p.

> "[In the desert] . . . lacking the camel's hump but with profound ingenuity, [man] devised a manner of moving water from where it was to where it had never been before. Meanwhile, those who stayed behind in the lush rain-country were busy turning their streams and rivers into sewers. . . ." This quote by the editors of Sierra Club Books is found in the foreword of the book; it sets the tone for the pages which follow. Three areas of the country (Texas, New York, and California) in which water diversion has a long history are investigated. The authors report what has taken place and what the various water agencies are now planning. The indictment against the dam builders is unremitting. Court-ordered halts on further damming have sometimes been effective, and the courtrooms will continue to be a battleground for the foreseeable future. Other alternatives, notably for New York, are presented.

Hall, Leonard. STARS UPSTREAM: LIFE ALONG AN OZARK RIVER. Rev. ed. Columbia: University of Missouri Press, 1969. 266 p. Paperbound.

> The stars referred to in the title are those reflecting from the

Current River and its main tributary, Jacks Fork in the Missouri Ozarks. This river story was instrumental in creating in Missouri the first national scenic riverway in the U.S. National Park System. The author is a long-time resident of the area; he writes of the history, wildlife, geology, and man's use and abuse of the river from the perspective of uncountable trips in canoes and John-boats.

Heuvelmans, Martin. THE RIVER KILLERS. Harrisburg, Pa.: Stackpole Books, 1974. 224 p. Preface.

Heuvelmans places the heaviest blame for what he terms the national tragedy of the despoilment of America's watersheds on the Civil Works Branch of the U.S. Army Corps of Engineers. He describes the methodology of the corps in securing project approval and financing despite strong public opposition. Documents written by various officials and intellectuals of national prominence are provided to substantiate the author's thesis. The remedy he recommends is abolishment of the corps.

Hurley, William D. ENVIRONMENTAL LEGISLATION. Springfield, Ill.: Charles C Thomas, 1971. ix, 81 p. Preface.

The federal government's role in halting pollution and improving the environment is the subject of this book. Pollution laws exist but are little understood. Hurley provides a detailed explanation of major air and water pollution laws and their enforcement.

Kauffmann, John M. FLOW EAST: A LOOK AT OUR NORTH ATLANTIC RIVERS. American Wilderness Series, vol. 3. New York: McGraw-Hill Book Co., 1973. 284 p.

Kauffmann looks at rivers from the James to those in Maine with a conservationist's eye. He notes the ravages of pollution and urbanization and the efforts underway or planned for cleansing the streams and controlling urban encroachment along them.

Landau, Norman J., and Rheingold, Paul D. THE ENVIRONMENTAL LAW HANDBOOK. New York: Ballantine Books, 1971. 508 p. Paperbound.

Landau and Rheingold are lawyers who have a background in environmental law. This handbook shows lawyers and laypersons practical ways in which law may be used for environmental protection. The authors begin with the premise that today's major battle against pollution is being fought in the courtroom by means of the private lawsuit. Such suits may be brought against a private polluter or the government. The steps to be taken and the tools needed to take legal action are described, with examples from earlier cases.

Leydet, Francois. TIME AND THE RIVER FLOWING: GRAND CANYON.
Abr. ed. San Francisco: Sierra Club, 1968. 160 p. Paperbound.

"In a sense, this book is a continuation of THE PLACE NO ONE
KNEW, by Eliot Porter. Each book tells about the same extraordinary river and its greatest canyons, Glen and Grand, both
fully deserving national park protection. . . ." This quote is
from the foreword. The Sierra Club is interested in keeping the
issue of canyon preservation before the public. One way the
organization does this is by publishing inexpensive, yet beauti-
fully illustrated books about the canyons. The message of the
book is that of a reasoned plea to save the remaining canyons.
The color photographs alone may be the best testimony of their
beauty.

Littlejohn, Bruce M., and Pimplott, Douglas H. WHY WILDERNESS: A RE-
PORT ON MISMANAGEMENT IN LAKE SUPERIOR PROVINCIAL PARK. Toronto: New Press, 1971. 127 p. Paperbound.

The intent of this report is to alert Canadians to the continuing
threat to the wilderness character of Lake Superior Provincial
Park, and to methods to combat this threat.

Maass, Arthur. MUDDY WATERS: THE ARMY ENGINEERS AND THE NA-
TION'S RIVERS. Harvard Political Studies series. 1951. Reprint. New York:
Da Capo, 1974. 320 p. Preface.

The U.S. Army Corps of Engineers develops rivers for flood control, navigation, irrigation, and other allied purposes. Maass
evaluates this work against several criteria or standards of administrative responsibility. The book contains a statement of
the corps's planning methodology. An elaborate case history of
California's Kings River projects documents many of Maass's con-
clusions.

Morgan, Arthur E. DAMS AND OTHER DISASTERS: A CENTURY OF THE
ARMY CORPS OF ENGINEERS IN CIVIL WORKS. Boston: Porter Sargent,
1971. 445 p. Preface.

Morgan is a civil engineer who has spent a lifetime battling the
U.S. Army Corps of Engineers. His book represents an attempt
to show that the training of the corps is unsuited to civil engineering needs, and that there have been consistent and disas-
trous failures by the corps in public works areas. Finally, Morgan
argues that the corps has avoided or prevented objective evaluation of its projects and has sought to keep the public ignorant
of the quality and the cost-to-benefit data documenting its work.

Nash, Roderick, ed. GRAND CANYON OF THE LIVING COLORADO. San
Francisco: Sierra Club, 1970. 143 p. Paperbound.

Like Francois Leydet's TIME AND THE RIVER FLOWING (see above), this Sierra Club publication argues for a greater Grand Canyon National Park. The wildwater enthusiast should note the chapter on "The Boatman's Canyon." There are scores of color photographs by Ernest Braun. Contributors of articles include David Brower, Colin Fletcher, Allen J. Malmquist, Roderick Nash, and Stewart Udall.

National Water Commission. WATER POLICIES FOR THE FUTURE. Port Washington, N.Y.: Water Information Center, 1973. 606 p. Preface.

The National Water Commission was established by a 1968 act of Congress. This final report addresses the policies America should adopt to enable finite water resources to provide the highest measure of utility while preserving and improving quality. The report contains many recommendations for improvement of policies dealing with protection, development, and use of water resources.

Norton, Boyd. SNAKE WILDERNESS. San Francisco: Sierra Club, 1972. 159 p.

Idaho's Snake River watershed may have more pristine wilderness and more unpolluted rivers than any other region in the forty-eight contiguous states. The Sierra Club is vitally interested in keeping it that way. This book is a record of the area's conservation battles. It is intended as a weapon in the fight for wilderness preservation. A thirty-page descriptive guide to the Snake wilderness is included.

Porter, Eliot. THE PLACE NO ONE KNEW: GLEN CANYON ON THE COLORADO. Sierra Club Exhibit Format Series, no. 5. San Francisco: Sierra Club, 1963. 170 p.

On 21 January 1963, the gates closed on Glen Canyon Dam. The canyon began to fill. Eventually the Colorado backed up beyond the mouth of the Dirty Devil River. Today's river-runners have only books such as Porter's with its seventy-two evocative color plates, to see something of what Major John Wesley Powell and relatively few others were ever privileged to see.

Texas Parks and Wildlife Department. TEXAS WATERWAYS: A FEASIBILITY REPORT ON A SYSTEM OF WILD, SCENIC, AND RECREATIONAL WATERWAYS IN TEXAS. Austin, Tex.: 1973. 64 p. Paperbound.

This is a companion volume to the Texas Parks and Wildlife Department's AN ANALYSIS OF TEXAS WATERWAYS (see chapter 8). The purpose of this publication differs somewhat in that it seeks to identify only candidate rivers for inclusion in a statewide system of wild, scenic, and recreational waterways. The physical attributes of twenty-eight waterways are briefly described. Color photographs are included.

U.S. Department of the Interior. National Park Service. PROPOSED BUFFALO NATIONAL RIVER, ARKANSAS. Washington, D.C.: 1968. 25 p. Paperbound.

> After Congress introduced legislation in 1967 naming the Buffalo a national river, the National Park Service restudied the river and offered this report of its findings. The report supports the legislation and the need to preserve the river and its recreational attributes. It is heavily illustrated and has a fold-out map.

Zwick, David, and Benstock, Marcy. WATER WASTELAND: RALPH NADER'S STUDY GROUP REPORT ON WATER POLLUTION. New York: Grossman Publishers, 1971. 511 p. Preface.

> This book is the formal report of a task force which, for twenty-one months, studied the nation's water pollution and the efforts to combat it. Five parts of the book present the case against pollution: "The Danger," "Polluters and Protectors," "Politics, Action, and Inaction," "Law and Order," and "The New Federalism." Part 6 makes three recommendations: (1) structure the laws to make government less susceptible to special interests, (2) place more power in the hands of the people, and (3) strike at the sources of illegitimate private influence.

Chapter 7

PICTORIAL WORKS

Crampton, C. Gregory. STANDING UP COUNTRY: THE CANYONLANDS OF UTAH AND ARIZONA. New York: Alfred A. Knopf, 1964. 219 p. Preface.

> More than one hundred photographs, sixteen of which are in color, illustrate this history of the remote Four Corners region of the southwestern United States. Crampton calls the area "Sandstone Country" and traces its recorded history from 1776. He writes of the men who have passed through this labyrinth of canyons. The book grew out of historical field studies undertaken prior to the flooding of Glen Canyon. Salvage was restricted to the canyon, but Crampton's interest is in the entire region. The book is the first popular history of the total canyon country; it is now in its third printing.

Gulick, Bill. SNAKE RIVER COUNTRY. Caldwell, Idaho: Caxton Printers, 1971. 211 p.

> This is a large volume containing a scholarly history of the Snake River watershed. The book is almost evenly divided between historical narrative and color photographs by Earl Roberge.

Hogan, Elizabeth, ed. RIVERS OF THE WEST. Menlo Park, Calif.: Lane Publishing Co., 1974. 223 p.

> Hundreds of pictures, some in color, constitute the major feature of this book. Rivers flowing west from the Rockies are categorized into four great drainage areas: Columbia, Colorado, Pacific Coast, and Great Basin. The history, uses, and abuses of the individual rivers are briefly discussed; however, these generalized comments are clearly secondary to the comprehensive pictorial presentation.

Mays, Buddy. WILDWATERS: EXPLORING WILDERNESS WATERWAYS. San Francisco: Chronicle Books, 1977. 143 p. Paperbound.

This work is almost equally divided between Mays's prose and his photographs (black and white). The opening chapter surveys the development of America's waterways as avenues of travel and commerce; accompanying illustrations are contemporary to the time discussed. The succeeding chapters contain the observations noted and photographs taken during trips down the Colorado, Rogue, Salmon, and Rio Grande rivers, and within the Boundary Waters Canoe Area.

Norton, Boyd. RIVERS OF THE ROCKIES. Chicago: Rand McNally and Co., 1975. 160 p.

Norton is a wilderness photographer and former Idaho river guide. There are eighty color photographs of western rivers, many of which he has personally run. Some nineteenth-century photographs from the Denver Public Library's Western History Department and other sources are included. Toward the end of the book is a chapter entitled "River People," which profiles some of the individuals whose livelihoods depend on flowing rivers.

Powell, John Wesley. DOWN THE COLORADO: DIARY OF THE FIRST TRIP THROUGH THE GRAND CANYON, 1869. Foreword by Don D. Fowler. New York: E.P. Dutton and Co., 1969. 168 p.

Powell's epic first trip is retold through his diary, contemporary drawings, and photographs. Throughout the book are dozens of full-page, color photographs by Eliot Porter. The foreword places the diary and illustrations in historical perspective. Porter's epilogue compares flooded Glen Canyon with the Grand Canyon, and the river and river-runners with impoundments and motor-boaters.

Pringle, Laurence. WILD RIVER. Philadelphia: J.B. Lippincott Co., 1972. 128 p.

Through narrative and color photographs, the reader of this book is instructed in North American stream ecology. The book describes the eco-systems of unpolluted, undammed, free-flowing rivers for the lay naturalist and outdoor recreationist. Rivers protected by the National Wild and Scenic Rivers Act are listed. There is a strong presentation advocating preservation of the remaining wild rivers. The sixty-seven photographs are by the author.

Reber, James Q. POTOMAC PORTRAIT. New York: Liveright, 1974. 96 p.

Photographs (all black and white) of the Potomac and surroundings are presented in this appreciation of the river by a long time canoeist and kayakist. The photographs are of the Potomac Gorge section of the river, from Great Falls to Little Falls. Part 1

displays the falls in varying seasons and flows, while part 2
shows the two-mile downriver section known as Mather Gorge.

RIVERS OF NORTH AMERICA. Waukesha, Wis.: Country Beautiful, 1973.
208 p.

Fifty-nine rivers in the United States have been selected for inclusion in this book, which features seventy color plates and
many more in black and white. The rivers were chosen for their
historical and commercial significance and for their beauty. A
chapter on wilderness rivers briefly describes the streams covered
by the 1968 National Wild and Scenic Rivers Act.

Smith, Kenneth L. THE BUFFALO RIVER COUNTRY. 3d ed. Little Rock,
Ark.: Ozark Society, 1976. 176 p. Paperbound.

River guide, regional history, geological and archeological reference, fishing guide--this book attempts to be all things to the
paddler. The Buffalo River is covered, from its source to the
confluence at White River. Liberal use of photographs make a
forceful statement on this unspoiled wilderness river in America's
heartland.

Spears, Borden, ed. WILDERNESS CANADA. Toronto: Clarke, Irwin and Co.,
1970. ix, 174 p.

The color photographs contained in this book give evidence of
the range and beauty of Canada's wilderness, most of which is
accessible by canoe. Eight articles, one of which describes a
canoe voyage by Pierre Elliott Trudeau, accompany what is essentially a pictorial work.

SUPERIOR-QUETICO CANOE COUNTRY. Virginia, Minn.: W.A. Fisher Co.,
1959. 48 p. Paperbound.

This book is primarily one of photographs of the Boundary Waters
Canoe Area. However, information is included on history, wildlife, canoe camping, and voyage starting points. A fold-out
historical map features the voyageur's highway of the fur-trade
era.

Watkins, Tom H. THE GRAND COLORADO: THE STORY OF A RIVER AND
ITS CANYONS. Palo Alto, Calif.: American West Publishing Co., 1969.
310 p.

The canyonlands of the Colorado River have seen 4,000 years of
human history. Nine contributing authors trace this panorama in
a work bringing together early photographs, documents, maps,
paintings, and the color photographs of Philip Hyde.

Chapter 8

WATERWAYS GUIDEBOOKS

Appalachian Mountain Club. THE A.M.C. NEW ENGLAND CANOEING GUIDE. 3rd ed. Boston: 1971. 619 p.

> This guide was developed from material in the 1935 publication, QUICK WATER AND SMOOTH (Brattleboro, Vt.: Stephen Daye Press), by John C. Phillips and Thomas D. Cabot. Arrangement of the rivers is by watershed. Each chapter begins with the major river of the watershed. Tributaries, if any, are listed next. Lakes are described as part of a stream or watershed. Coastal rivers are arranged by area. A total of sixteen watersheds and coastal areas are presented. The information includes appropriate topographic map order numbers, access, length of stream segments, carries, hazards, stream flow, and occasional reference to local history and legend. Despite its 600 pages, the book still fits into an average pocket. Three removable maps are provided. A new, two-volume edition in preparation, THE A.M.C. RIVER GUIDE, will supersede this guidebook (see above). However, the current edition will continue to be sold until both volumes of the new guidebook are in print. Volume 1 will cover northeastern New England, and volume 2, the watersheds of the central and southern parts of the region.

_____. A.M.C. RIVER GUIDE. Vol. 1, NORTHEASTERN NEW ENGLAND. Boston: 1976. 186 p. Preface.

> This guide supersedes the Appalachian Mountain Club's NEW ENGLAND CANOEING GUIDE (see below). It is a completely new book, not a revised edition. While the scope of the new guide remains almost the same, all materials have been reviewed, and reflect changes which have taken place since 1971. Tidewater descriptions are no longer given. Included are interpretive materials on the watersheds, maps, charts, and photographs. Volume 2 is being prepared and will cover watersheds in central and southern New England. The Appalachian Mountain Club has announced that neither volume 1 nor 2 will be offered for sale until both are in print.

Aquardo, Chip. CANOEING THE BRANDYWINE: A NATURALIST'S GUIDE.
Chadds Ford, Pa.: Tri-County Conservancy of the Brandywine, 1973. 61 p.
Paperbound.

>   As suggested by the subtitle, this is more a guide to the regional
>   flora and fauna than a river guidebook; however, one is given
>   basic information for Brandywine trip planning. Possible runs are
>   suggested as are canoe rental agencies and river access points.
>   Sketch maps are provided.

Arighi, Scott, and Arighi, Margaret S. WILDWATER TOURING: TECHNIQUES
AND TOURS. New York: Macmillan Co., 1974. 352 p. Preface.

>   The book was written to answer questions about the unique prob-
>   lems presented by touring on rapids-filled rivers. The authors are
>   also concerned with promoting river touring as a means of dem-
>   onstrating that our remaining free-flowing rivers are a recreational
>   resource to be treasured. The book is arranged in three parts.
>   The first section instructs in the art of tour planning and prepara-
>   tion. It is divided into chapters on evaluating river difficulty;
>   choosing cotourers, river craft, and accessories; and selecting food
>   and equipment. In part 2, one finds information on running the
>   river and camping. Part 3 is a guide to nine trips on six north-
>   western U.S. rivers: the Rogue, Grande Ronde, John Day, Main
>   and Middle Fork Salmon, and the Owyhee. The trip descriptions
>   give information on recommended boat type, rating rapids, gra-
>   dient, best season, and trip length. This information is followed
>   by a general discussion of the trip and a mile-by-mile log. Sketch
>   maps are included.

Batchelor, Bruce T. YUKON CHANNEL CHARTS: STERNWHEELER-STYLE
STRIP MAPS OF THE HISTORIC YUKON RIVER. Whitehorse, Yukon Territory,
Canada: Star Printing Co., 1975. 55 p. Paperbound.

>   With the cooperation of the Yukon Territorial government, the
>   author has reproduced sixty-four strip maps in the style of the
>   old river-pilot charts. The Klondike run, 460 miles from White-
>   horse to Dawson, is the section of the river which has been
>   mapped. Aerial photographs and recent surveys were used to
>   chart the river to scale. Channels, bars, and islands are pre-
>   sented as they were at the end of the 1974 season. Included
>   with the maps are stories and photographs of the river and the
>   people living nearby. Interspersed throughout are advertisements
>   for canoes, snowmobiles, and a variety of visitor services.

Belknap, Bill, and Belknap, Buzz. CANYONLANDS RIVER GUIDE. Boulder
City, Nev.: Westwater Books, 1974. 63 p. Paperbound.

>   The canyonlands referred to in the title are those in southeastern
>   Utah through which the Colorado and Green rivers flow. The
>   guidebook is a series of strip maps, including topographical de-

tail based on maps produced by the U.S. Geological Survey.
The guide is divided into sections on the smooth water of Lake
Powell, the lower Green, the Colorado from Moab to the confluence and the sixty-two miles from Westwater to Moab, and
Cataract Canyon. Parallel to the maps, information on mileage,
rapids, and elevation is given. Throughout the guide are photographs and historical information. The book is also available in
a waterproof edition.

Belknap, Buzz. GRAND CANYON RIVER GUIDE. Boulder City, Nev.: Westwater Books, 1969. 47 p. Paperbound.

This guide covers the section of the Colorado River lying within
the Grand Canyon, from Lees Ferry to Lake Mead, and is composed of a series of strip maps. The maps are made to the scale
of 1-to-40,000 miles and are based on those drawn by the U.S.
Geological Survey in 1924 and 1962. Adjacent to the maps are
the mileage from Lees Ferry; names of major rapids with ratings
on the one to ten scale; river elevation; timely photographs of
people, places, and things; and, often, a quote about the river
and its surroundings by John Wesley Powell. The guide is also
available in a waterproof edition.

Benner, Bob. CAROLINA WHITEWATER: A CANOEIST'S GUIDE TO WESTERN
NORTH CAROLINA. 2d ed. Morganton, N.C.: Western Piedmont Community
College, 1976. Distributed by Morganton, N.C.: Pisgah Providers. x, 164 p.
Spiralbound.

This guide is intended for the open-canoe paddler; much of the
water described is suitable for the novice. The river-guide portion of the book is divided into five sections, four of which describe rivers in neighboring counties of North Carolina; the fifth
covers rivers outside of this area. A total of fifty-four streams
are included. Typical information on a stream includes a general
description, location and access, gauge location, and an estimate
of the difficulties. The table for each stream gives drop, difficulty rating, distance, time, scenery, and water quality. Other
information includes advice about winter canoeing, safety, and
the legal rights of canoeists.

A BOATER'S GUIDE TO THE UPPER YUKON RIVER. Rev. ed. Anchorage:
Alaska Northwest Publishing Co., 1976. ix, 78 p. Paperbound.

Those wishing to discover the rich history of the Yukon, either
through reading or making the actual river trip, are the intended
audience for this book. The run downriver is described in five
sections in the guidebook: Bennett Lake to Whitehorse (with a
Teslin River side trip), Whitehorse to Carmacks, Carmacks to Dawson City (with a Pelly River side trip), Dawson City to Fort Yukon,
and beyond Fort Yukon. Sketch maps are included.

Boy Scouts of America. Order of the Arrow Colonneh Lodge. "Camping and Canoeing Guidebook." Houston, Tex.: 1971. vi, 299 p. Preface. Mimeographed.

> This guidebook has two distinct sections, the second of which has the greatest application to wilderness waterways as it presents forty-six trips on ten Texas streams. The concentration is on waterways in southeastern Texas; however, this is being expanded to include many rivers outside this region in a second edition currently in preparation. Map information for the listed trips includes the name of the appropriate U.S. Geological Survey topographic map and county map. Sketch maps are included as an aid to general location and planning. On these maps, river mileage is recorded which roughly corresponds with the mile-by-mile description of the run given on facing pages. The Neches, Angelina, Trinity, Brazos, Colorado, Guadalupe, Rio Grande, and Pecos rivers, Village Creek, and Armand's Bayou are the waterways covered in the guide.

Burdge, Ray E. "Floating, Fishing and Historical Guide to Yellowstone State Waterway." Billings, Mont.: By the author, n.d. 55 p. Mimeographed.

> This guidebook gives information on the section of Montana's Yellowstone River between Gardiner and the mouth of the Big Horn River. There are twenty-six strip maps presenting fair detail, including mileage, road access, and river obstacles. Opposite the maps, textual information describes historical points of interest along the way.

Burmeister, Walter F. THE CONNECTICUT RIVER AND ITS TRIBUTARIES. Appalachian Waters, no. 6. Oakton, Va.: Appalachian Books, forthcoming.

_____. THE DELAWARE AND ITS TRIBUTARIES. Appalachian Waters, no. 1. Oakton, Va.: Appalachian Books, 1974. vii, 274 p. Paperbound.

> This is the first in a series of ten guidebooks (see all the citations for Burmeister, Walter F.). Each volume deals with a river system or grouping of river systems. The term "Appalachian" is one of convenience, as the guidebooks incorporate waterways from Maine to Florida. The first four books in the series have been published, and the remaining six are either in preparation or in press. The author admits a bias toward the kayakist and decked canoeist. However, all streams have been rated using the International Scale of Difficulty, and there is an ample range of water for the open canoeist within Class 1 or 2. Burmeister sees his series as not only serving the paddler but also the secondary reference needs of hiker, bicyclist, motorist, and naturalist. Information on individual waterways is standard throughout the series and includes tabular data on distances between selected points, drop in feet, time in hours, degree of difficulty,

scenery rating, water levels, river width, and U.S. Geological
Survey map name. Detailed explanations are given under paragraphs headed: "Danger Points," "Water Conditions," and "Com-
mentary." Also common to the series is introductory material on
the total river system, and a removable map of that system. The
map is of a scale that is little help in practical trip planning.
This first guide, to the Delaware drainage, contains information
on forty-six streams in New York, Pennsylvania, New Jersey,
and Delaware.

_____. THE HUDSON RIVER AND ITS TRIBUTARIES. Appalachian Waters,
no. 2. Oakton, Va.: Appalachian Books, 1974. viii, 488 p. Paperbound.

This guidebook contains information on ninety-five Hudson River
System streams in New York, New Jersey, Vermont, Massachusetts, and Connecticut. See the annotation under Burmeister,
Walter F., THE DELAWARE AND ITS TRIBUTARIES above, for a
general description of the full Appalachian Waters series.

_____. THE LOWER OHIO, TENNESSEE, AND CUMBERLAND AND THEIR
TRIBUTARIES. Appalachian Waters, no. 7. Oakton, Va.: Appalachian Books,
forthcoming.

_____. MAINE AND NEW HAMPSHIRE RIVERS. Appalachian Waters, no. 10.
Oakton, Va.: Appalachian Books, forthcoming.

_____. THE POTOMAC RIVER AND ITS TRIBUTARIES. Appalachian Waters,
no. 8. Oakton, Va.: Appalachian Books, forthcoming.

_____. THE SOUTHEASTERN U.S. RIVERS. Appalachian Waters, no. 4.
Oakton, Va.: Appalachian Books, 1976. viii, 850 p. Paperbound.

This guide contains information on 228 streams in fourteen separate
drainage basins in Virginia, North Carolina, South Carolina,
Georgia, and Florida. See the annotation under Burmeister,
Walter F., THE DELAWARE AND ITS TRIBUTARIES above, for
a general description of the full Appalachian Waters series.

_____. THE SUSQUEHANNA RIVER AND ITS TRIBUTARIES. Appalachian
Waters, no. 3. Oakton, Va.: Appalachian Books, 1975. viii, 600 p. Paperbound.

The Susquehanna guide contains information on 182 streams in
Pennsylvania, New York, and Maryland. See the annotation
under Burmeister, Walter F., THE DELAWARE AND ITS TRIBU-
TARIES, above, for a general description of the full Appalachian
Waters series.

Waterways Guidebooks

_____. THE UPPER OHIO RIVER BASIN. Appalachian Waters, no. 5. Oakton, Va.: Appalachian Books, forthcoming.

_____. WESTERN AND CENTRAL NEW ENGLAND RIVERS. Appalachian Waters, no. 9. Oakton, Va.: Appalachian Books, forthcoming.

Burrell, Bob, and Davidson, Paul. WILDWATER WEST VIRGINIA: A PADDLER'S GUIDE TO THE WHITEWATER RIVERS OF THE MOUNTAIN STATE. 2d ed. Parsons, W.Va.: McClain Printing Co., 1975. 160 p. Preface. Paperbound.

> This second edition of the guidebook contains the latest information on three out-of-state rivers--the Youghiogheny, Savage, and Casselman--plus the more than seventy other whitewater streams within West Virginia. Although the guide is a collective effort of members of the West Virginia Wildwater Association, the authors have themselves paddled more than 2,000 river miles since the first edition was published in 1972. This has resulted in the addition of new runs and the occasional reevaluation of runs described previously. The stated intention of the book is to introduce the intermediate paddler to some different whitewater. In addition to a general discussion of the river, history, and surroundings, specific paddling data include international difficulty classification, trip time estimate, difficulties, gauge location, shuttle information, and the appropriate quadrangle name for U.S. Geological Survey maps.

CANOEING THE WILD RIVERS OF NORTHWESTERN WISCONSIN. 1969. Reprint. Eau Claire: Wisconsin Indian Head Country, 1977. Paperbound.

> This is a waterproof guidebook with maps and descriptions of the Brule, Eau Claire, Totogatic, Namekagon, St. Croix, Yellow, and Clam rivers. The descriptive portion provides information on the history of the locale, campsites, fishing, wildlife, rapids, and access roads.

Canoe Sport British Columbia. BRITISH COLUMBIA CANOE ROUTES: A GUIDE TO NINETY-TWO CANOE TRIPS IN BEAUTIFUL BRITISH COLUMBIA. Rev. ed. New Westminster, British Columbia: Nunaga Publishing Co., 1974. 111 p. Paperbound.

> Since publication of the first edition of this guide in 1971, much information has been updated, expanded, and through several subsequent editions, refined into its present form. Yet another revision is in progress, with publication scheduled for 1977. The ninety-two trips suggested are organized into geographical regions. The majority of the trips are in southwestern provincial waters. A typical trip report includes information on name, location, International River Classification, length, river width, time required, camping facilities, National Topographic System map, access, and one or more paragraphs of description. There are

infrequent maps and sketches of specific rapids. The recommended trips are intended for all classes of paddlers in all kinds of paddle craft.

CANOE TRAILS OF NORTH-CENTRAL WISCONSIN. Madison: Wisconsin Tales and Trails, 1973. 64 p. Paperbound.

Wisconsin river guides and canoeing enthusiasts collected and wrote the material in this guidebook. Drafting and editing was done by the U.S. Soil Conservation Service through the Headwaters Pri-Ru-Ta Resource Conservation and Development Project. River runs that have been mapped include the Chippewa, Flambeau, Couderay, Jump, Turtle, Manitowish, Yellow, Thornapple, Deertail, and Main. Thirty-nine strip maps show hazards, rapids (rated on a scale of one to four) access, landmarks, and campsites. A narrative describing the river parallels each map.

CANOE TRAILS OF NORTHEASTERN WISCONSIN. Madison: Wisconsin Tales and Trails, 1972. 72 p. Paperbound.

This guidebook offers descriptions (including fishing and history), maps, rapids location (with ratings), access, mileage, and campsites for sixty-nine trips on sixteen rivers: the Brule, Deerskin, Embarrass, Manitowish, Menominee, Oconto, Pelican, Peshtigo, Pike, Pine, Popple, Prairie, Spirit, Tomahawk, Wisconsin, and Wolf.

Carter, Randy. CANOEING WHITEWATER RIVER GUIDE. 8th ed. Oakton, Va.: Appalachian Books, 1974. viii, 267 p. Preface. Paperbound.

The purpose of the guide is to give the canoeist an idea of what to expect from ninety-five whitewater rivers in Virginia, eastern West Virginia, North Carolina, and the Great Smoky Mountains area. Specific trip data include a table listing average gradient, difficulty, distance, time, scenery, depth, and width. More detailed information follows under the headings: "favorable winds," "maps," "type of river," "water conditions," "danger points," "marker stations," "fish," and "description." The book is written for the canoeist, but it will also apply to the kayakist when water height increases a foot or more. Sketch maps of varying scale and quality are provided. There is also a section on general canoeing, camping, and fishing information.

Cawley, James S., and Cawley, Margaret. EXPLORING THE LITTLE RIVERS OF NEW JERSEY. 3d ed. New Brunswick, N.J.: Rutgers University Press, 1971. xi, 251 p. Preface.

The Cawleys, lifelong canoeists, cruised the entire length of the seventeen streams described in this guidebook. The present edition features all new photographs. In addition to river descriptions and sketch maps, the folklore, history, canoe liveries, camping areas, and natural histories of the surroundings are presented. The authors show that, while New Jersey may be ribbed by freeways and bracketed by Philadelphia and New York, peaceful waterways still exist.

Center, Robert M., ed. INTERPRETIVE GUIDE OF THE AMERICAN, STANISLAUS, AND TUOLUMNE RIVERS. Oakland, Calif.: American River Touring Association, 1975. iv, 85 p. Preface. Paperbound.

The purpose of this guide is to provide a single source of interpretive information for the three rivers of the title. By and for boatmen and women it is a guide which does not concentrate on the rivers as much as on their surroundings and the past and present inhabitants of these surroundings. There are sketch maps for each river which show side canyons and access points. Mile-by-mile river logs are given only for the Stanislaus and Tuolumne. Chapters are devoted to the geology, caves, plants, animals, Indians, and prospectors of the region.

Clark, Fogle C. BUFFALO NATIONAL RIVER GUIDE. University, Miss.: Recreational Publications, 1976. Map.

This guide is a detailed, 24 x 36 inch, colored topographic map with river notes--for practical descriptive purposes, a river guidebook in a sheet-map format. While the map is not waterproof, it is printed on heavy stock and folds to a convenient 6 x 8 inches. The runnable 130 miles of the river are described--from Boxley Bridge to Buffalo City. Information given in the notes includes distance, gradient, gauge location, and minimum practical water level. A narrative section describing river conditions and other more general information is presented next to the appropriate mileage indication. Sections on camping, paddling technique, and river reading have been included. Other brief notes are given on fishing, water level and quality, archaeology, history, caves, canoe rentals, and trip suggestions.

_____. OZARK SCENIC RIVERWAYS GUIDE. University, Miss.: Recreational Publications, 1977. Map.

Two maps, on both sides of a 24 x 36 inch sheet, show Missouri's Current, Jacks Fork, and Eleven Point rivers. This guide is similar in format to BUFFALO NATIONAL RIVER GUIDE (see above). The maps show access, distance, gradient, topography, springs, caves, and campgrounds. The accompanying notes detail points of interest, hazards, major springs, caves, canoe liveries, history, water level, fishing, and more.

Colwell, Robert. INTRODUCTION TO WATER TRAILS IN AMERICA. Harrisburg, Pa.: Stackpole Books, 1973. 221 p. Paperbound.

This guide lists water trails located within a three-hour drive of 125 major cities, plus some others somewhat more distant. The author has systematized waterways information into categories of difficulty, season, location, access, transportation services, canoe rentals, accommodations, medical assistance, fishing, recreation, and sources for further information. Some of the suggested trips are described in a subsequent outline. Sketch maps accompany a majority of the descriptions.

Connecticut River Watershed Council. THE CONNECTICUT RIVER GUIDE. Rev. ed. Easthampton, Mass.: 1971. 87 p. Paperbound.

Boating enthusiasts operating every type of craft use the Connecticut River and its tributaries. The scope of this guide is broad because of this; it attempts to include a wide boating readership. There are chapters on river use by kayak, canoe, motorboat, sailboat, and yacht. Competent canoeists have been responsible for compiling the canoe information portion of the guide. The river is described in logical segments, from its source at the New Hampshire-Canada border to mile zero at Saybrook Breakwater light. Separate chapters provide information on applicable U.S. Geological Survey maps, campsites, access points, fishing, and nature study. Another chapter describes some of the whitewater tributaries of the Connecticut: White River, West River, Millers River, Westfield River, and Salmon River. Three removable maps, and the guidebook itself, are printed on high-strength paper and fit inside a waterproof plastic envelope.

Corbett, H. Roger, Jr. BLUE RIDGE VOYAGES: ONE AND TWO DAY RIVER CRUISES; MARYLAND, VIRGINIA, WEST VIRGINIA. Blue Ridge Voyages, vol. 2. 2d ed. Oakton, Va.: Appalachian Books, 1972. iv, 84 p. Preface. Paperbound.

This is a continuation of number 1 of the Blue Ridge Voyages series (see below); the format and type of information are essentially the same. This volume lists ten additional trips within acceptable driving distance of Washington, D.C. There is an emphasis on the Smoke Hole region of West Virginia. The trips cited are along the Potomac and its south branch, Cedar Creek, Catoctin Creek, Cacapon River, Monocacy River, and Antietam River. Two walking trips are suggested for those canoeing in the Smoke Hole region.

_____. ONE DAY CRUISES IN VIRGINIA AND WEST VIRGINIA. Blue Ridge Voyages, vol. 3. Dunn Loring, Va.: Louis J. Matacia, 1972. vi, 116 p. Preface. Paperbound.

Ten day trips for beginning and intermediate canoeists are presented in this guide. Eight trips are in Virginia, two in West Virginia. All trips are within a three-hour drive of Washington,

D.C. The Virginia trips are along the Hughes, Shenandoah, Rappahannock, North and South Anna rivers, and Passage and Goose creeks. West Virginia trips are along the Upper Lost River and Sleepy Creek. Maps and detailed descriptions are given for each trip. Rapids are indicated on the maps, and other points of caution are conveyed in the text.

Corbett, H. Roger, Jr., and Matacia, Louis J., Jr. BLUE RIDGE VOYAGES: ONE AND TWO DAY RIVER CRUISES; MARYLAND, VIRGINIA, WEST VIR-GINIA. Blue Ridge Voyages, vol. 1. 3d ed. Oakton, Va.: Appalachian Books, 1972. v, 75 p. Paperbound.

Ten trips are presented in this guidebook. All are within a 150-mile drive of Washington, D.C. Sketch maps are provided for each trip. Some of these maps are drawn to a scale somewhat difficult to read; however, the appropriate topographic quadrangle map name is given for ease in ordering from the U.S. Geological Survey. Recommended trip dates are given based on stream flow. Streams included are the Rappahannock, Antietam, Thornton, Potomac, Shenandoah, and Cedar. (See also Corbett, above.)

Council, Clyde C. SUWANNEE COUNTRY: A CANOEING, BOATING, AND RECREATIONAL GUIDE TO FLORIDA'S IMMORTAL SUWANNEE RIVER. Sara-sota, Fla.: Council Co., 1976. 60 p. Paperbound.

The Suwannee River rises in the Okefenokee Swamp and meanders 220 miles through Georgia and Florida to the Gulf of Mexico. The author writes that he has included all the information he "can find or remember" about the river. This information is a product of canoe trips, aircraft over-flight, and other research. Strip maps form the core of the guide. Along the sides of the maps are positioned scores of photographs interspersed with in-formational paragraphs on local history and canoe camping sug-gestions. The maps show mileage, access, camp and picnic sites, and the locations of the many large, stream-side springs.

DeHart, Don, and DeHart, Vangie. A GUIDE OF THE YUKON RIVER. Chey-enne, Wyo.: Cheyenne Litho, 1971. 47 p. Paperbound.

Seventy strip maps present 1,160 miles of the river, from White-horse to Tanana. An opening caveat, dated 25 February 1976, cautions the reader on the inaccuracy of the maps due to con-stant shifting of sand and gravel bars. The authors have tried to preserve the flavor of the 1898 gold-rush charts by including cabins, buildings, and other early sites of human habitation.

Denis, Keith. CANOE TRAILS THROUGH QUETICO. Quetico Foundation Series, no. 3. Toronto: Quetico Foundation, 1959. Distributed by Toronto: University of Toronto Press. ix, 84 p. Paperbound.

Fifteen routes are described in this guidebook. The descriptions vary from one paragraph to several pages in length. Trip time and distance by both water and portage are given in every instance. The most suitable trips for beginners are presented in detail, with portages and campsites pinpointed. The history of the region and the quality of the fishing receive occasional mention. A separate, large map with a scale of two miles to the inch shows all routes. Typical equipment and food for a Quetico trip are recommended in an introductory chapter.

Duncanson, Michael E. A CANOEING GUIDE TO THE INDIAN HEAD RIVERS OF WEST CENTRAL WISCONSIN. Virginia, Minn.: W.A. Fisher Co., 1976. 61 p. Paperbound.

The physical features for the fifty river maps in this guide were taken from U.S. Geological Survey topographic maps. The maps were drawn with the canoeist in mind, with "downstream" always at the top of the page. Access, campsites, rapids, points of interest, and mileage are shown. An index map guides the reader to the page presenting a particular segment of the river. A descriptive text accompanies each segment; the descriptions briefly mention the history of the area. Rapids are rated on a one-to-four scale. The more difficult rapids are enlarged on the map by means of an inset. Points of interest and access location comments are the result of the author's personal observations. The rivers, or parts of rivers, included are the Chippewa, Eau Claire, Red Cedar, Hay, Chetek, Buffalo, Trempealeau, Black, St. Croix, and Mississippi.

_____. CANOE TRAILS OF SOUTHERN WISCONSIN. Madison: Wisconsin Tales and Trails, 1974. i, 64 p. Paperbound.

This guide is intended to facilitate the selection of a route for a day's canoe outing or a week's journey. The author, a freelance cartographer, prepared the maps from U.S. Geological Survey topographic maps as well as on-the-river observation. Water areas are shown in blue. Access, camping, obstacles, mileage, and points of interest are indicated. Rapids are rated on a scale of one to four, based on average water levels. The descriptions accompanying the maps give information on fishing, scenery, and history. There are additional general observations about each route.

_____. A PADDLER'S GUIDE TO THE BOUNDARY WATERS CANOE AREA. Virginia, Minn.: W.A. Fisher Co., 1976. 76 p. Paperbound.

Duncanson has provided detailed maps of thirty-one wilderness canoe routes in the Superior National Forest of the Boundary Waters Canoe Area. Descriptions of each trip accompany the maps. The guidebook lists the regulations governing the area as well as

information on regional history and geography. Other information is given on portage lengths and campsites. The work is
illustrated with photographs.

Dwyer, Ann. CANOEING WATERS OF CALIFORNIA. Kentfield, Calif.:
GBH Press, 1973. 95 p. Preface. Paperbound.

The Merced, Kings, Kern, and lower Colorado rivers, thirty-
eight lakes, and several tidewater possibilities are southern canoe-
trip additions to the author's original work on northern California
canoeing waters. The new information should be welcome to
those who have had difficulty finding material on southern waters.
A typical trip description includes a sketch map and brief information on the best season, shuttle time, and necessary paddling
skill. A subsequent paragraph presents an overview of the run.
An evaluation of the favorable and unfavorable qualities of each
trip are also included. (Bear are listed under both categories.)

Esslen, Rainer. BACK TO NATURE IN CANOES: A GUIDE TO AMERICAN
WATERS. Frenchtown, N.J.: Columbia Publishing Co., 1976. 345 p.
Paperbound.

This is a comprehensive guidebook naming flat-water paddling
possibilities throughout the United States. There are, of course,
many regional and single-trip guidebooks, but these are sometimes difficult to verify and locate. Esslen has gathered into
one reference work an enormous amount of information on a multitude of waterways. Of necessity, the information is brief, but
most of the essential data are given, including name, location,
access, trip length, and rental locations. At the end of each
state or regional chapter, sources for detailed trip planning information are cited.

Evans, Laura, and Belknap, Buzz. DESOLATION RIVER GUIDE. Boulder City,
Nev.: Westwater Books, 1974. 56 p. Paperbound.

The two hundred miles of the Green River, from Split Mountain
Canyon to the town of Green River, Utah, are covered in this
guide. Desolation Canyon is somewhat past midpoint on the
downriver journey. Strip maps, drawn to scale from U.S. Geological Survey sources by Belknap, are the heart of the guide.
The maps are divided into four groups: Uinta Basin, north; Uinta
Basin, south; Desolation Canyon; and Gray Canyon. Material
appearing parallel to the maps includes mileage from Green
River, names of rapids, and photographs and information appropriate to that particular section of the river. The guide is also
available in a waterproof edition.

_____. DINOSAUR RIVER GUIDE. Boulder City, Nev.: Westwater Books,
1973. 64 p. Paperbound.

The Yampa and Green, as they flow through Dinosaur National Monument and Flaming Gorge National Recreation Area, are the subject rivers of this guide. The guidebook is a series of strip maps drawn to scale by Belknap from various maps of the Geological Survey and U.S. Forest Service. The first map is of Flaming Gorge Reservoir, and shows campgrounds, distances, and access roads. Succeeding maps show the rivers by section: Red Canyon, Browns Park, Canyon of Lodore, Whirlpool Canyon, Split Mountain Canyon, and the lower Yampa River. Material on and adjacent to the maps includes elevation and topographic detail, rapids, mileage, photographs, and condensed quotations from Major John Wesley Powell's 1875 report, entitled EXPLORA-TION OF THE COLORADO RIVER OF THE WEST AND ITS TRI-BUTARIES (see chapter 5). The guide is available in a water-proof edition.

Farmington River Watershed Association. THE FARMINGTON RIVER AND WATERSHED GUIDE. Avon, Conn.: 1970. iii, 60 p. Preface. Paperbound.

This guidebook is almost evenly divided into descriptions of nine canoe runs and other information on the area included in the watershed--fishing, wildlife, geology, and ornithology. Access, mileage, approximate trip times, portages, and rapids ratings (international scale) are given for each run. Hazards are em-phasized. A protective, heavy-plastic book pouch is provided.

Fédération Québécoise de Canot-Kayak. GUIDE DES RIVIÈRES DU QUEBÉC. Montreal: Messageries du Jour, 1973. 228 p. Preface. Paperbound.

This is a comprehensive guide to paddling Quebec's rivers. An English translation is in preparation. The province is divided into ten hydrographic regions; the guide is arranged to correspond to these regions. At the beginning of each section are a map and list of rivers in the region; descriptions of the individual river trips follow. A typical river description contains informa-tion on location and access, difficulty on the international scale, portages, campsites, topographic map names, and confluence with other streams. Additional information on canoe camping, food, equipment, and sources of local information for trip planning is given.

Foshee, John H. ALABAMA CANOE RIDES AND FLOAT TRIPS. Huntsville, Ala.: Strode Publishers, 1975. 263 p. Paperbound.

This guide contains maps and descriptions of fifty-two day trips on twenty-five of Alabama's smaller rivers. Fifteen other streams which the author has never paddled are briefly described in the appendix. There is a section presenting information on clothing, equipment, and safety.

Furrer, Werner. KAYAK AND CANOE TRIPS IN WASHINGTON. Lynnwood, Wash.: Signpost Publications, 1971. 32 p. Preface. Paperbound.

This booklet is a companion guide to the author's subsequent volume, WATER TRAILS OF WASHINGTON (see below). Both booklets have similar contents and format. This guide describes fifteen trips on lakes and rivers requiring intermediate paddling skills.

_____. WATER TRAILS OF WASHINGTON. Lynnwood, Wash.: Signpost Publications, 1973. 31 p. Preface. Paperbound.

Nineteen day trips are chosen for inclusion in this guide intended for the beginning paddler. Sketch maps are provided. Sufficient detail is given for adequate trip preparation, including road access, distance, international difficulty rating, average gradient, and name of the corresponding U.S. Geological Survey topographic map.

Gabler, Ray. NEW ENGLAND WHITE WATER RIVER GUIDE. New Canaan, Conn.: Tobey Publishing Co., 1975. iv, 236 p. Preface. Paperbound.

Sixty-two whitewater trips in Connecticut, Maine, Massachusetts, New Hampshire, New York, and Vermont are described in this guide. Descriptions are detailed and include distance, average and maximum drop, difficulty, scenery, stream flow, gauge location, shuttle mileage, access, and a sketch map. Practicing safety in heavy water is stressed throughout.

Garren, John. OREGON RIVER TOURS. Portland, Oreg.: Binford and Mort, 1974. ix, 120 p. Paperbound.

This guidebook may be regarded as one of the limited number of its genre worthy of emulation. It features thirteen tours on eleven rivers. Some of the river descriptions first appeared in 1973 as articles in NORTHWEST MAGAZINE. Trips described are along the Clackamas, upper and lower Deschutes, Grande Ronde, John Day, McKenzie, North and South Santiam, Owyhee, Rogue, Sandy, Snake, and Umpqua rivers. Garren has chosen to rate rapids as either major or minor, with international Class 3 and above being major; however, the trip logs are so precise that this uncommon rating method may not be a disadvantage. Estimated time between selected rapids is given as well as an equation to calculate relative drift time in raft, drift boat, canoe, or kayak. Maps are drawn to scale and show access, mileage, camping, reference points, and roads. The narrative segments of the individual tour descriptions are extensive.

Grinnell, Lawrence I. CANOEABLE WATERS OF NEW YORK STATE AND VICINITY. New York: Pageant Press, 1956. viii, 349 p.

Grinnell's book is dated, but it does have the advantage of presenting a great amount of information in one comprehensive volume. Most of the data is in tabular form. Although the more isolated waterways change slowly, it may be advisable (being mindful of the ubiquitous dam builder) to consult Grinnell first and then to follow with a look into a more recent guide covering a specific portion of the state.

Hamblin, W. Kenneth, and Rigby, J. Keith. GUIDEBOOK TO THE COLO-RADO RIVER, PART 1: LEES FERRY TO PHANTOM RANCH IN GRAND CAN-YON NATIONAL PARK. Brigham Young University Geology Studies, Studies for Students, no. 4. 2d ed. Provo, Utah: Brigham Young University, Department of Geology, 1969. 84 p. Preface. Paperbound.

This guidebook was written as a result of several years' experience taking geology students down the Colorado River. Anyone wishing to understand canyon geology may find the book useful. It is written in a manner allowing for a self-conducted trip. Aerial photographs have been used in place of maps. The names of side canyons and other land forms are superimposed on the photographs as is the mileage downstream from Lees Ferry. Descriptions of geologic formations are shown in river-log fashion. Further information explains how the rocks respond to erosion and describes the environment in which the rocks are accumulated. This guide is the first in a geological series on the rivers of the Colorado Plateau along which boat trips are feasible. To date, three guides have been published. They cover the middle and lower Colorado from Moab to Lake Mead. Part 2 is cited below; part 3 is cited in this section, under Rigby, J. Keith.

_____. GUIDEBOOK TO THE COLORADO RIVER, PART 2: PHANTOM RANCH IN GRAND CANYON NATIONAL PARK TO LAKE MEAD, ARIZONA-NEVADA. Brigham Young University Geology Studies, Studies for Students, no. 5. Provo, Utah: Brigham Young University, Department of Geology, 1969. ii, 126 p. Preface. Paperbound.

This guide is the second in a geological series on the rivers of the Colorado Plateau along which boat trips are feasible. It continues part 1 and completes the geological description of the Grand Canyon. For a general description of the contents, see the annotation above. To date, three guides have been published; part 3 is cited in this section under Rigby, J. Keith.

Harris, Thomas. DOWN THE WILD RIVERS: A GUIDE TO THE STREAMS OF CALIFORNIA. 2d ed. San Francisco: Chronicle Books, 1973. 223 p. Paperbound.

This is a California river guide intended for the family recreational paddler. The rivers most suited to the abilities of the

family paddler have the most exhaustive descriptions. The Kla-
math, Trinity, and Eel are described almost in their entirety,
and have been placed first in the book. Following these rivers
are trip descriptions for Sierra Nevada rivers and Sacramento
Valley and coastal rivers--twenty-two in all. Since this is a
selective guidebook, some rivers are not mentioned and others
are given only cursory attention. Sketch maps show access,
mileage, landmarks, side streams, and campsites. The river descriptions are broken into logical trip segments and have information on length, class (international rating scale), running time,
U.S. Geological Survey quadrangle map name, and a mile-by-
mile narration of the run.

Hawksley, Oscar. MISSOURI OZARK WATERWAYS. Rev. ed. Jefferson
City: Missouri Conservation Commission, 1976. 114 p. Preface. Paperbound.

Hawksley has canoed more than 3,500 miles on Ozark waterways.
Data from these trips have been distilled into this guidebook to
about thirty-seven major float streams in the Missouri Ozark high-
lands. Maps are clearly drawn and present acceptable detail.
Mile-by-mile descriptions parallel the map pages. Difficulty
ratings are expressed according to the international scale. Topographic map quadrangles are listed in the order of their use,
from headwaters to stream mouth.

Hayes, Philip T. YAMPA RIVER SUPPLEMENT TO VOLUME 1. River Runners'
Guide to the Canyons of the Green and Colorado Rivers, with Emphasis on
Geologic Features, vol. 1, supplement. Denver: Powell Society, 1971.
23 p. Paperbound.

This guide was published as a supplement to the Green River
guide, FROM FLAMING GORGE DAM THROUGH DINOSAUR
CANYON TO OURAY, by Hayes and Elmer S. Santos (see below). Both the Hayes/Santos and Hayes guides have been superseded by a revised edition by Hayes and George C. Simmons,
RIVER RUNNERS' GUIDE TO DINOSAUR NATIONAL MONU-
MENT AND VICINITY (see below).

Hayes, Philip T., and Santos, Elmer S. FROM FLAMING GORGE DAM
THROUGH DINOSAUR CANYON TO OURAY. River Runners' Guide to the
Canyons of the Green and Colorado Rivers, with Emphasis on Geologic Features, vol. 1. Powell Centennial, vol. 1. Denver: Powell Society, 1969.
40 p. Paperbound.

The centennial of Major John Wesley Powell's pioneer exploration of the Green and Colorado rivers was celebrated in 1969
by the Powell Society with the publication of four river guidebooks, of which this was the first. The three companion volumes (all of which are cited below, in this section) are: LABY-
RINTH, STILLWATER, AND CATARACT CANYONS and DESO-

LATION AND GRAY CANYONS, both by Felix E. Mutschler; and MARBLE GORGE AND GRAND CANYON by George C. Simmons and David L. Gaskill. This guide and its Yampa River supplement (see above) have been superseded by a revised edition by Hayes and George C. Simmons, RIVER RUNNERS' GUIDE TO DINOSAUR NATIONAL MONUMENT AND VICINITY (see below).

Hayes, Philip T., and Simmons, George C. RIVER RUNNERS' GUIDE TO DINOSAUR NATIONAL MONUMENT AND VICINITY, WITH EMPHASIS ON GEOLOGIC FEATURES. Rev. ed. Denver: Powell Society, 1973. 78 p. Paperbound.

This volume is a revision of volume 1 of the Powell Centennial series published under the auspices of the U.S. Geological Survey. This revised edition combines volume 1 (see above) and the YAMPA RIVER SUPPLEMENT TO VOLUME 1 (see above) and new material. The parts of the rivers described are those from Flaming Gorge Dam to Ouray, on the Green, and Deerlodge Park to Echo Park, on the Yampa. Approximately one half of this river mileage lies within Dinosaur National Monument. The guide is arranged in segments which correspond to customary river-trip access points. The nongeologist should have no problem with the log-type descriptions of formations and deposits. There are numerous nontechnical, geological cross-section sketches and photographs of the surroundings. Sketch maps show river mileage, side canyons, campsites, and access points. A glossary of geological terms is included. Three companion volumes comprise the Powell Centennial Series (all are cited below, in this section): LABYRINTH, STILLWATER, AND CATARACT CANYONS and DESOLATION AND GRAY CANYONS, both by Felix E. Mutschler; and MARBLE GORGE AND GRAND CANYON by George C. Simmons and David L. Gaskill. RIVER RUNNERS' GUIDE TO CANYONLANDS NATIONAL PARK AND VICINITY, WITH EMPHASIS ON GEOLOGIC FEATURES (see below) is Mutschler's revision of LABYRINTH, STILLWATER, AND CATARACT CANYONS.

Hedges, Harold, and Hedges, Margaret. BUFFALO RIVER CANOEING GUIDE. Rev. ed. Little Rock, Ark.: Ozark Society, 1973. 14 p. Paperbound.

The Buffalo River rises in the Boston Mountains of northwest Arkansas and flows 150 miles to its White River confluence. Approximately 133 miles are navigable by canoe or kayak. The authors have divided the river into fourteen segments, the longest being the twenty-four miles from Rush Creek to Buffalo City. Descriptions of the runs are in narrative form and include information on access, rapids, mileage, gradient, flow, and the sights and history of the surroundings. Paddler's services (canoe rentals, shuttle service, supplies) and appropriate U.S. Geological Survey maps are listed on the booklet's last page.

Hedges, Margaret, and Hedges, Harold. THE MIGHTY MULBERRY: A CA-
NOEING GUIDE. Little Rock, Ark.: Ozark Society, 1974. 16 p. Paperbound.

> This booklet describes the most canoeable fifty miles of the
> plunging Mulberry River of northwestern Arkansas. Since only
> one large-scale map is provided, the prospective river-runner
> may be interested to note the appropriate quadrangle maps cited
> in the introduction. River description is in narrative form.

Huser, Verne, and Belknap, Buzz. SNAKE RIVER GUIDE. Boulder City, Nev.:
Westwater Books, 1972. 72 p. Paperbound.

> The upper Snake River from the south entrance to Yellowstone
> National Park, through Grand Teton National Park to the town
> of Alpine, Wyoming, comprises the scope of this guide. The
> book is a series of strip maps drawn by Belknap from U.S. Geo-
> logical Survey, National Park Service, Forest Service, and Bu-
> reau of Reclamation data. The maps show rapids, mileage,
> campgrounds, roads, towns, and adjacent topographic detail.
> Material which parallels the maps include photographs and his-
> torical data. Maps of south Jackson and Jenny lakes are also
> given. The guide may be purchased in a waterproof edition.

Illinois Department of Conservation. ILLINOIS CANOEING GUIDE. Springfield, Ill.: 1975. 67 p. Paperbound.

> This guidebook was compiled from reports submitted by canoeists,
> representatives of state agencies, and scientists throughout Illi-
> nois. Trips with a duration varying from one day to a week or
> more are suggested. Twenty-four waterways are included. Two-
> color maps are drawn to scale, but do not give much detail;
> the maps show symbols for access, obstructions, points of interest,
> and campsites. River descriptions, however, are fairly detailed.

Indiana Department of Natural Resources. INDIANA CANOE GUIDE. Indianapolis: 1975. 108 p. Paperbound.

> This guide was produced from information gathered by Indiana
> Department of Natural Resources employees and others knowledge-
> able about Indiana waterways. Data on 1,300 miles of streams
> were collected and divided into trips lasting one day. Twenty-
> one waterways are mapped to scale, with access roads and points
> of interest marked. Description of the day trips includes dis-
> tance, access, picnic areas, and location of medical facilities.
> The names of appropriate U.S. Geological Survey maps are pro-
> vided.

Jamieson, Paul. ADIRONDACK CANOE WATERS: NORTH FLOW. Glens
Falls, N.Y.: Adirondack Mountain Club, 1975. 299 p. Paperbound.

Many Adirondack waterways remain remarkably wild and clean. This guide describes more than seven hundred miles of canoeing in the St. Lawrence River basin and Lake Champlain basin. No sketch maps are provided, but U.S. Geological Survey maps are cited and the descriptions are extensive. Use of the pocket-sized guide is simplified by the provision of an extensive index.

Jenkinson, Michael. WILD RIVERS OF NORTH AMERICA. New York: E.P. Dutton and Co., 1973. 413 p.

Only wilderness rivers or sections thereof, essentially unmarked by man's hand, have been chosen for inclusion in this volume. Jenkinson laments the diminishing number of such rivers, yet he has discovered that there are enough wild rivers remaining on this continent to fill a sizeable guidebook. A major portion of the work is devoted to the history and guide notes for nine waterways: the Rogue, Salmon, Urique, Colorado, Suwannee, Yukon, Buffalo, Rio Grande, and the route of the voyageurs. Included is a feature not often encountered in river guides--information on seldom-run Central American and Mexican rivers, such as the Urique, Coco, Patuca, Usumacinta, and the Rio Grande de Santiago. In all, 115 trips are described in widely varying detail, with abundant photographs throughout.

Jones, Charles, and Knab, Klaus. AMERICAN WILDERNESS, A GOUSHA WEEKEND GUIDE: WHERE TO GO IN THE NATION'S WILDERNESS, ON WILD AND SCENIC RIVERS AND ALONG THE SCENIC TRAILS. San Jose, Calif.: Gousha Publications, 1973. iv, 212 p. Paperbound.

This guide lists ninety-nine hikes and river trips which may be taken through America's national wilderness and primitive areas, and on scenic trails and along the rivers included in the Wild and Scenic Rivers Act. The rivers described are the first eleven covered by the act: the Allagash, Clearwater-Lochsa-Selway, Eleven Point, Feather Middle Fork, Rio Grande, Rogue, St. Croix, Salmon Middle Fork, and Wolf. A standard block of information is given for each river, including runnable season, length, campsites, guides and rentals, difficulty description, and address for additional information. Similar information is presented in the hiking portion of the book.

Kemmer, Rick. A GUIDE TO PADDLE ADVENTURE: HOW TO BUY CANOES, KAYAKS, AND INFLATABLES; WHERE TO TRAVEL; AND WHAT TO PACK ALONG. New York: Vanguard Press, 1975. 319 p. Preface.

The possible strength of this work lies in its potential to aid the novice in selecting the right canoe, kayak, or inflatable. Approximately 70 percent of the book is, in fact, a buyer's guide to paddle craft, accessories, and camp gear. Information on boat models, length, beam, depth, weight, price, and material is presented in columns for easy comparison, as is data on paddles and other equipment. A section on suggested trips in the United States and Canada is also given. Some maps are included, but they seem to be intended more for illustrative purposes than for utility in trip planning.

Kissner, Jakob, ed. FABULOUS FOLBOT HOLIDAYS. 4th ed. Charleston, S.C.: Creative Holiday Guides, 1976? 308 p. Paperbound.

The folbot, or "foldboat," is a European adaptation of the kayak, first introduced in America in 1935. The book contains finely lithographed color photographs showing the company's products in a variety of uses and locations. Since the book is essentially promotional, the cost is low. There is introductory material on paddling and sailing technique. In addition to its illustrations, the book is most noteworthy for its collection of almost eighty narratives of paddling vacations throughout the Western Hemisphere which were taken by the author and others.

Knudson, George E. "Guide to the Upper Iowa River." Decorah, Iowa: Luther College, 1970. vi, 57 p. Mimeographed.

Seven day trips are described for a hundred-mile portion of the Iowa River, from Lime Springs to the Mississippi. The trips vary in length from ten to twenty miles. Strip maps of each segment are provided; the maps include a key to symbols showing river conditions, access, wildlife, campsites, and geological and historical points of interest. The descriptive portion of the book emphasizes the flora and fauna as well as the history and geology of the region bordering the river.

Makens, James C. MAKEN'S GUIDE TO U.S. CANOE TRAILS. Irving, Tex.: Le Voyageur Publishing Co., 1971. 110 p. Paperbound.

Nine hundred canoeable waterways are listed in this guidebook. Information on trips is very rudimentary, ranging from brief to fleeting. The "brief" entries give waterway name, location, access, dangers, difficulty, and distance. The "fleeting" ones may list only name and general location. Waterways are listed alphabetically under state headings, with all states except Hawaii represented. There is an index by waterway name. The apparent intent of the author is to have this guide used as a first source of reference. Other guidebooks almost certainly will need to be consulted in any trip-planning process. In this regard, Makens provides a selective list of state and regional waterways guides.

Marks, Henry, and Riggs, Gene B. RIVERS OF FLORIDA. Atlanta: Southern Press, 1974. 116 p. Paperbound.

This is a concise guide offering fifty-two pages of general description on twelve rivers: the Saint Marys, Saint Johns, Miami, Lostman's, Peace, Hillsborough, Weeki Wachee, Withlacooche, Suwannee, Saint Marks, Ochlockonee, and Apalachicola. Remaining pages contain photographs of the rivers and neighboring landmarks.

Martin, Charles. SIERRA WHITEWATER: A PADDLER'S GUIDE TO THE RIVERS OF CALIFORNIA'S SIERRA NEVADA. Sunnyvale, Calif.: Fiddleneck Press, 1974. 192 p. Paperbound.

This guide is arranged in four parts. Part 1 introduces Sierra paddling, including how to get started, organizing a trip, and safety precautions. The next two parts describe seventy-four runs on eighteen rivers. A typical description contains brief information on shuttle, length of run, gradient, difficulty, and U.S. Geological Survey maps. Several following paragraphs discuss the run in more detailed terms. Part 4 presents a short history of the development of the rivers, and an argument for preservation of free-flowing rivers as a wilderness and recreational resource. Fifty-two professionally drafted maps and sixty-three action photographs illustrate the book. An appendix lists the names of California river conservation organizations.

Matacia, Louis J., and Cecil, Owen S. BLUE RIDGE VOYAGES: AN ILLUSTRATED CANOE LOG OF THE SHENANDOAH RIVER AND ITS SOUTH FORK. Blue Ridge Voyages, no. 4. Oakton, Va.: Louis J. Matacia, 1974. 184 p. Paperbound.

The Shenandoah, from its headwaters to Harpers Ferry, is thoroughly documented in this guidebook. Water level is critical on this river; the general rule is that low flow dictates trips on the northern portions. Maps giving mileage, obstructions, rapids, and access points are provided. The work is illustrated with photographs. Suggestions are given for one-week, three-day, and two-day trips. Alternate trips for high water conditions are proposed.

Meyer, Joan, and Meyer, Bill. CANOE TRAILS OF THE JERSEY SHORE. New Jersey Recreation Series. Ocean, N.J.: Specialty Press, 1974. v, 73 p. Preface. Paperbound.

The authors have personally canoed all routes presented in this guide. Included are trips on eight of the Jersey shore's most popular streams: Batsto, Cedar, Great Egg Harbor, Mamasquan, Mullica, Oswego, Tom's, and Wading. The distances, time requirements, river conditions, camping areas, natural qualities, and local history are explained. Sketch maps show the access roads and campgrounds. There is a directory of local canoe rental agencies.

Minnesota Department of Natural Resources. MINNESOTA VOYAGEUR TRAILS.
1970. Reprint. St. Paul, Minn.: 1972. 48 p. Paperbound.

> About 5 percent of Minnesota is water. The outflow from the
> state is in three directions: east to the Gulf of the St. Lawrence,
> south to the Gulf of Mexico, and north to Hudson Bay. This
> chaos of water presents an almost infinite number of choices for
> the paddler. The guide describes a selection of sixteen rivers
> and the Boundary Waters Canoe Area. The rivers are: Big
> Fork, Cannon, Cloquet, Crow Wing, Des Moines, Kettle, Little
> Fork, Minnesota, Mississippi, Crow, Red Lake, Root, Rum,
> Snake, St. Croix, and St. Louis. Descriptions of trips are
> mile-by-mile. Accompanying maps show access, rapids, mile-
> age, campsites, points of interest, and more. A general water-
> way description includes the addresses of local contacts who act
> in a clearinghouse capacity to dispense current information.

Mittenthal, Suzanne Meyer. THE BALTIMORE TRAIL BOOK. Baltimore, Md.:
Greater Baltimore Group, Sierra Club, 1970. Distributed by Oakton, Va.:
Appalachian Books. xi, 163 p. Paperbound.

> As the title suggests, this is primarily a foot-trail book. It
> maps and describes forty hikes; however, eight canoe trips are
> also listed. Listings give distance, access, attractions, and
> other advice. The usefulness of the sketch maps may be se-
> verely reduced due to blurring of copy.

Montagne, John De la. WILDERNESS BOATING ON YELLOWSTONE LAKES.
Bozeman: Montana State College, 1961. 31 p. Paperbound.

> The lakes described in this guide are the Upper Yellowstone,
> Shoshone, and Lewis. All are contained in Yellowstone Na-
> tional Park and all are limited to hand-propelled boats. Sketch
> maps are included, showing access trails and lake-use zones.
> The opening section of the book presents material on suitable
> equipment and canoeing technique.

Mutschler, Felix E. DESOLATION AND GRAY CANYONS. River Runners'
Guide to the Canyons of the Green and Colorado Rivers, with Emphasis on
Geologic Features, vol. 4. Powell Centennial, vol. 4. Denver: Powell
Society, 1969. 85 p. Paperbound.

> This guide is one of four volumes published as a Powell cen-
> tennial commemorative project under the auspices of the U.S.
> Geological Survey. It is intended for the river-runner new to
> the canyons. The area covered is from Ouray to Green River,
> Utah--a distance of about 128 miles. The nongeologist should
> have no problem with the mile-by-mile descriptions of forma-
> tions and deposits. There are numerous cross-section sketches
> and photographs of the surroundings. Sketch maps show river
> mileage, side canyons, and access points. A glossary of geo-

logical terms is included. There are three companion volumes in the Powell Centennial Series (all are cited in this section): FROM FLAMING GORGE DAM THROUGH DINOSAUR CANYON TO OURAY by Philip T. Hayes and Elmer S. Santos; LABYRINTH, STILLWATER, AND CATARACT CANYONS by Felix E. Mutschler; and MARBLE GORGE AND GRAND CANYON by George C. Simmons and David L. Gaskill. RIVER RUNNERS' GUIDE TO DINOSAUR NATIONAL MONUMENT AND VICINITY (see above) by Philip T. Hayes and George C. Simmons; and RIVER RUNNERS' GUIDE TO CANYONLANDS NATIONAL PARK AND VICINITY (see below) by Felix E. Mutschler, are revised editions of Powell Centennial volumes 1 and 2 respectively.

_____. LABYRINTH, STILLWATER, AND CATARACT CANYONS. River Runners' Guide to the Canyons of the Green and Colorado Rivers, with Emphasis on Geologic Features, vol. 2. Powell Centennial, vol. 2. Denver: Powell Society, 1969. 79 p. Paperbound.

The area in Utah from Green River to Hite is described in this guidebook. It is one of four volumes published in the Powell Centennial Series prepared under the auspices of the U.S. Geological Survey. This work is now out of print. A revised edition, published in 1977 has the title RIVER RUNNERS' GUIDE TO CANYONLANDS NATIONAL PARK AND VICINITY, WITH EMPHASIS ON GEOLOGIC FEATURES (cited immediately below). The river-running nongeologist should have no problem with the descriptions of formations and deposits or with the numerous geological cross-section sketches and photographs of the surroundings. Sketch maps show river mileage, side canyons, and access points. A glossary of geological terms is given. There are three companion volumes in the Powell Centennial Series (all are cited in this section): FROM FLAMING GORGE DAM THROUGH DINOSAUR CANYON TO OURAY by Philip T. Hayes and Elmer S. Santos; MARBLE GORGE AND GRAND CANYON by George C. Simmons, and David L. Gaskill; and DESOLATION AND GRAY CANYONS by Felix E. Mutschler. RIVER RUNNERS' GUIDE TO DINOSAUR NATIONAL MONUMENT AND VICINITY, WITH EMPHASIS ON GEOLOGIC FEATURES (see above) is Philip T. Hayes's and Elmer S. Santos's revision of FROM FLAMING GORGE DAM THROUGH DINOSAUR CANYON TO OURAY.

_____. RIVER RUNNERS' GUIDE TO CANYONLANDS NATIONAL PARK AND VICINITY, WITH EMPHASIS ON GEOLOGIC FEATURES. 2d ed. Denver: Powell Society, 1977. 99 p. Paperbound.

This volume replaces Mutschler's now out-of-print LABYRINTH, STILLWATER, AND CATARACT CANYONS (listed immediately above). It has been expanded to include the sixty-five-mile

portion of the Colorado River from Moab, Utah, to the confluence with the Green River. As with the previous edition
and all the Powell Society guidebooks, a nontechnical, mile-
by-mile log is the principal feature within which is described
the canyon geology and the rivers. Sketch maps show river
mileage, side canyons, geologic features, and access points.
A glossary of geological terms is included. There are four
volumes in the Powell Centennial Series (all are cited in this
section): FROM FLAMING GORGE DAM THROUGH DINO-
SAUR CANYON TO OURAY by Philip T. Hayes and Elmer S.
Santos; MARBLE GORGE AND GRAND CANYON by George
C. Simmons and David L. Gaskill; DESOLATION AND GRAY
CANYONS and LABYRINTH, STILLWATER, AND CATARACT
CANYONS both by Felix E. Mutschler. RIVER RUNNERS'
GUIDE TO DINOSAUR NATIONAL MONUMENT AND VICIN-
ITY, WITH EMPHASIS ON GEOLOGIC FEATURES (see above)
is Philip T. Hayes's and Elmer S. Santos's revision of FROM
FLAMING GORGE DAM THROUGH DINOSAUR CANYON TO
OURAY.

Nickels, Nick. "Canada Canoe Routes." Lakefield, Ontario: Canoecanada,
1973. 198 p. Preface. Mimeographed.

Nickels, who is from the Kawartha Lakes region of Ontario,
has been a canoeist-outdoorsman for more than fifty years. Much
of the material in this book has been incorporated into his most
recent guidebook, CANOE CANADA (cited below). Trip suggestions are grouped by province or territory. The information
provided is very limited and is intended only as a first point of
reference in investigating touring possibilities in the Canadian
wilderness.

_____. CANOE CANADA. Toronto: Van Nostrand Reinhold, 1976. vi,
278 p. Preface. Paperbound.

Six hundred canoe routes throughout Canada are very briefly
outlined as to length, trip time, access, maps available, and
portages. The more popular trips have detailed descriptions
following the outline. The book concludes with chapters on
map comprehension, canoe techniques, and camping. The author has incorporated selected information into this book from
his earlier works: SOUTHERN ONTARIO/QUEBEC CANOE
ROUTES (Lakefield, Ont.: Trent Publishing Co., n.d.), CAN-
ADA CANOE AND CAMP FACTPACK (Lakefield, Ont.: Nickels, 1972), and "Canada Canoe Routes" (the latter is cited
above). "Canada canoe routes data service," a supplemental
custom service promising much additional information, is offered
by the author for a fee.

Nolen, Ben M., ed. TEXAS RIVERS AND RAPIDS. Humble, Tex.: Nolen, 1974. 128 p. Paperbound.

Primarily a canoeing guide to Texas waterways, the reader will also find material on the Buffalo and Cossatot rivers (Arkansas), the Illinois (Oklahoma), the Arkansas (Colorado), and the Rio Concho (Mexico). In all, twenty-nine trips are mapped and described. The maps vary in scale and quality, and all lack detail. However, access points, mileage, camping facilities, and hazards are usually indicated. Also included are fundamental paddling tips and items of regional interest, such as Texas canoe competition dates. A significant portion of the book is given over to advertising by local canoe liveries and equipment manufacturers.

North Central Canoe Trails. WISCONSIN'S NORTH CENTRAL CANOE TRAILS. Rev. ed. Ladysmith, Wis.: 1967. ii, 28 p. Paperbound.

The Chippewa, Flambeau, south fork of the Flambeau, Jump, and Yellow rivers are featured on strip maps in this guide. There are twenty-eight carefully drawn maps, with hazards, rapids, campsites, landmarks, and access points located. Difficult stretches of water are shown in enlarged detail. The maps are based on aerial photographs and are drawn to a four-inch-per-mile scale. No accompanying descriptions of the runs are included. Rapids difficulty is rated on a scale of one to four.

Nova Scotia Camping Association. "Canoe Routes of Nova Scotia." Halifax, Nova Scotia: 1967. 112 p. Mimeographed.

This guidebook is composed of trips suggested by N.S.C.A. canoeists for a Nova Scotia centennial project called Operation Exploration. A total of forty-three trips are described. Each description makes reference to distance, time, difficulty (in a ranking of "no problem" to "hazardous"), topographic map name, access, rapids, water level, identification points, and more. With each trip description is a sketch map with numbers keyed to the corresponding paragraph of text.

Ontario Voyageurs Kayak Club. "Ontario Voyageurs River Guide." Toronto: 1970. 150 p. Mimeographed.

Descriptions of many of southern Ontario's whitewater rivers are contained in this guidebook prepared by members of the club. Sketch maps are provided with the river descriptions. Most of the rivers included have flows of Class 3 and above, reflecting the principal whitewater orientation of the O.V.K.C.

Palmer, Timothy T. SUSQUEHANNA WATERWAY: THE WEST BRANCH IN LY-COMING COUNTY. Williamsport, Pa.: Lycoming County Planning Commission, 1975. x, 56 p. Paperbound.

By strict definition, this is not a river guidebook. It is, however, descriptive of the west branch of the Susquehanna. The
book was prepared by the Lycoming County Planning Commission
to show present and past uses of the river and to suggest ways
to plan for future use. Of more immediate interest to the canoeist, perhaps, will be the chapters on river-related recreation
and the canoeing experiences of the author.

Palzer, Bob, and Palzer, Jody. WHITEWATER, QUIETWATER: A GUIDE TO
THE WILD RIVERS OF WISCONSIN, UPPER MICHIGAN, AND N.E. MINNE-
SOTA. 2d ed. Two Rivers, Wis.: Evergreen Paddleways, 1975. 157 p.
Paperbound.

The first edition of this guide had its partial beginning in two
Wisconsin Hoofers Outing Club booklets: GUIDE TO WHITE-
WATER IN THE WISCONSIN AREA (Madison: Wisconsin Hoofers
Outing Club, 1967), by Andres Peekna, and WATER SAFETY
CODE (Madison: Wisconsin Hoofers Outing Club, n.d.), by
Bob Palzer (neither title is cited in this bibliography). Seven
hundred fifty miles of wild rivers have been mapped and described. Trips are presented as one-day runs between automobile
access points. In this fashion, trips of many days may be planned
by linking a number of runs. Runs on twenty-nine rivers are
fully mapped and described; an additional ten rivers are not
mapped. The two-color maps are drawn in sufficient detail to
show rapids, access, campsites, and other information. The trip
descriptions provide information on access, mileage, time requirements, river width, gradient, difficulty, and flow. Perhaps
one-fifth of the book is devoted to a discussion of equipment,
technique, safety, organizations, competition, and other canoe-
related information.

Parks Canada. WILD RIVERS: SASKATCHEWAN. Wild Rivers Series, no. 1.
Ottawa: Department of Indian Affairs and Northern Development, Parks Canada, 1974. 66 p. Paperbound.

The first book in a ten-volume series of Canadian river guides,
this work describes five trips of varying length down the Clearwater, Fond du Lac, Churchill, and Sturgeon-Weir. Amply illustrated with photographs and maps, the guide provides a reliable description of rapids, portages, native plants and animals,
fishing tips, and geography. Reliability of a fair degree may be
assumed because the book is the result of findings of an official
Parks Canada survey. Other titles being prepared for the series
are: ALBERTA, THE BARRENLANDS, CENTRAL BRITISH CO-
LUMBIA, THE JAMES BAY/HUDSON BAY REGION, LABRADOR
AND NEWFOUNDLAND, NORTHWEST MOUNTAINS, QUEBEC
NORTH SHORE, SOUTHWESTERN QUEBEC AND EASTERN ON-
TARIO, and YUKON TERRITORY. Several of these may al-
ready be in print. Many descriptions of individual rivers within

the various regions are available in mimeographed form. A number are listed under the appropriate province or territory in chapter 12, which cites free or inexpensive waterways pamphlets and maps.

Patterson, Barbara McMartin. WALKS AND WATERWAYS: AN INTRODUC-TION TO ADVENTURE IN THE EAST CANADA CREEK AND THE WEST BRANCH OF THE SACANDAGA RIVER SECTIONS OF THE SOUTHERN ADIRONDACKS. Glens Falls, N.Y.: Adirondack Mountain Club, 1974. 171 p. Paperbound.

There are five Adirondack regions covered in this pocket-sized hiking and canoeing guidebook. The hiking trails receive some-what more coverage than the canoeing waters. A separate, cartographer-drawn map is provided. Shown on the map are number keys which refer to descriptions of the trips.

Pewe, Troy Lewis. COLORADO RIVER GUIDEBOOK: A GEOLOGIC AND GEOGRAPHIC GUIDE FROM LEES FERRY TO PHANTOM RANCH, ARIZONA. Tempe: Arizona State University Press, 1969. 78 p. Paperbound.

This book was prepared as a guide for geology student groups using the Colorado canyons as a laboratory. It is intended as an introductory guide to the region. Pewe is a professor in the Department of Geology at Arizona State University. Geological (and some historical) information is listed and mapped according to mileage downstream from the mouth of the Paria River. Black and white photographs of strata illustrate the work. A revised edition is in preparation.

Piggott, Margaret H. DISCOVER SOUTHEAST ALASKA WITH PACK AND PADDLE. Seattle, Wash: The Mountaineers, 1974. 269 p. Paperbound.

Canoe and kayak trips in the tidal waters of southeastern Alaska are described, as are hiking expeditions in the region. Special note is taken of the hazards attendant with paddling tide, squall, and iceberg-prone waters. The natural and human history of the region is included. Sketch maps are provided. Access by steamer, rail, highway, and air is shown.

Rigby, J. Keith, et al. GUIDEBOOK TO THE COLORADO RIVER, PART 3: MOAB TO HITE, UTAH, THROUGH CANYONLANDS NATIONAL PARK. Brigham Young University Geology Studies, Studies for Students, no. 6. Provo, Utah: Brigham Young University, Department of Geology, 1971. 91 p. Pref-ace. Paperbound.

The Colorado River, from Moab to the upper reaches of Lake Powell, is the coverage of this guidebook. It is the third in a geological series on the rivers of the Colorado Plateau along which boat trips are feasible. Parts 1 and 2 describe the geology of the Grand Canyon portion. For a full description of the contents, see Hamblin, W. Kenneth, and Rigby, J. Keith, this section.

Robinson, William M., Jr. MARYLAND-PENNSYLVANIA COUNTRYSIDE CANOE TRAILS: CENTRAL MARYLAND TRIPS. Oakton, Va.: Appalachian Books, 1974. iii, 34 p. Paperbound.

The Gunpowder and Patapsco rivers, Muddy Creek, and several flatwater trips are outlined in this Baltimore-area guide. In all, nine river runs are described. Information given for each run includes access, distance, difficulty, best season, and a pollution rating. There are no maps in the book; however, the names of the necessary U.S. Geological Survey quadrangle maps are included.

Satterfield, Archie. THE YUKON RIVER TRAIL GUIDE. Harrisburg, Pa.: Stackpole Books, 1975. 159 p. Paperbound.

This guide is limited to a description of only that portion of the Yukon River between Lake Bennett and Dawson City--a stretch of some six hundred miles. The duration of such a journey is estimated to be two weeks with a motor-driven vessel. None of the many strip maps are to scale, but the mileage numbers included are said to be accurate. There is a listing of all Canada National Topographic System maps needed for the trip. Other planning advice is included. The photographs from the gold-rush era are reproduced from those in the Asahel Curtis Collection at the Washington State Historical Society Museum. In addition to his observations about the Yukon and its people and history, Satterfield provides brief descriptive summaries of tributary streams suitable for canoe and kayak.

Schweiker, Roioli. CANOE CAMPING VERMONT AND NEW HAMPSHIRE RIVERS: A GUIDE TO 600 MILES OF RIVERS FOR A DAY, WEEKEND, OR WEEK OF CANOEING. Edited by Catherine J. Baker. Somersworth: New Hampshire Publishing Co., 1977. vi, 91 p. Paperbound.

Trips are listed by watershed. They have been selected for accessibility by good roads and the probability of having sufficient water throughout the summer in at least part of the run. The descriptions assume basic canoeing knowledge and include sketch maps; a brief introduction to the river; a summary table listing cumulative miles, break points, international scale difficulty rating, and special difficulties; and detailed descriptions of the trip. These descriptions usually cover observations on campsites, fishing, side hikes, picnic areas, and historical sites.

Schwind, Richard. WEST COAST RIVER TOURING: ROGUE RIVER CANYON AND SOUTH. Beaverton, Oreg.: Touchstone Press, 1974. 221 p. Preface. Paperbound.

This detailed and carefully researched guide describes the west-coast rivers from the Rogue to the Salinas, all of which have their sources in the coastal mountain ranges. The guide includes both easy and difficult descents down nearly every creek or river with a minimum of one hundred square miles of drainage area. Virtually all of the 1,700 miles of rivers described have been run one or more times by the author. Part 1 presents general material on equipment and technique as well as several pages of river-flow tables and prediction methods. Part 2 explains the runs. A feature is the recommendation made for the type of craft (kayak, canoe, raft, or dory) best-suited for a particular river run. Further information includes location, rapids classification (international scale), topographic maps needed, average optimum-flow date, length of run, scenery rating, and area of drainage. Sketch maps show sections of the rivers and access roads.

Scott, Ian, and Kerr, Mavis. CANOEING IN ONTARIO. Toronto: Greey de Pencier Publications, 1975. 80 p. Paperbound.

The beginning and intermediate canoe campers are the primary audience toward which this book is directed. More than half of the book explains canoe paddling and camping techniques. The remainder contains a directory of waterways touring information, which lists access, campsites, rental agencies, and further information sources keyed to eleven regional maps.

Sea Explorers. Ship 648, comps. CANOEING IN LOUISIANA. Edited by John W. Thieret. Lafayette, La.: Lafayette Natural History Museum, 1972. iv, 62 p. Preface. Paperbound.

This booklet is a guide to trips on twelve waterways: Whiskey Chitto Creek, Calcasieu River, Bayou Teche, Vermilion River, Atchafalaya Basin, Bogue Chitto River, Amite River, Tangipahoa River, Kisatchie Bayou, Bayou Dorcheat, Lake Bistineau, and Saline Bayou. Sketch maps show nearby roads and campsites. Reports on the trips are arranged under standard headings of location, history, description, access, and distance.

Simmons, George C., and Gaskill, David L. MARBLE GORGE AND GRAND CANYON. River Runners' Guide to the Canyons of the Green and Colorado Rivers, with Emphasis on Geologic Features, Powell Centennial, vol. 3. Denver: Powell Society, 1969. 132 p. Paperbound.

This geological guidebook is one of four volumes published in the Powell centennial series under the auspices of the U.S. Geological Survey. The area covered is from Lees Ferry to Pierces Ferry at Lake Mead, a distance of 279 miles. The nongeologist should have no problem with the mile-by-mile descriptions of formations and deposits. There are numerous geological cross-section sketches and photographs of the canyons. Sketch maps show river mileage, side canyons, and access points. A glossary of geological terms is given. There are three companion volumes

in the Powell Centennial Series (all are cited in this section):
FROM FLAMING GORGE DAM THROUGH DINOSAUR CAN-
YON TO OURAY by Philip T. Hayes and Elmer S. Santos;
LABYRINTH, STILLWATER, AND CATARACT CANYONS, and
DESOLATION AND GRAY CANYONS, both by Felix E. Mut-
schler. RIVER RUNNERS' GUIDE TO DINOSAUR NATIONAL
MONUMENT AND VICINITY (see above) by Philip T. Hayes
and George C. Simmons; and RIVER RUNNERS' GUIDE TO
CANYONLANDS NATIONAL PARK AND VICINITY (see above)
by Felix E. Mutschler, are revised editions of Powell Centennial
volumes 1 and 2 respectively.

Spindt, Katherine M., and Shaw, Mary, eds. CANOEING GUIDE: WEST-
ERN PENNSYLVANIA AND NORTHERN WEST VIRGINIA. 6th ed. Pittsburgh,
Pa.: American Youth Hostels, Pittsburgh Council, 1975. viii, 168 p. Paper-
bound.

Within an easy drive of Pittsburgh are many good paddling
streams and lakes having wilderness characteristics. The center-
piece of this guidebook is the section on description of trips
along rivers in the Beaver, Allegheny, and Monongahela water-
sheds--plus a "miscellaneous" streams section. Technical information (length, class, gradient, volume, and level) is given in
tabular form above narrative which explains the river and suggests shuttles. The identifying names for gauge stations and
U.S. Geological Survey topographic maps are given. The authors have assigned a "scenic value rating" and a "pollution
rating" for each run.

Texas Explorers Club. "Suggested River Trips Through the Rio Grande River
Canyons in the Big Bend Region of Texas." Rev. ed. Temple, Tex.: 1971.
30 p. Mimeographed.

The combining of notes taken during many trips by members of
the Texas Explorers Club resulted in the compilation of this guide.
The notes begin at Presidio and trace the run downstream, through
eleven canyons, to Langtry. The information is limited to descriptions of the main canyon runs, how to get there, and special points of interest in each canyon. No detailed maps are
provided, although the appropriate U.S. Geological Survey maps
are named. The notes contain many practical suggestions on
what to do with shuttle cars, photographic vantage points, and
areas of interest near the river.

Texas Parks and Wildlife Department. Trail and Waterways Section. AN
ANALYSIS OF TEXAS WATERWAYS: A REPORT ON THE PHYSICAL CHARAC-
TERISTICS OF RIVERS, STREAMS, AND BAYOUS IN TEXAS. Austin, Tex.:
1972. 240 p. Paperbound.

The nature of Texas rivers is diverse. Eastern Texas rivers are bordered by pines, slow-moving, and serene. Central rivers have a steeper gradient with stretches of whitewater, while western Texas rivers cut canyons through arid lands and often provide a true wilderness experience. The book describes hundreds of miles of rivers. Many rivers are mapped in accurate detail. The information presented is the result of on-site inspection as well as input from other sources. The agency was attempting to determine the feasibility of establishing a state-wide system of recreational waterways. A total of eighty-two waterways are described, either fully or in part. An index map and key to symbols is included. (See also Texas Parks and Wildlife Department, chapter 6.)

Thomas, Eben. HOT BLOOD AND WET PADDLES: A GUIDE TO CANOE RACING IN MAINE AND NEW HAMPSHIRE. Hallowell, Maine: Hallowell Printing Co., 1974. viii, 188 p. Paperbound.

As the title states, this is a racing guide, not a guide for the canoe cruiser. However, there is useful river information here for those who do not race. Sections of fourteen New England rivers are sketch-mapped, showing locations of rapids and carriers. Car routes to the rivers and accommodations in the vicinity are given. Those who do race will discover a concentration of information on registration, rules, classes, locations, participants, dates, and times.

_____. NO HORNS BLOWING: A GUIDE TO CANOEING 10 GREAT RIVERS IN MAINE. Hallowell, Maine: Hallowell Printing Co., 1973. ix, 134 p. Paperbound.

Allagash, Bow, Dead (north branch), Machais, Narraguagus, St. Croix, St. John, Saco, Cobbossee, and a circle trip in the West Grand Lake area are the ten canoeing rivers covered. Descriptions of the rivers are full and incorporate maps and many photographs. Hints are given about trip selection, equipment organization, and menu planning. Since much of Maine's back country is owned by paper companies, permit procedures for travel, fires, and campsites within these areas are explained. U.S. Geological Survey topographic quadrangle maps are identified; rapids are rated on the international scale.

_____. THE WEEKENDER: A GUIDE TO FAMILY CANOEING. Hallowell, Maine: Hallowell Printing Co., 1975. vi, 134 p. Paperbound.

A sequel to the author's NO HORNS BLOWING (cited above) this guide suggests ten additional Maine river trips suitable for beginning whitewater paddlers. There is also a guide to Class 2 and 3 wilderness trips for the more experienced paddler. Each trip description contains general information on the river and surrounding area, sketch map, water volume, shuttle routes,

topographic maps, and any fire and camping permits needed.
There is an introductory section on basic strokes, river-running
technique, rapids, and safety.

Thomson, John Seabury. POTOMAC WHITE WATER: A GUIDE TO SAFE
CANOEING ABOVE WASHINGTON, SENECA TO LITTLE FALLS. Oakton,
Va.: Appalachian Books, 1974. 44 p. Paperbound.

The guide is intended for experienced whitewater canoeists unfamiliar with the upper Potomac. This section of the river is
defined as the twenty miles between Seneca and Little Falls,
with Great Falls approximately in the middle. There is a large-
scale, removable map provided, which shows the total run in
good detail. Six of the rapids are particularly discussed as are
the various river-access points.

Truesdell, William G. A GUIDE TO THE WILDERNESS WATERWAY OF THE
EVERGLADES NATIONAL PARK. Coral Gables, Fla.: University of Miami
Press, published in cooperation with the Everglades Natural History Association.
1969. 64 p. Paperbound.

A park naturalist prepared this guidebook through the mangroves
and sawgrass of the Everglades. There are twenty-seven maps
based on charts and aerial photographs. The actual water route
has been marked for its one-hundred-mile length. Both guidebook and waterway trail have been designed for use by canoeists
of modest experience.

Ungnade, Herbert E. GUIDE TO THE NEW MEXICO MOUNTAINS. 2d ed.
Albuquerque: University of New Mexico Press, 1972. 235 p.

While this is primarily a mountaineering guide, there is one
chapter on New Mexico river-running, with contributions by
J.H. Fretwell. Included are brief descriptions of runs down
six rivers: the Rio Grande, Pecos, Chama, San Juan, Gila,
and Canadian.

Vierling, Philip E. ILLINOIS COUNTRY CANOE TRAILS: DES PLAINES
RIVER. Chicago: Illinois Country Outdoor Guides, 1976. 72 p. Paperbound.

_____. ILLINOIS COUNTRY CANOE TRAILS: DU PAGE RIVER, KANKAKEE
RIVER, AUX SABLE CREEK, DES PLAINES RIVER. Chicago: Illinois Country
Outdoor Guides, 1975. 84 p. Paperbound.

_____. ILLINOIS COUNTRY CANOE TRAILS: FOX RIVER, MAZON RIVER,
VERMILION RIVER, LITTLE VERMILION RIVER. Chicago: Illinois Country
Outdoor Guides, 1974. 80 p. Paperbound.

This guide by Vierling and the two cited directly above are almost identical in format and arrangement. Descriptions of the
runs are done in detail and with precision; sketch maps are keyed
to the descriptions. The guidebooks also present a summary of
the historical, scientific, and cultural aspects of the rivers' en-
virons. The scale of difficulty chosen for rating the runs is one
of the author's own creation: "riffles, rapids, and hazardous
rapids." Enlarged sketches of major rapids are provided.

Weber, Sepp. WILD RIVERS OF ALASKA. Anchorage: Alaska Northwest
Publishing Co., 1976. vi, 170 p. Paperbound.

Alaska has many of the world's diminishing count of truly wilderness rivers, almost all of which may be negotiated by small
boats. Weber has chosen fifty-three wild rivers for inclusion
in his guidebook. Descriptions of the trips are brief. Maps
describing each trip are drawn to scale with hazards, portages,
distances, whitewater classification, and road or air access indicated. Five rivers (Noatak, Aniak, Porcupine, Copper, and
Chilikadrotna) have been chosen for detailed description. It
seems evident that Weber writes from close experience and understanding of these waterways. The many captioned, color
photographs give an indication of the character of the rivers and
of the surrounding area. Some pages are devoted to explaining
the necessities of choosing the right craft and equipment, preparation, and transportation.

Wheat Ridge High School. Jefferson County. Colorado. "River Rats' Guide
to the Green and Yampa Rivers: Dinosaur National Monument, Colorado-Utah."
Denver: Colorado Outward Bound School, 1972. 24 p. Mimeographed.

This guidebook has little material on the specific act of running
the rivers. Rather, it is a guide to the natural world of the
area, with generalized descriptions and drawings of the geology,
flora, fauna, prehistory, and history of Dinosaur National Monument.

YOUGHIOGHENY RIVER GUIDE. Columbus, Ohio: Rich Designs, 1975.
Map.

Pennsylvania's Youghiogheny may be the most popular whitewater
river in the United States. State parks personnel counted more
than 3,000 boaters per weekend during the summer of 1976. This
river guide is actually a 25 x 38 inch map containing photographs
and descriptions of the runs and rapids between Casselman River
confluence and the town of Stewarton. It is a hybrid publication--
both map and guidebook in a sheet-map format. Fifteen major
rapids are featured in enlargements superimposed on the two-color
map. Several short paragraphs on area camping, lodging, hiking,
fishing, and wildlife complete the guide.

Chapter 9
BASIC LIST OF RECOMMENDED BOOKS

The list below represents an attempt to identify, from more than 350 books cited in this information guide, a small, representative group comprising a "library list" of recommended titles for the business or institution library, or for a personal library. All twenty-three books in the list are currently in print, many in paperbound editions.

Selection has been difficult, made more so by the comparatively recent growth in the quality and number of wilderness waterways books. The list reflects the consequence of applying objective book-judging criteria with respect to authoritativeness, accuracy, arrangement, scope, format, and use of illustrative material. Reflected, too, are my own biases about what constitutes a good book. I place such subjective responses under the term "readability."

The descriptive annotation for each work cited (excluding the one presently in hand) may be found elsewhere in this book. It was not feasible to list waterways guidebooks outside of those with a most general character. In the case of specific guidebooks, one or more covering a waterway or region in which you have a special interest would, of course, be the most appropriate choice. In this regard, the waterways guidebooks chapter presents a full range of possibilities.

American National Red Cross. CANOEING. 2d ed., rev. Garden City, N.Y.: Doubleday and Co., 1977. 452 p. Paperbound. (see chapter 2.)

_____. LIFESAVING, RESCUE, AND WATER SAFETY. Garden City, N.Y.: Doubleday and Co., 1974. 240 p. Paperbound. (see chapter 3.)

Bolz, John Arnold. PORTAGE INTO THE PAST: BY CANOE ALONG THE MINNESOTA-ONTARIO BOUNDARY WATERS. Minneapolis: University of Minnesota Press, 1960. vi, 181 p. (see chapter 5.)

Recommended Books

Bunnelle, Hasse, and Thomas, Winnie. FOOD FOR KNAPSACKERS AND OTHER TRAIL TRAVELERS. A Sierra Club Totebook. San Francisco: Sierra Club Books, 1971. 144 p. Paperbound. (see chapter 3.)

Davidson, James West, and Rugge, John. THE COMPLETE WILDERNESS PADDLER. New York: Alfred A. Knopf, 1976. 284 p. (see chapter 3.)

Dickerman, Pat. ADVENTURE TRAVEL U.S.A. 3d ed. New York: Adventure Guides, 1976. 224 p. Paperbound. (see chapter 1.)

Esslen, Rainer. BACK TO NATURE IN CANOES: A GUIDE TO AMERICAN WATERS. Frenchtown, N.J.: Columbia Publishing Co., 1976. 345 p. Paperbound. (see chapter 8.)

Evans, Robert Jay, and Anderson, Robert R. KAYAKING: THE NEW WHITE-WATER SPORT FOR EVERYBODY. An Environmental Sports Book. Brattleboro, Vt.: Stephen Greene Press, 1975. 192 p. Paperbound. (see chapter 4.)

Hazen, David. THE STRIPPER'S GUIDE TO CANOE BUILDING. 3d ed. San Francisco: Tamal Vista Publications, 1976. 95 p. Paperbound. (see chapter 4.)

Houston, C. Stuart, ed. TO THE ARCTIC BY CANOE, 1819-1821: THE JOURNAL AND PAINTINGS OF ROBERT HOOD, MIDSHIPMAN WITH FRANKLIN. Montreal: McGill-Queen's University Press, 1974. 250 p. (see chapter 5.)

Lathrop, Theodore G. HYPOTHERMIA: KILLER OF THE UNPREPARED. Rev. ed. Portland, Oreg.: The Mazamas, 1975. 29 p. Paperbound. (see chapter 3.)

McGinnis, William W. WHITEWATER RAFTING. Toronto: Fitzhenry and Whiteside; New York: Quadrangle Press/New York Times Book Co., 1975. 379 p. (see chapter 3.)

McPhee, John. THE SURVIVAL OF THE BARK CANOE. New York: Farrar, Straus and Giroux, 1975. 145 p. (see chapter 5.)

Manley, Atwood. RUSHTON AND HIS TIMES IN AMERICAN CANOEING. Syracuse, N.Y.: Syracuse University Press, 1968. 223 p. (see chapter 5.)

Mead, Robert Douglas. THE CANOER'S BIBLE. Outdoor Bible Series. Garden City, N.Y.: Doubleday and Co., 1976. 176 p. Paperbound. (see chapter 3.)

Nickels, Nick. CANOE CANADA. Toronto: Van Nostrand Reinhold, 1976. vi, 278 p. Paperbound. (see chapter 8.)

Olsen, Larry Dean. OUTDOOR SURVIVAL SKILLS. 4th ed. Provo, Utah: Brigham Young University Press, 1973. 203 p. (see chapter 3.)

Rutstrum, Calvin. THE WILDERNESS ROUTE FINDER. New York: Macmillan Co., 1967. x, 214 p. (see chapter 3.)

Thomas, Dian. ROUGHING IT EASY: A UNIQUE IDEABOOK FOR CAMPING AND COOKING. Provo, Utah: Brigham Young University Press, 1974. 215 p. Paperbound. (see chapter 3.)

_____. ROUGHING IT EASY 2. New York: Warner Books, 1977. 223 p. Paperbound. (see chapter 3.)

Urban, John T. A WHITEWATER HANDBOOK FOR CANOE AND KAYAK. Boston: Appalachian Mountain Club, 1965. vii, 77 p. Paperbound. (see chapter 2.)

Walbridge, Charles. BOATBUILDER'S MANUAL: HOW TO BUILD FIBERGLASS CANOES AND KAYAKS FOR WHITEWATER. 2d ed. Penllyn, Pa.: Wildwater Designs, 1974. iii, 70 p. Paperbound. (see chapter 4.)

Part 2

OTHER MEDIA

(FILMS, PERIODICALS, PAMPHLETS)

INTRODUCTION

Media other than books constitute significant sources of information about wilderness waterways. The visual media of motion pictures, filmstrips, and slides have a unique capacity to entertain and instruct. Some are available for a rental fee, while others cost only the postage (usually with the stipulation that they be shown only to groups). Most provincial and state agencies willingly loan films depicting their lakes, rivers, and water recreation facilities. Representative of this type of film is SUWANEE ADVENTURE, listed in chapter 10. One may discover many others by contacting provincial or state departments of commerce or tourism. Some manufacturers and retailers of canoes, kayaks, rafts, and equipment have films for loan. To learn the distributor of any Canadian film, write to: Canadian Film Institute, c/o Film Canadiana, 1762 Carling Avenue, Ottawa, Ontario K2A 1C9.

The three-letter code in the first line of each film citation refers to the producer or distributor of the material. A directory immediately following the film listings gives producer-distributor name, address, and telephone number.

Unquestionably, periodicals are the best sources of current information. The national canoeing, kayaking, and rafting magazines present a continually updated overview of recent developments, race results, environmental concerns, new products, and other news. Club newsletters are invaluable for keeping current on regional and local people, issues, and events. The list in chapter 11 is complete regarding the national magazines. Newsletters are extremely difficult to locate, verify, and cite with total bibliographic accuracy; consequently, that list is certainly far from complete. Many clubs publish a newsletter, even if infrequently. A good method for tapping these information resources is by individual inquiry. Chapter 18 lists clubs by province and state.

Material contained in brochures, folders, pamphlets, and maps can be important in trip planning. Indeed, they are sometimes the only sources of data on a remote waterway or region. A representative number of these materials have been cited in chapter 12. Although they were in print at the time this book was in preparation, be reminded of the ephemeral nature of these publications. Inquiries about the most recent pamphlets and maps on an area should be addressed to the appropriate agency or interest group in that area. (Part 3 of this book presents an extensive listing of agencies and organizations which are potential sources for this kind of information.)

Chapter 10
MOTION PICTURES, FILMSTRIPS, SLIDES

VISUAL MEDIA LISTING

ACROSS THE CONTINENT BY CANOE. NCF, 1971. Slides.

35mm, 90 min., color. Using three projectors and three screens, Clinton Waddell narrates the longest canoe trip ever completed in a single season. Waddell and Verlin Kruger traveled 7,000 miles from Montreal to the Bering Sea between 17 April and 10 October 1971. The slides of this trip are shown and narrated by Waddell, personally. For more information concerning this personal presentation, contact: Clinton Waddell, North Central Forest Experiment Station, 1992 Folwell Avenue, St. Paul, Minnesota 55108. (612) 645-0841.

ADVENTURE RIVERS. ART, n.d. Motion picture.

16mm, 30 min., sound, color. An introduction to rafting and shore camping is provided, featuring the Grand Canyon's Colorado and other rivers.

ALPS OF THE RIVER TARA. ART, n.d. Slides.

35mm, 35 min., 140 slides, color. This slide program may be conducted by a member of the American River Touring Association.

BE WATER WISE: BOATING. Training film no. TF-5129B. AIR, 1960. Motion picture.

16mm, 20 min., sound, color. Safe methods for canoeing, outboard motorboating, sailing, and skiing are demonstrated. Marine traffic regulations, emergency measures, and courtesy codes are reviewed. Free loan.

BIRCH BARK CANOE. QPB, n.d. Motion picture.

16mm, 15 min., sound, color. Tete-de-Boule Indians of the Upper St. Maurice region build a birch-bark canoe. Free loan.

BOATING FEVER. EKC, 1970. Motion picture.

16mm, 18 min., sound, color. This film shows all types of boats in action--outboards, inboards, sailboats, yachts, and kayaks shooting the rapids. Free loan.

BUILDING A KAYAK. NFB, 1968. Motion picture.

16mm, 55 min., sound, color. This film is issued in two parts. Part 1 follows two Eskimo men as they build a kayak from scraps of trader's wood, seal skins, and sinew; it shows them cutting, joining, and binding the kayak. Part 2 continues the discussion of kayak construction and shows the women sewing skins, soaking the frame and skins, and covering the kayak.

BUSH FIRST AID, PART 1. MLP and SEF, 1967. Motion picture.

16mm, 10 min., sound, color. How to assemble a practical first aid kit and how to use it for almost any emergency are shown.

BUSH FIRST AID, PART 2. MLP and SEF, 1967. Motion picture.

16mm, 10 min., sound, color. The subject matter is how to treat an accident victim in the bush, using only material which is readily available.

BY NATURE'S RULES. ASF, n.d. Motion picture.

16mm, 27 min., sound, color. This film addresses hypothermia in its various forms, such as exposure, immersion, heart arrest, freezing, and exhaustion. The film covers prevention as well as treatment. Free loan.

CANOE. NFB, n.d. Motion picture.

16mm, ? min., sound, color. The canoe and a variety of canoeing activities are depicted.

CANOE CHURCHILL. SAM, 1973. Motion picture.

16mm, 25 min., sound, color. A canoe voyage down the Churchill River in Saskatchewan is the subject of this film.

CANOE COUNTRY. NFB, 1949. Motion picture.

16mm, 13 min., sound, color. This film tells the story of a

Cincinnati family vacationing in the Canadian North in an eighteen-foot canoe along the route of the fur traders.

CANOE COUNTRY SASKATCHEWAN. SAM, 1973. Motion picture.

16mm, 27 min., sound, color. The "Canoe Country" of the title is the Churchill River.

CANOEING. NFB, 1969. Filmstrip.

35mm, 37 fr., color. This is the revised version of a 1965 filmstrip of the same title. It describes techniques for canoeing, shows how to pack the canoe, and how to enter and leave the canoe safely. Captions are included. The French version of the filmstrip is entitled LE CANOTAGE.

CANOEING THE BIG COUNTRY. CTF and NFB, 1966. Motion picture.

16mm, 14 min., sound, color. Scenes taken on a seventy-mile canoe trip through Bowron Lake Park in the Caribou country of British Columbia are shown.

CANOEING THE SUPERIOR COAST. ART, n.d. Motion picture.

16mm, 10 min., sound, color. Giant fur-trader canoes are shown against the backdrop of the Lake Superior coast and Voyageur National Park.

CANOEING THE TREMBLING EARTH. WKY, 1975. Motion picture.

16mm, 25 min., sound, color. The experiences of a group of high school students on a week-long canoe trip through the Okefenokee Swamp of Georgia and northern Florida are depicted.

CANOES. EMC, 1974. Motion picture.

16mm, 8 min., sound, color. Canoe construction and use are described.

CANYON RIVERS OF UTAH. ART, n.d. Slides.

35mm, 30 min., color. This slide program may be conducted by a member of the American Rivers Touring Association. The slides show the canyons of the Colorado River, including Westwater, Cataract, and Canyonlands National Park.

DANGER RIVER. MFE, n.d. Motion picture.

16mm, ? min., sound, color. The film takes the viewer down the rapids of the Colorado River "in a rowboat."

DISTRESS SIGNALS, PART 1. MLP and SEF, 1967. Motion picture.

> 16mm, 10 min., sound, color. This film explains that fire and smoke are the most effective distress signals; it shows in detail how to construct weatherproof signal beacons.

DISTRESS SIGNALS, PART 2. MLP and SEF, 1967. Motion picture.

> 16mm, 10 min., sound, color. The preparation and use of international distress signals, using peeled logs, are illustrated. Aerial shots show their effectiveness.

DROWN-PROOFING. AFP and UIL, n.d. Motion picture.

> 16mm, 14 min., sound, color. This film is the winner of six film awards. It teaches the technique of staying afloat in deep water for an indefinite length of time.

EUROPEAN FLAT WATER PADDLERS. NPC, 1971. Motion picture.

> 16mm, 30 min., no sound, color. This film is issued in three parts of equal length. These films are accompanied by a thirty-five page technical report on stroke analysis. They show styles and training methods of expert European flat-water paddlers.

FIRE MAKING AND SHELTERS. MLP and SEF, 1967. Motion picture.

> 16mm, 10 min., sound, color. How to select a site, choose timber for fire, and build a rainproof shelter in two hours are shown in detail.

FIRST AID. ARC, 1958. Motion picture.

> 16mm, 29 min., sound, color. Issued in two parts, the film shows eight individuals with different problems which require first aid; it explains in detail what to do about each case. Part 1 covers dressings and bandages, artificial respiration, shock, and burns. Part 2 discusses bleeding, poisoning, broken bones, and common emergencies.

FIRST AID: ARTIFICIAL RESPIRATION. ARC, 1965. Motion picture.

> 16mm, 28 min., sound, black and white. Diagrams and live demonstrations are used to show the mouth-to-mouth, chest-pressure arm-lift, and back-pressure arm-lift methods of artificial respiration.

FIRST AID FOR INJURIES CAUSED BY HEAT AND COLD. MCG, 1959. Filmstrip.

> 35mm, 39 fr., black and white. This film demonstrates and

explains first aid treatment for simple burns and scalds, sunburn, chemical burns, sunstroke, heat exhaustion, heat cramps, frost-bite, and freezing. A guide is included.

FIRST AID FOR SHOCK AND ARTIFICIAL RESPIRATION. ARC, 1965. Motion picture.

16mm, 28 min., sound, black and white. How to administer first aid for shock and how to give artificial respiration are shown.

FLOAT PARTY: DOWN THE RIVER. The Wonderful World of Sport, Boating Series. AFI and SPI, n.d. Motion picture.

16mm, 5 min., sound, color. A group raft trip is filmed against an idyllic river background.

FUNDAMENTAL CANOEING. MLP and SEF, 1967. Motion picture.

16mm, 10 min., sound, color. How to launch, paddle, portage, load, and enter a canoe safely are shown, as well as what to do if a canoe capsizes.

GOLD RUSH RIVERS OF CALIFORNIA. ART, n.d. Slides.

35mm, 30 min., color. This slide program may be conducted by a member of the American Rivers Touring Association. The Stanislaus, Tuolumne, and American rivers of the Sierra are featured.

GRAND CANYON. ART, n.d. Slides.

35mm, 30 min., slides, color. This slide program may be conducted by a member of the American Rivers Touring Association. The presentation shows the canyon's rapids and monumental grandeur.

THE GRAND CANYON. SIC, 1967. Motion picture.

16mm, ? min., sound, color. The film was made with Martin Litton of Grand Canyon Dories, as part of a campaign to stop the damming of the Colorado River.

GRAND CANYON BY DORY. GCD, n.d. Motion picture.

16mm, 85 min., no sound, color. Natural history and dories combine in this film of the world's most famous canyon river. The tremendous hydraulics of the Colorado capsize more than one of Martin Litton's boats.

THE GREAT CANADIAN CANOE. NSR, 1974. Motion picture.

16mm, 10 min., sound, color. This film depicts war canoe races on Dartmouth Lakes and includes highlights from national championships and club regattas. It gives information about equipment and course requirements, rules, and techniques of the sport.

GUADALUPE SHOW. KXA, 1972. Motion picture.

16mm, 27 1/2 min., sound, color. This film about Texas's Guadalupe River was nominated that state's outstanding documentary. While this motion picture was shot on 16mm film, it is not available for loan in this format. It is available on either two-inch video tape, or 3/4-inch video cassette.

HEADWATERS OF THE AMAZON. ART, n.d. Slides.

35mm, 122 slides, 30 min., color. This slide program may be conducted by a member of the American Rivers Touring Association. This presentation is outside the scope of North American wilderness waterways, but because of its exotic subject it may be considered by groups looking for an unusual program. The Napo, Nanay, and Urubamba rivers in Peru and Columbia's Rio Magdalena and Caribbean seascapes are depicted, as well as the Inca ruins at Machu Picchu.

HELL'S CANYON: WHITEWATER THRILLS ON IDAHO'S SNAKE RIVER. ICD, 1961. Motion picture.

16mm, 26 min., sound, color. A small group of people are followed as they raft through Hell's Canyon. The trip begins at Homestead and ends at Lewiston, Idaho.

IDAHO MOUNTAIN RIVERS. ART, n.d. Slides.

35mm, 70 slides, 30 min., color. This slide program may be conducted by a member of the American Rivers Touring Association. The program is about the Middle and Main Salmon, which flow through the Idaho Primitive Area.

JOURNEY TO THE RAGGED EDGE. Travis Prewitt, n.d. Motion picture.

16mm, 120 min., sound, color. This film features Kathy and Travis Prewitt's 600-mile canoe journey across the Arctic barrens in Canada's Northwest Territories. Inquiries about the film may be addressed to: Jay Pritchett, Arctic Explorations, Whitworth College, Spokane, Washington 99251.

KAYAK. PYF, 1971. Motion picture.

16mm, 8 min., sound, color. The skilled kayakist is portrayed as he works with the river to experience the thrill of being in the center of a force which is both kinetic and aesthetic.

KAYAK. ABC, 1975. Motion picture.

16mm, 19 min., sound, color. Five people are followed as they float down the Colorado River and encounter some very large rapids.

KAYAKING ON THE LOWER SALMON. KUI, n.d. Motion picture.

16mm, 18 min., sound, color. The exuberance of whitewater kayaking is evident in this film about a day on the river with a group of college students.

LADY OF THE RAPIDS. TCF, 1962. Motion picture.

16mm, 11 min., sound, color. The adventures of Georgie White are depicted as she shoots the rapids of the Colorado River on its course through the Grand Canyon.

LAKE AND RIVER KAYAKING. MLP and SEF, 1973. Motion picture.

16mm, 14 min., sound, color. An expert kayakist demonstrates the proper handling of paddle and kayak in smooth and white-water.

THE LAKES AND RIVERS OF ARKANSAS. APT, 1967. Motion picture.

16mm, 28 min., sound, color. The water recreations of skiing, swimming, boating, and canoeing are shown. Free loan.

LOWER CANYONS OF THE RIO GRANDE. KXA, n.d. Motion picture.

16mm, ? min., sound, color. This area is Texas's least-known, and is rated by some as the third-most-scenic wild river canyon in North America. The production shows the arguments over wild river status and real estate development.

LURE OF THE LONELY LAND. SPL, 1971. Motion picture.

16mm, 90 min., sound, color. A 1,200-mile canoe journey by Jay Pritchett and Jack West through Manitoba and parts of the Northwest Territories to Hudson Bay is the subject of this documentary. Pritchett was responsible for the camera work.

MOUTH TO MOUTH ARTIFICIAL RESPIRATION WITH THREE METHODS OF POSITIONING THE HEAD. EBE, 1968. Motion picture.

8mm, 3 min., no sound, color. This loop film demonstrates the correct way to give mouth-to-mouth respiration to a victim, and shows how to position the head.

1976 OLYMPIC CANOE AND KAYAK RACES. MAN, 1976. Motion picture.

16mm, 113 min., no sound, black and white. This slow-motion film was photographed at more than four times normal speed, to facilitate coaching and stroke analysis.

1964 TOKYO TRAINING FILM. NPC, 1964. Motion picture.

16mm, 30 min., no sound, black and white. This film is issued in three parts of equal length. In slow motion, the various styles of some of the world's top paddlers are shown as they train for the 1964 Olympics.

NORTH COUNTRY WATERWAYS. STO, n.d. Slides.

35mm, 30 min., color. This slide program may be conducted by a member of the American Rivers Touring Association. A group follows the wilderness route of the voyageurs in historical Montreal canoes and "Huck Finn" rafts. The setting is the Wisconsin-Minnesota northern lakes region.

ONE RIVER DOWN. JDR, 1977. Motion picture.

16mm, 30 min., sound, color. James West Davidson and John Rugge canoe an unidentified river in Labrador's barrens. The name and location of the river are not divulged, pending its protection by Canadian authorities.

OREGON'S ROGUE RIVER. ART, n.d. Slides.

35mm, 70 slides, 30 min., color. This slide program may be conducted by a member of the American River Touring Association. The program presents the Rogue's rapids, fern-laden side canyons, and mountain forests.

PADDLE AND PORTAGE. CTF and NFB, 1966. Motion picture.

16mm, 12 min., sound, color. A paddler with thirty-five years of experience is featured as he demonstrates the art of canoeing, from basic strokes to advanced techniques. Demonstrations of canoe rescue and water safety are included.

PADDLING KAYAKS AND CANOES. NPC, n.d. Motion picture.

16mm, 40 min., sound, black and white. The first reel demonstrates Olympic-style canoeing; the second shows flat-water kayak paddling. Both start with an introduction for beginners and follow through to world class and Olympic paddlers.

PLANNING FOR FLOODS. An Environmental Defense Fund film. ASF, n.d.
Motion picture.

> 16mm, ? min., sound, color. This film presents the environ-
> mentalist's argument of the reasons structural answers to the prob-
> lem of flooding do not work.

POLICY CENTER SLIDE SHOW ON EFFECTS OF DAMS. EPC, n.d. Slides.

> 35mm, 15 min., color. A set of forty slides depicts some of the
> effects of dams on farmland, wildlife, and the community. The
> slides may be reproduced for inclusion in other programs.

PORTAGE. IFB, n.d. Motion picture.

> 16mm, 21 min., sound, color. A record of canoe building and
> of the Indian trapper and explorer. PORTAGE is also available as
> two separate films: HOW INDIANS BUILD CANOES and TRAP-
> PERS AND TRADERS.

PULSE OF LIFE. PYF, n.d. Motion picture.

> 16mm, 27 min., sound, color. This film illustrates recent de-
> velopments in resuscitation methods. Included are mouth-to-
> mouth breathing and external heart compression techniques.

QUABOG RIVER SUITE. ?, 1974. Motion picture.

> Super 8mm, 12 min., sound, color. Shows a group of young
> people as they run parts of the Quabog River on rubber rafts.
> Produced by John T. Donoghue.

QUETICO. CON, n.d. Motion picture.

> 16mm, 22 min., sound, color. This film highlights Quetico
> Provincial Park and gives an introduction to the idea of taking
> a canoe trip.

RAPIDS OF THE COLORADO. PYF, n.d. Motion picture.

> 16mm, 15 min., sound, color. Scenes from a trip down the
> Colorado River are shown.

RESCUE AND SELF RESCUE (CANOE). HEK, 1968. Motion picture.

> Super 8mm, 3 min., no sound, color. This cartridge-loop film
> demonstrates rescue and self-rescue methods to be followed when
> a canoe has overturned.

RIVER BUSTERS. SOS, n.d. Motion picture.

> 16mm, 22 min., sound, color. Two college boys fight their way up the "River of No Return" in a battle against the Salmon and Snake rivers of Idaho. Free loan.

ROGUE RIVER COUNTRY. AUD, 1962. Motion picture.

> 16mm, 28 min., sound, color. The recreational opportunities and wealth of natural resources found in the Rogue River valley of southwestern Oregon are reviewed. The film shows the river's effect on the economy and the character of its watershed, and includes views of the scenery and boat trips through the rapids.

RUN THE WILD COLORADO. JCS, 1969. Motion picture.

> 16mm, 28 min., sound, color. This film records ten days of whitewater adventure by a group challenging the rapids of the Colorado River.

SACRAMENTO RIVER LOGUE. ART, n.d. Motion picture.

> 16mm, 15 min., sound, color. This film presents a "Huck Finn" adventure, with music by the San Francisco Folk Music Society.

SURVIVAL, MOUNTAIN AND DESERT. A Department of Defense training film, no. AF-TF-5571A. AIR, n.d. Motion picture.

> 16mm, ? min., sound, color.

THE SURVIVAL KIT, PART 1. MLP and SEF, 1967. Motion picture.

> 16mm, 10 min., sound, color. This film shows the first day of survival in the wilderness, and explains how a small kit is designed to combat the seven enemies of survival.

THE SURVIVAL KIT, PART 2. MLP and SEF, 1967. Motion picture.

> 16mm, 10 min., sound, color. The second day of survival in the wilderness is depicted, with an explanation of how the survival kit continues to keep one alive (see above citation).

SURVIVAL STRESS. A Department of Defense training film, no. AF-TF-1-5375. AIR, n.d. Motion picture.

> 16mm, ? min., sound, color. This film shows survival's psychological effect.

SURVIVAL THROUGH WILD PLANTS. Audiovisual Instructional Devices Co., 1971. Filmstrip.

35mm, 162 fr. (4 filmstrips), color. This film shows methods for searching out and preparing wild plants that are healthful as well as appetizing, such as milkweed, bayberry, mustard, and chicory. It is issued with four phonotapes in cassette.

SUWANNEE ADVENTURE. FDC, n.d. Motion picture.

16mm, 14 min., sound, color. Two women explore the Suwannee's 170 miles of natural beauty across northern Florida to the Gulf of Mexico. Free loan.

THE THERMAL WILDERNESS. SAC, n.d. Motion picture.

16mm, ? min., sound, color. This film shows the effect of heat on a victim. Free loan.

A TIME TOGETHER. COR, 1974. Motion picture.

16mm, 14 min., sound, color. A father-son relationship is described as well as how it changed when they spent time together on a canoeing trip.

TO KAYAK. DIC, n.d. Motion picture.

16mm, 33 min., sound, color. This film attempts to answer the question "what is kayaking all about?" All aspects are covered, including equipment, construction, safety, getting started, cruising, and racing. Action shows a slalom on the Savage River in Maryland and the Gull River in Ontario as well as downriver racing on West Virginia's Cheat River. A Canadian wilderness cruise sequence is included.

TRAPS AND SNARES. MLP and SEF, 1967. Motion picture.

16mm, 10 min., sound, color. How to catch small game is shown. The film includes construction details and the operation of traps and snares by an expert Indian trapper.

TUKTU AND THE BIG KAYAK. NFB and FIL, 1969. Motion picture.

16mm, 14 min., sound, color. This is a children's adventure film about Tuktu, a Netsilik Eskimo boy. It shows the construction of a kayak.

THE UNCALCULATED RISK. ARC and RNP, 1977. Motion picture.

16mm, 15 min., sound, color. The dangerous aspects of whitewater river running are stressed in this film available from local Red Cross chapters, stock no. 321578.

UPPER IOWA. NEI, n.d. Slides.

> 35mm, 20 min., color. This presentation consists of one hundred numbered slides illustrating the scenery, canoeing, wildlife, and historical and archaeological sites. Free loan.

UPPER IOWA. BLB and NBW, 1969. Motion picture.

> 16mm, 50 min., sound, color. This film makes a plea for preservation of the upper Iowa River. Free loan.

WATER RESCUE. AFP and UIL, n.d. Motion picture.

> 16mm, 12 min., sound, color. How to rescue and revive nearvictims of drowning in boat, canoe, sailboat, and pool situations are explained.

WHERE THE LOON SCREAMS. Life Support Technology, 1970. Motion picture.

> An expedition to the Canadian Arctic is followed; extensive survival studies are conducted and a search is made for the prehistoric musk-ox.

WHITEWATER. ARC, 1971. Motion picture.

> 16mm, 11 min., sound, color. Whitewater canoeing and slalom and downriver racing on the Nantahala River in the Smoky Mountains are shown. The film explains basic racing rules and shows all types of craft in actual competition. Free loan.

WHITEWATER. CFI, 1975. Motion picture.

> 16mm, 24 min., sound, color. This film is a documentary of the first annual Great Canadian River Race.

WHITEWATER. FIL, 1976. Motion picture.

> 16mm, 24 min., sound, color. The importance of precautions and preparation when participating in whitewater sports involving canoes, kayaks, and rafts are pointed out in this film.

WHITEWATER, BLUE WATER. CFM, 1974. Motion picture.

> 16mm, 14 min., sound, color. This film concerns Canada's first whitewater school for kayaking and canoeing, located on the Madawaska River in northern Ontario.

WHITEWATER PA. PSU, 1977.

> 16mm, 37 min., sound, color. Pennsylvania rivers are the scene

for this film of paddling instruction, slalom, and plain fun.
Safety is stressed throughout.

WHITEWATER SELF-DEFENSE: THE ESKIMO ROLL. RNP, n.d. Motion picture.

Super 8mm, 14 min., sound, color. All the complexities of the
Eskimo roll are demonstrated through the use of creative camera
work. The film uses members of the U.S. whitewater team as
the demonstrators.

WHITEWATER SLALOM. SAF, 1967. Motion picture.

16mm, 18 min., sound, color. Canoe and kayak slalom racing
in the eastern section of the United States are discussed. The
film explains the various paddle strokes and rules of slalom racing, and includes scenes from the National Canoe and Eastern
Kayak Championships held on Vermont's West River.

THE WHY AND HOW OF STANDARD FIRST AID. ARC, 1965. Motion picture.

16mm, 28 min., sound, black and white. This film is based on
the Red Cross standard first aid course and is designed to develop
good safety attitudes. It describes the first aid skills used in
caring for victims of accidents and sudden illness.

WILDERNESS QUEST. BFC, n.d. Motion picture.

16mm, 28 min., sound, color. An account of travel by canoe,
foot, and horse through picturesque wilderness is given. Free
loan.

WILDERNESS RIVER TRAIL. AFS and SIC, 1952. Motion picture.

16mm, 28 min., sound, color. The Yampa and Green rivers
of Dinosaur National Monument are explored on a float trip,
showing the unique canyon country and the excitement and
pleasure of river travel in the canyonlands of western America.

WILD RIVER. EBE, 1965. Motion picture.

16mm, 14 min., sound, color. This film shows the beauty of
wild river regions and explains the value of rivers for recreation
and as havens for wildlife. It describes how water resources
may be polluted by refuse, oil, and chemicals, and stresses the
need for conservation.

WILD RIVER. FIL, NGS, and UIL, 1970. Motion picture.

16mm, 52 min., sound, color. A family is followed as they
explore, in rafts and kayaks, the middle fork of the Salmon

river as it flows through Idaho, and as they travel through the Florida Everglades. The beauty of nature and importance of conservation are emphasized.

WILD WATER. ?, 1971. Motion picture.

16mm, 20 min., sound, color. This film follows the U.S. kayak and canoe team, from training sessions on the Mascoma River in New Hampshire to competition at the 1971 World Kayak and Canoe Championships in Merano, Italy.

PRODUCERS AND DISTRIBUTORS
(Listed by three-letter code)

ABC American Broadcasting Companies
1330 Avenue of the Americas
New York, New York 10019
(212) 581-7777

AFI American Film Institute
Kennedy Center
Washington, D.C. 20566
(202) 833-9300

AFP American Film Productions
1540 Broadway
New York, New York 10036
(212) 582-1900

AFS Associated Film Service
3607 West Magnolia, Suite M
Burbank, California 91505
(213) 467-1171

AIR U.S. Air Force
Audio Visual Service
Central Audio Visual Library
Norton Air Force Base, California
92409

APT Arkansas Department of Parks
and Tourism
149 Capitol Building
Little Rock, Arkansas 72201
(501) 371-2535

ARC American National Red Cross
17th and D Streets, N.W.
Washington, D.C. 20006
(202) 737-8300

ART American River Touring
Association
1016 Jackson Street
Oakland, California 94607
(415) 465-9355

ASF Association-Sterling Films
(Main Office)
866 Third Avenue
New York, New York 10022
(212) 935-4210

AUD U.S. National Audio Visual
Center
National Archives and Records
Service
8th Street and Pennsylvania
Avenue, N.W.
Washington, D.C. 20408
(202) 963-6411

BFC Boyd Film Co.
1569 Selby Avenue
St. Paul, Minnesota 55104
(612) 644-7317

BLB   Blackhawk Broadcasting Co.
East 4th and Franklin Streets
Waterloo, Iowa 50703
(319) 234-4401

BSA   Boy Scouts of America
Supply Division, AV Department
New Brunswick, New Jersey 08901
(201) 249-6000

EMC   British Columbia Provincial
Educational Media Centre
4455 Juneau Street
Burnaby, British Columbia   V5C 4C4
(604) 294-5151

CBC   Canadian Broadcasting Corp.,
English Services Division
P.O. Box 500, Station A
Toronto, Ontario M5W 1E6
(416) 925-3311

CBC   Canadian Broadcasting Corp.,
French Services Division
P.O. Box 6000
Montreal, Province of Quebec
H3C 3A8
(514) 285-3211

CFD   Canadian Film Development Corp.
C.P. 71 Tour de la Bourse, Suite 2220
Montreal, Province of Quebec
H4Z 1A8
(514) 283-6363

CFD   Canadian Film Development Corp.
111 Avenue Road, Suite 602
Toronto, Ontario M5R 3J8
(416) 966-6436

CFI   Canadian Film Institute
1762 Carling Avenue
Ottawa, Ontario K2A 1C9
(413) 729-6193

CFM   Canadian Film-Makers
Distribution Center
341 Bloor Street, W., Room 204
Toronto, Ontario M5S 1W8
(416) 921-2259

CNH   Canadian Department of
National Health and Welfare
Film Library
Brooke Claxton Building
Ottawa, Ontario KIA OK9

CON   Contemporary Films (McGraw-
Hill)
1221 Avenue of the Americas
New York, New York 10020
(212) 997-6761

COR   Coronet Films
65 East South Water Street
Chicago, Illinois 60611
(312) 332-7676

CTF   Canadian Travel Film Library
(U.S. Distribution)
1251 Avenue of the Americas
New York, New York 10019
(212) 586-2400

DIC   Peg Dice
2022 Day Street
Ann Arbor, Michigan 48104

EBE   Encyclopedia Britannica Educational Corp.
425 North Michigan Avenue
Chicago, Illinois 60611
(312) 321-6800

EKC   Eastman Kodak Co.
Audio Visual Library Distribution
343 State Street
Rochester, New York 14650
(716) 458-1000

EPC Environmental Policy Institute
317 Pennsylvania Ave., S.E.
Washington, D.C. 20003
(202) 544-8200

FDC Florida Department of Commerce
Audio Visual Library
Collins Building
Tallahassee, Florida 32304
(904) 488-6300

FIL Films Incorporated (Main Office)
1144 Wilmette Avenue
Wilmette, Illinois 60091
(312) 256-4730

GCD Grand Canyon Dories
P.O. Box 5585
Stanford, California 94305
(415) 851-0411

HEK Herbert Kerkow
South Quaker Hill
Pawling, New York 12564
(914) 855-1394

ICD Idaho Department of Tourism and
Industrial Development
108 State House
Boise, Idaho 83720
(208) 384-2470

IFB International Film Bureau
332 South Michigan Avenue
Chicago, Illinois 60604
(312) 427-4545

JCS Jack's Camera Shop
614 St. Joe Street
Rapid City, South Dakota 57701
(605) 343-5837

JDR James West Davidson and
John Rugge
c/o P.O. Box 281
Chestertown, New York 12817

KUI KUID-TV
University of Idaho
Moscow, Idaho 83843
(208) 885-6723

KXA KXAS-TV
c/o Tom McDonald
P.O. Box 1780
Fort Worth, Texas 76101
(817) 429-1550

MAN Motion Analysis
P.O. Box 52
Buchanan, Michigan 49107
(616) 695-9637

MCG McGraw-Hill Book and Educational Services Group
Film Division
1221 Avenue of the Americas
New York, New York 10020
(212) 997-1221

MFE Mogull's Film Exchange
235 West 46th Street
New York, New York 10036
(212) 757-1414

MLP Moreland-Latchford Productions
299 Queen Street, W.
Toronto, Ontario M5V 1Z9
(416) 362-2011

MLP Moreland-Latchford Productions
(U.S. Distribution)
1051 Clinton Street
Buffalo, New York 14206
(716) 855-3122

NAS National Science Film Library
Canadian Film Institute
1762 Carling Avenue
Ottawa, Ontario K2A 2H7

NBW National Bank of Waterloo
c/o William J. Rickert
100 East Park Avenue
Waterloo, Iowa 50704
(319) 291-5200

NCF North Central Forest Experiment
Station
c/o Clinton Waddell
1992 Folwell Avenue
St. Paul, Minnesota 55108
(612) 645-0841

NEI North East Iowa Council on
Outdoor Resources
c/o George Knudson
Luther College
Decorah, Iowa 52101

NFB National Film Board
150 Kent Street
Ottawa, Ontario KIA OM9

NFB National Film Board
(U.S. Distribution)
1251 Avenue of the Americas
New York, New York 10019
(212) 586-2400

NGS National Geographic Society
17th and M Streets, N.W.
Washington, D.C. 20036
(202) 296-7500

NPC NPC
Route 1, Box 83
Buchanan, Michigan 49107

NSR Nova Scotia Department of
Recreation
P.O. Box 864
Halifax, Nova Scotia B3J 2V2

PSU Pennsylvania State University TV
WPSX-TV
201 Wagner Building
University Park, Pennsylvania 16802
(814) 865-9531

PYF Pyramid Films
P.O. Box 1048
Santa Monica, California
90406
(213) 828-7577

QPB Quebec Publicity Bureau
(U.S. Distribution)
17 West 50th Street
New York, New York 10020
(212) 581-0770

RNP Russ Nichols Productions
P.O. Box 192
Lemont, Pennsylvania 16851

SAC Safeco Insurance Co.
Safeco Plaza
Seattle, Washington 98185
(206) 545-5000

SAF Sanderling Films
2401 Washington Street
Canton, Massachusetts 02021

SAM Saskatchewan Media Corp.
University of Regina
Regina, Saskatchewan S4S OA2
(306) 584-4111

SEF Sterling Educational Films
241 East 34th Street
New York, New York 10016
(212) 683-6300

SIC Sierra Club
1050 Mills Tower
San Francisco, California
94104
(415) 981-8634

SOS Solana Studios
4365 North 27th Street
Milwaukee, Wisconsin 53216
(414) 445-2222

SPL Spokane Public Library
West 906 Main Avenue
Spokane, Washington 99201
(509) 838-3361

SPI Sports Illustrated
Time-Life Building
New York, New York 10020
(212) 586-1212

STO Duncan Storlie
5375 Eureka Road
Excelsior, Minnesota 55331

TCF Twentieth Century-Fox Film Corp.
P.O. Box 900
Beverly Hills, California 90213
(213) 277-2211

UIL University of Illinois
Visual Aids Service
1325 South Oak Street
Champaign, Illinois 61822
(217) 333-1360

WKY WKYC-TV
1403 East 6th Street
Cleveland, Ohio 44114
(216) 696-1100

YFL Yukon Regional Library
Film Library
P.O. Box 2703
Whitehorse, Yukon Territory Y1E

Chapter 11
PERIODICALS

CANOEING, KAYAKING, AND RAFTING MAGAZINES

THE AMERICAN CANOEIST. Vol. 1-32? North Hollywood, Calif.: American Canoe Association, 1941-72? Quarterly.

> For more than thirty years this magazine served as the official organ of the American Canoe Association (ACA). Several years ago it ceased publication. The ACA now reports activities in its official publication, CANOE (see below).

AMERICAN WHITEWATER: THE JOURNAL OF THE AMERICAN WHITEWATER AFFILIATION. San Bruno, Calif.: American Whitewater Affiliation, 1955-- . Bimonthly.

> Members of the American Whitewater Affiliation receive a sub-scription to this magazine. It is intended for the kayakist, but virtually every issue includes an article on canoeing and perhaps another on a conservation theme, such as preservation of free-flowing rivers. Regular features are book reviews, product re-views, directory of affiliates, letters, and obituaries. Business office: P.O. Box 321, Concord, New Hampshire 03301.

CANOE: MAGAZINE OF THE AMERICAN CANOE ASSOCIATION. St. Paul, Minn.: Webb Co., 1973-- . Bimonthly.

> This magazine has a circulation of about twenty-two thousand, making it the largest American paddling publication. In addition to articles on touring, poling, and canoe competitions, there is usually an article or two about kayaking. Regular departments include book reviews, camping, letters, and conservation. The American Canoe Association annual canoe and kayak racing schedule is listed in the spring issue. Business office: 1999 Shepard Road, St. Paul, Minnesota 55116.

CANOE: THE OFFICIAL PUBLICATION OF THE CANADIAN CANOE ASSO-
CIATION. Vanier City, Ontario: Canadian Canoe Association, 1976-- .
Quarterly.

> This new Canadian Canoe Association publication has a heavy
> emphasis on organized canoeing, especially racing. Not re-
> markably, volume 1 gives an in-depth report on canoeing at the
> 1976 Olympic Games. There is thorough coverage of the results
> of national paddling competition. Business office: 333 River
> Road, Vanier City, Ontario KIL 8B9.

CANOE NEWS: OFFICIAL PUBLICATION OF THE UNITED STATES CANOE
ASSOCIATION. Milwaukee, Wis.: U.S. Canoe Association, 1968-- . Bimonthly.

> This magazine is included with membership in the U.S. Canoe
> Association (USCA). Before separate publication began with
> volume 10, CANOE NEWS came as an insert in the magazine
> entitled WILDERNESS CAMPING. Recent focus of the articles
> has been on providing information about water management proj-
> ects. The general tone of the publication is casual. Various
> issues include racing and cruising schedules for USCA-sanctioned
> competition. Business office: 9021 F North 91st Street, Mil-
> waukee, Wisconsin 53224.

OAR AND PADDLE. Idaho Falls, Idaho: M. O. Carnes, 1974. Semiannual.

> A magazine specializing in canoe, kayak, and raft touring,
> OAR AND PADDLE ceased publication after only one year's
> issues. This is unfortunate, for there was a good range of ma-
> terial on wilderness paddling as well as extensive use of black
> and white and color illustrations. Some libraries will retain
> this short-lived publication in their periodical backfiles.

RIVERWORLD. Mountain View, Calif.: World Publications, 1974-- .
9 issues/year.

> As the title suggests, this magazine is intended for the river-
> runner--whether by canoe, kayak, or raft. Departments include
> fishing, wild foods, classifieds, and nature observation. The
> list of contributing editors and special contributors reads like a
> paddling who's who. With volume 4, the magazine changes
> from a monthly to publication nine times a year--February to
> October. DOWNRIVER. Business office: P.O. Box 366,
> Mountain View, California 94040.

CANOEING, KAYAKING, AND RAFTING NEWSLETTERS

AMERICAN RIVERS CONSERVATION NEWSLETTER. 317 Pennsylvania Avenue, S.E. Washington, D.C. 20003. Monthly.

BY-WAYS. American Youth Hostels, Metropolitan Chicago Council, 2210 North Clark Street, Chicago, Illinois 60614. Irregular.

HUT. Minnesota Canoe Association, 9th and Cedar Streets, St. Paul, Minnesota 55108. Bimonthly.

ILLINOIS PADDLING COUNCIL NEWSLETTER. 2316 Prospect Avenue, Evanston, Illinois 60201. Monthly.

LOOKING DOWNSTREAM. American River Touring Association, 1016 Jackson Street, Oakland, California 94607. Quarterly.

MUIR VIEWS. Sierra Club, John Muir Chapter, River Touring Section, 2604 North Murray Avenue, No. 107, Milwaukee, Wisconsin 53211. Bimonthly.

NEW YORK-NEW JERSEY RIVER CONFERENCE NEWSLETTER. 1 Red Cross Place, Brooklyn, New York 11201. Quarterly.

RIO GRANDE GURGLE. c/o Helen F. Redman, Route 1, Box 177, Santa Fe, New Mexico 87501. 1969-- . Bimonthly.

SIGNPOST NEWSLETTER. Signpost Publications, 16812 36th Avenue, W., Lynnwood, Washington 98036. 1966-- . 16 issues/year.

THE WANDER PADDLER. Wander Paddlers Guild, 724 Poplar Street, Coquitlam, British Columbia V3J 3S3. Quarterly.

WILD WATER SPLASHES. West Virginia Wildwater Association, 2737 Daniels Avenue, South Charleston, West Virginia 25303. Monthly.

WISCONSIN CANOE ASSOCIATION NEWSLETTER. 10915 North Sherwood Drive, Mequin, Wisconsin 53092. Irregular.

SELECTED PERIODICALS WITH REGULAR OR OCCASIONAL
CANOEING, KAYAKING, AND RAFTING COVERAGE

APPALACHIA JOURNAL. Appalachian Mountain Club, 5 Joy Street, Boston, Massachusetts 02108. 1876-- . Semiannual.

ARCTIC EXPLORER. TravelArctic, Yellowknife, Northwest Territories X1A 2L9. Monthly.

THE BEAVER: A MAGAZINE OF THE NORTH. Hudson's Bay House, Winnipeg, Manitoba R3C 2R1. 1920-- . Quarterly.

CANADIAN GEOGRAPHICAL JOURNAL. Royal Canadian Geographical Society, 488 Wilbrod Street, Ottawa, Ontario K1N 6M8. 1930-- . 11 issues/year.

MARIAH: QUARTERLY JOURNAL OF WILDERNESS EXPEDITION. Mariah Publications, 3401 West Division Street, Chicago, Illinois 60651. 1976-- . Quarterly.

NATIONAL GEOGRAPHIC MAGAZINE. National Geographic Society, 17th and M Streets, N.W. Washington, D.C. 20036. 1888-- . Monthly.

NORTHEAST OUTDOORS. David Zackin, 95 North Main Street, Waterbury, Connecticut 06702. 1968-- . Monthly.

OUTDOOR CANADA. Outdoor Canada Magazine, Ltd., 181 Eglinton Ave., E., Suite 201, Toronto, Ontario M2J 1X3. 1972-- . Bimonthly.

OUTDOOR ILLINOIS. Dan Malkovich, 320 South Main Street, Benton, Illinois 62812. 1963-- . Monthly.

OUTDOOR JOURNAL. Outdoor Journal Publications, 303 Goldstream Ave., Victoria, British Columbia V9B 2W4. 1974-- . Weekly.

OUTSIDE. Straight Arrow Publishers, 625 Third Street, San Francisco, California 94107. 1977-- . Monthly.

PRAIRIE CLUB BULLETIN. Prairie Club, 6 East Monroe Street, Room 1507, Chicago, Illinois 60603. 1915-- . Monthly (September-June).

SIGNPOST MAGAZINE. Signpost Publications, 16812 36th Avenue, W., Lynnwood, Washington 98036. 1966-- . 16 issues/year.

WILDERNESS CAMPING. Fitzgerald Communications, 1597 Union Street, Schenectady, New York 12309. 1971-- . Bimonthly.

WISCONSIN TRAILS: MAGAZINE OF LIFE IN THE BADGER STATE. Wisconsin Tales and Trails, P.O. Box 5650, Madison, Wisconsin 53705. 1960-- . Quarterly.

Chapter 12

FREE OR INEXPENSIVE WATERWAYS AND CAMPING
BOOKLETS AND MAPS

CANADA

ALBERTA

Alberta Department of Recreation, Parks, and Wildlife
10004 104th Avenue
Edmonton, Alberta   T5J OK5

"Lesser Slave Lake"

Travel Alberta
10255 104th Street
Edmonton, Alberta   T5J 1B1

"Travel Alberta Canoe"

BRITISH COLUMBIA

Department of Recreation and Travel Industry
Parks Branch
Parliament Buildings
Victoria, British Columbia   V8W   2Y9

"Bowron Lake Provincial Park"
"Strathcona Provincial Park"
"Tweedsmuir Provincial Park"
"Wells Gray Provincial Park"

LABRADOR (See NEWFOUNDLAND)

MANITOBA

Manitoba Department of Mines, Resources, and Environmental Management
139 Tuxedo Boulevard, Box 11
Winnipeg, Manitoba   R3C OV8

"Bloodvein River Charted"
"Canoeing on the Souris"

Manitoba Department of Tourism, Recreation, and Cultural Affairs
Parks Branch
200 Vaughan Street
Winnipeg, Manitoba   R3C OP8

"Canoe Trips in Manitoba"
"Frances Lake Canoe Route"
"Grass River Canoe Route"
"Kantunigan Route"
"Little Grand Rapids Canoe Routes"
"The Middle Track and Hayes River Route"
"Mistik Creek Canoe Route"
"Riviere aux Rats Canoe Route"
"Sasaginnigak Canoe Country"
"Whitemouth River Canoe Route"
"Winnipeg River Routes"

NEW BRUNSWICK

New Brunswick Department of Tourism
P.O. Box 6000
Fredericton, New Brunswick   E3B 5H1

"Guide to Canoe Tripping, New Brunswick"
"New Brunswick River Routes Map List"

NEWFOUNDLAND and LABRADOR

Canadian Department of Indian Affairs and Northern Development
400 Laurier Avenue, W.
Ottawa, Ontario   K1A OH4

"Wild Rivers Surveys" (Goose, Lloyds-Exploits, Main, Ugjoktok,
Naskaupi)

Newfoundland Tourist Services Division
Elizabeth Towers
St. John's, Newfoundland

"Suggested Newfoundland Canoe Routes"

NORTHWEST TERRITORIES

Canadian Department of Indian Affairs and Northern Development
Conservation Group
400 Laurier Avenue, W.
Ottawa, Ontario   K1A OH4

"Wild River Surveys" (Coppermine, Hanbury and Thelon, Hare, Mountain, Natla and Keele, South Redstone, Snare)

Canadian Department of the Environment
Information Branch
Ottawa, Ontario K1A OH3

"Canoe Routes to Hudson Bay"

Royal Canadian Geographical Society
488 Wilbrod Street
Ottawa, Ontario K1N 6M8

"Fresh Water Northwest Passage" (by Eric Morse)
"Summer Travel in the Canadian Barren Lands" (by Eric Morse)

TravelArctic
Northwest Territories Division of Tourism
Yellowknife, Northwest Territories X1A 2L9

"Across the Barrens by Canoe" (by Orris Herfindahl)
"Canoe Canada's Arctic Northwest Territories"
"Canoeing in the Northwest Territories"
"The Liard River Area"
"Nahanni National Park"
"The South Nahanni River"

NOVA SCOTIA

Nova Scotia Communications and Information Centre Book Store
P.O. Box 637
Halifax, Nova Scotia

"Canoe Route Maps" (for individual trips)

Nova Scotia Department of Tourism
P.O. Box 456
Halifax, Nova Scotia B3J 2R5

"Canoe Cape Breton"
"Canoe Waterways of Nova Scotia--Index"

ONTARIO

Northern Ontario Tourist Outfitters Association
Rural Route 1
Alban, Ontario P0M 1A0

"NOTOA Member Camps Directory"

Ontario Ministry of Industry and Tourism
900 Bay Street
Toronto, Ontario   M7A 1S6

> "Ontario/Canada Camping: Where to Go and How to Get There"

Ontario Ministry of Natural Resources
Division of Parks
Whitney Block, Queen's Park
Toronto, Ontario   M7A 1W3

> "Algonquin Provincial Park Canoe Routes Map"
> "Algonquin Provincial Park Map"
> "Mattawa Provincial Park"
> "Northern Ontario Canoe Routes"
> "Quetico Provincial Park Canoe Routes"
> "Quetico Provincial Park Map"
> "Wild River Parks" (Chapleau-Nemegosenda, Lady Evelyn,
>   Mattawa, Mississagi, and Winisk rivers)

Ontario Ministry of Natural Resources
Information Branch
Room 5314, Whitney Block, Queen's Park
Toronto, Ontario   M7A 1W3

> "Answering Your Questions about Canoeing in Ontario"
> "Conservation Areas in Ontario Map"
> "New Regulations Affecting Users of the Algonquin Provincial
>   Park Interior"
> "What You Should Know about Overnight Camping in North-
>   western Ontario"

Rockwood Outfitters
31 Yorkshire Street, S.
Guelph, Ontario   N1H 4Z9

> "Grand River Canoe Route" (Elora to Kitchener)
> "Grand River Canoe Route" (Kitchener to Galt)
> "Grand River Canoe Route" (Galt to Brantford)
> "Grand River Canoe Route" (Brantford to Caledonia)
> "Grand River Canoe Route" (Caledonia to Lake Erie)
> "Magnetawan River"
> "Moon River Canoe Trip"
> "Muskoka-Gibson Rivers"
> "Saugeen River Canoe Route" (Walkerton to Southampton)

PRINCE EDWARD ISLAND

Prince Edward Island Tourist Information Centre
P.O. Box 940
Charlottetown, Prince Edward   C1A 7M5

"Camping on Prince Edward Island"

QUEBEC

Quebec Department of Tourism, Fish, and Game
150 est boulevard Saint-Cyrille
Quebec, Province of Quebec   G1R 4Y3

"Camping Quebec"
"Canoe Camping on Jacques-Cartier River"
"Chochocouane River Canoe-Camping Map"
"Parks and Reserves of Quebec"
"Parks of Quebec: Activities and Rates"
"Reserve La Verendrye Canoe Camping"
"Reserve La Verendrye Map"
"Reserve Papineau-Labelle Canoe Camping Routes Map"

SASKATCHEWAN

Canadian Department of Indian Affairs and Northern Development
Conservation Group
400 Laurier Avenue, W.
Ottawa, Ontario   K1A OH4

"Wild River Surveys" (Clearwater, Fond du Lac, and Churchill rivers)

Meadow Lake Region Canoeing Program
P.O. Box 70
Dorintosh, Saskatchewan   SOM OTO

"The Meadow Lake Region Canoeing Program"

Saskatchewan Department of Tourism and Renewable Resources
P.O. Box 7105
Regina, Saskatchewan   S4P OB5

"Canoe Saskatchewan" (listing fifty route booklets)
"Saskatchewan Canoe Trips, Number 1" (Ile-a-la-Crosse, Churchill
    River to Otter Lake)
"Saskatchewan Canoe Trips, Number 21" (Sulphide, Freda, Freestone,
    Hebden, Contact, and Lynx lakes)

YUKON TERRITORY

Canadian Department of Indian Affairs and Northern Development
400 Laurier Avenue, W.
Ottawa, Ontario   K1A OH4

"Wild Rivers Surveys" (Bell, Bennett-Nares-Tagish-Atlin-Marsh, Big Sal-
    mon, Firth, Klondike, MacMillan, Nisutlin, Ogilvie, Peel, Pelly,
    Porcupine, Ross, Sixty Mile, Stewart, Teslin, White, and Yukon rivers)
"Yukon Canoe Travel Information"

UNITED STATES

ALABAMA

Alabama Department of Conservation and Natural Resources
Administration Building
Montgomery, Alabama 36104

"The Beautiful Cahaba River"
"Fishing Scenic Little River"
"Float Fishing on the Sipsey River"
"Float Fishing the Tallapoosa Offers Many Thrills, Scenery"

ALASKA

U.S. Department of the Interior
Bureau of Land Management
P.O. Box 2511
Juneau, Alaska 99801

"Alaska's Gulkana Basin"
"Alaska's Gulkana Float Trips"
"Alaska's River Trails, Southern Region"
"Historic Eagle and Alaska's Taylor Highway"
"Recreation along Alaska's Denali Highway"
"Recreation along Alaska's Steese and Elliott Highways"

U.S. Department of the Interior
Bureau of Sport Fisheries and Wildlife
P.O. Box 1287
Juneau, Alaska 99801

"Swan Lake Canoe Route"

ARIZONA

Arizona Office of Tourism
State Capitol
Phoenix, Arizona 85007

"Grand Canyon River Runners Directory"
"River Running: Arizona, Colorado, Utah"

ARKANSAS

Arkansas Department of Parks and Tourism
149 State Capitol
Little Rock, Arkansas 72201

"Arkansas Camping Guide"
"Arkansas Little Red River Trout Fishing"

"Arkansas White River Trout Fishing"
"The Buffalo River, Arkansas"
"Spring River and South Fork of Spring River"

Bluff City Canoe Club
P.O. Box 4523
Memphis, Tennessee 38104

"Mid-South River Guide" (Arkansas, Missouri, Tennessee)

U.S. Department of Agriculture
Forest Service
Ouachita National Forest
Hot Springs, Arkansas 71901

"Ouachita River Float Trip"

CALIFORNIA

U.S. Department of Agriculture
Forest Service
Six Rivers National Forest
710 E Street
Eureka, California 95501

"Six Rivers National Forest"

COLORADO

U.S. Department of Agriculture
Forest Service
Rio Grande National Forest
Monte Vista, Colorado 81144

"Rio Grande National Forest"

U.S. Department of Agriculture
Forest Service
Uncompahgre National Forest
Delta, Colorado 81416

"Uncompahgre National Forest"

U.S. Department of Agriculture
Forest Service
White River National Forest
Steamboat Springs, Colorado 80477

"White River National Forest"

Booklets and Maps

CONNECTICUT

Connecticut Department of Environmental Protection
Public Information and Education
State Office Building
Hartford, Connecticut 06115

    "Connecticut Canoeing Guide"

FLORIDA

Coastal Plain Area Tourism Council
P.O. Box 1223
Valdosta, Georgia 31601

    "Suwannee River Canoe Trail"
    "Withlacoochee River Canoe Trail"

Florida Department of Natural Resources
Crown Building
Tallahassee, Florida 32304

    "Guide to Florida Canoe Trails"

U.S. Department of Agriculture
Forest Service
P.O. Box 1050
Tallahassee, Florida 32302

    "Alexander Springs Recreation Area, Ocala National Forest"
    "Juniper Creek Canoe Run, Ocala National Forest"

U.S. Department of the Interior
National Park Service
Everglades National Park
P.O. Box 279
Homestead, Florida 33030

    "Everglades National Park Canoe Trail Guide"

GEORGIA

Coastal Plain Area Tourism Council
P.O. Box 1223
Valdosta, Georgia 31601

    "Canoe Guide to the Suwannee, Withlacoochee, and Alapaha Rivers"

Georgia Department of Community Development
P.O. Box 38097
Atlanta, Georgia 30334

    "Canoe Guide to the Alapaha River Trail"

"Canoe Guide to the Scenic Satilla River"
"Historical St. Marys River Canoe Guide"
"Suwannee River Canoe Trail Guide"

U.S. Department of Agriculture
Forest Service
P.O. Box 1437
Gainesville, Georgia 30501

"Canoeing on the Chattooga"

U.S. Department of the Interior
Division of Wildlife Refuges
Okefenokee National Wildlife Refuge
P.O. Box 117
Waycross, Georgia 31501

"Wilderness Canoeing in Okefenokee National Wildlife Refuge"

IDAHO

Idaho Department of Fish and Game
600 South Walnut Street, Box 25
Boise, Idaho 83707

"Idaho Lakes and Reservoirs"
"Mountain Lakes of Idaho"

U.S. Department of Agriculture
Forest Service
St. Joe National Forest
P.O. Box 310
Coeur d'Alene, Idaho 83814

"St. Joe River Float Trips"

U.S. Department of Agriculture
Forest Service
Salmon National Forest
Salmon, Idaho 83467

"The Salmon--River of No Return"

U.S. Department of the Interior
Bureau of Land Management
Resource Area Headquarters
Route 3
Cottonwood, Idaho 83522

"Lower Salmon River Guide"

Booklets and Maps

ILLINOIS

Chicagoland Canoe Base
4019 North Narragansett Avenue
Chicago, Illinois 60634

"Chicagoland Canoe Trails"

U.S. Army
Corps of Engineers, North Central Division
536 South Clark Street
Chicago, Illinois 60605

"Illinois Waterway"
"Mississippi River" (Cairo, Illinois, to Minneapolis, Minnesota)

INDIANA

Indiana Department of Natural Resources
Division of Outdoor Recreation
612 State Office Building
Indianapolis, Indiana 46204

"Indiana Canoe Guide, Summary of Contents"

IOWA

Iowa Conservation Commission
300 4th Street
Des Moines, Iowa 50319

"Iowa Canoe Trips"

U.S. Department of the Army
Army Corps of Engineers
1800 Federal Office Building
Kansas City, Missouri 64106

"Rathbun Lake"

KANSAS

U.S. Army
Corps of Engineers
1800 Federal Office Building
Kansas City, Missouri 64106

"Kanopolis Lake"
"Melvern Lake"
"Milford Lake"
"Perry Lake"

"Pomona Lake"
"Tuttle Creek Lake"
"Wilson Lake"

KENTUCKY

Kentucky Department of Public Information
Capitol Annex
Frankfort, Kentucky 40601

"Guide to Canoeing Streams of Kentucky"

U.S. Department of Agriculture
Forest Service
Daniel Boone National Forest
100 Vaught Road
Winchester, Kentucky 40391

"Daniel Boone National Forest Canoeing Guide" (Red River)
"Summary of Boating Streams in Daniel Boone National Forest"

U.S. Department of the Interior
National Park Service
Mammoth Cave National Park
Mammoth Cave, Kentucky 42259

"Mammoth Cave National Park Map" (Green River)

LOUISIANA

Louisiana Wildlife and Fisheries Commission
400 Royal Street
New Orleans, Louisiana 70160

"Streams and Stream Preservation--Justification for a Scenic
Rivers Program in Louisiana"

MAINE

Great Northern Paper Co.
6 State Street
Bangor, Maine 04106

"Sportsman's Map" (Allagash, Chesuncook, Chamberlain)

Maine Department of Conservation
Bureau of Parks and Recreation
State Office Building
Augusta, Maine 04330

"Allagash Wilderness Waterway"

Booklets and Maps

Moor and Mountain
63 Park Street
Andover, Massachusetts 01810

     "Baxter State Park Map"
     "East of Allagash Map"
     "East of Katahdin Map"
     "Moosehead--Allagash Map"
     "Mt. Desert Island Trails and Waterways Map"
     "Rangeley Lakes Region Map"
     "St. John--Allagash Wilderness Map"
     "Washington County Map"

Rangeley Lakes Region
Chamber of Commerce
Rangeley, Maine 04970

     "Canoe Routes" (Rangeley Lakes--Azicoos)

St. Croix Paper Co.
Woodland, Maine 04694

     "Sportsman's Map" (Grand Lake)

Scott Paper Co.
Winslow, Maine 04901

     "Sportsman's Map" (Moosehead--Upper Kennebec)

MARYLAND

Gray, Thomas L.
11121 Dewey Road
Kensington, Maryland 20795

     "Canoeing Streams of the Potomac and Rappahannock Basins"

Maryland Department of Economic and Community Development
Division of Tourist Development
2525 Riva Road
Annapolis, Maryland 21401

     "Canoe Rentals"

MASSACHUSETTS

Charles River Watershed Association
2391 Commonwealth Avenue
Auburndale, Massachusetts 02166

     "Charles River Canoe Guide"

New England Electric System
20 Turnpike Road
Westborough, Massachusetts 01581

"Down River" (Connecticut River)

Westfield River Watershed Association
P.O. Box 232
Huntington, Massachusetts 01050

"Westfield River Map"

MICHIGAN

Huron-Clinton Metropolitan Authority
3050 Penobscot Building
Detroit, Michigan 48226

"Clinton River Canoeing Maps"
"Huron River Canoeing Maps"

Michigan Department of Natural Resources
Stevens T. Mason Building
Lansing, Michigan 48926

"Canoeing in Michigan"
"Michigan's Natural Rivers Program"

Michigan Grand River Watershed Council
3322 West Michigan Avenue
Lansing, Michigan 48917

"Grand River Map"

Recreational Canoeing Association
P.O. Box 265
Baldwin, Michigan 49304

"Let's Go Canoeing" (rental guide)

South Branch Canoe Livery Association
Roscommon, Michigan 48653

"Wilderness Canoe Trail" (Au Sable, south branch)

U.S. Department of Agriculture
Forest Service
Cadillac, Michigan 49601

"Huron National Forest Map"
"Manistee National Forest Map"

U.S. Department of Agriculture
Forest Service
Ottawa National Forest
Ironwood, Michigan 49938

"Sylvania Recreation Area Map"

U.S. Department of the Army
Army Corps of Engineers
630 Federal Building
Detroit, Michigan 48226

"Great Lakes Map"

West Michigan Tourist Association
136 Fulton, E.
Grand Rapids, Michigan 49502

"Canoeing in West Michigan"

MINNESOTA

Aitkin County Park Commission
Court House
Aitkin, Minnesota 56431

"The Mighty Mississippi"

Bigfork River Canoe Trail
P.O. Box 356
Bigfork, Minnesota 56628

"Bigfork River Canoe Trail"

Crow Wing Trails Association
P.O. Box 210
Sebeka, Minnesota 56477

"Crow Wing River"

Ely Chamber of Commerce
30 South 1st Avenue, E.
Ely, Minnesota 55731

"Quetico-Superior Wilderness Canoe Routes"

Le Seur City Administrator
218 Main Street, S.
Le Seur, Minnesota 56058

"The Minnesota River"

Minnesota Department of Natural Resources
Centennial Building
St. Paul, Minnesota 55155

"Kettle River Guide"
"Minnesota Canoe Trails"
"Minnesota's Wild and Scenic Rivers"
"Mississippi Headwaters Canoe Route"
"North Fork of the Crow River Guide"

"Rum River Guide"
"St. Croix River" (Danbury to U.S. Highway 8)
"St. Croix River" (U.S. Highway 8 to the Mississippi)
"St. Louis River Canoe Route"
"Snake River Guide"

Muller Boat Co.
Taylor Falls, Minnesota 55084

"St. Croix River"

Pine County Soil and Water Conservation District
Hinckley, Minnesota 55037

"Kettle River Canoe Route"

Root River Canoe Trails Association
P.O. Box 548
Rushford, Minnesota 55971

"Root River Canoe Trail"

U.S. Department of Agriculture
Forest Service
Chippewa National Forest
Cass Lake, Minnesota 56633

"Chippewa National Forest" (Turtle and Rice rivers)

U.S. Department of Agriculture
Forest Service
Superior National Forest
P.O. Box 338
Duluth, Minnesota 55801

"BWCA Entrance Points"
"BWCA User Distribution Program"

U.S. Department of the Interior
Fish and Wildlife Service
Upper Mississippi River Wild Life and Fish Refuge
P.O. Box 226
Winona, Minnesota 55987

"Upper Mississippi River Wild Life and Fish Refuge"

U.S. Department of the Interior
National Park Service
Voyageurs National Park
P.O. Box 50
International Falls, Minnesota 56649

"Voyageurs National Park"

Booklets and Maps

MISSISSIPPI

U.S. Department of Agriculture
Forest Service
De Soto National Forest
P.O. Box 1291
Jackson, Mississippi 39505

"Black Creek Float Trip"

U.S. Department of Agriculture
Forest Service
P.O. Box 245
Rolling Fork, Mississippi 39159

"Little Sunflower River"

U.S. Department of the Army
Army Corps of Engineers
P.O. Box 60
Vicksburg, Mississippi 39181

"Mississippi River" (Cairo, Illinois, to the Gulf of Mexico)

MISSOURI

Bluff City Canoe Club
P.O. Box 4523
Memphis, Tennessee 38104

"Mid-South River Guide" (Arkansas, Missouri, Tennessee)

Missouri Department of Conservation
P.O. Box 180
Jefferson City, Missouri 65101

"Current River Map"

Missouri Geological Survey
P.O. Box 250
Rolla, Missouri 65401

"Lake and Reservoir Map of Missouri"

Three Rivers Tourist Association
P.O. Box 322
Winona, Missouri 65588

"Three Rivers of the Ozarks" (Current, Eleven Point, Jacks Fork)

U.S. Department of the Army
Army Corps of Engineers
601 East 12th Street
Kansas City, Missouri 64106

"Pomme de Terre Lake"
"Stockton Lake"

U.S. Department of the Interior
Fish and Wildlife Service
Mingo National Wildlife Refuge
Puxico, Missouri 63960

"Black Mingo Nature Area"

U.S. Department of the Interior
National Park Service
Van Buren, Missouri 63965

"Ozark National Scenic Riverways"

MONTANA

Montana Fish and Game Department
Sam W. Mitchell Building
Helena, Montana 59601

"Missouri River Map"
"Montana's Popular Float Streams"
"Timeless River--the Wide Missouri"
"Yellowstone State Recreational Waterway" (Gardiner to Pompey's
    Pillar)

U.S. Department of Agriculture
Forest Service
Helena National Forest
616 Helena Avenue
Helena, Montana 59601

"Gates of the Mountains River Guide"

U.S. Department of the Interior
National Park Service
1709 Jackson Street
Omaha, Nebraska 68101

"Missouri River, 1893 Historical Map" (Fort Benton to Fort Peck
    Lake)

NEBRASKA

Nebraska Game and Parks Commission
P.O. Box 30370
Lincoln, Nebraska 68503

"Canoeing Nebraska"
"Nebraskaland Boating Guide"

149

U.S. Department of the Army
Army Corps of Engineers
601 East 12th Street
Kansas City, Missouri 64106

     "Harlan County Dam and Multi-Purpose Reservoir"

U.S. Department of the Army
Army Corps of Engineers
P.O. Box 103, Downtown Station
Omaha, Nebraska 68101

     "Lewis and Clark Lake"
     "Lewis and Clark Trail"
     "Salt Valley in Nebraska"

NEVADA

Nevada Department of Economic Development
State Capitol
Carson City, Nevada 89701

     "Your Guide to Camping in Nevada"

Tahoe Sierra Development
P.O. Box T, Incline Village
Lake Tahoe, Nevada 89450

     "Lake Tahoe Map"

U.S. Department of the Interior
Bureau of Land Management
Carson City, Nevada 89701

     "Indian Creek Reservoir Recreation Site"

U.S. Department of the Interior
National Park Service
Lake Mead National Recreation Area
601 Nevada Highway
Boulder City, Nevada 89005

     "Lake Mead and Lake Mohave Guide"

NEW HAMPSHIRE

Vermont Environmental Conservation Agency
Division of Recreation
5 Court Street
Montpelier, Vermont 05602

     "Canoeing on the Connecticut River"

White Mountains Region Association
P.O. Box K
Lancaster, New Hampshire   03584

> "Summer Canoeing and Kayaking in the White Mountains of
> New Hampshire"

NEW JERSEY

Delaware River Basin Commission
P.O. Box 360
Trenton, New Jersey   08603

> "Delaware River Maps"
> "Shooting Rapids on the Upper Delaware"

New Jersey Department of Environmental Protection
Bureau of Parks
P.O. Box 1420
Trenton, New Jersey   08625

> "Canoeing in New Jersey"
> "Wharton State Forest Map"

Upper Raritan Watershed Association
P.O. Box 44
Far Hills, New Jersey   07931

> "Raritan River Guide"

NEW MEXICO

Base Camp
121 San Francisco
Santa Fe, New Mexico   87501

> "Rafting, Kayaking, and Canoeing on the Rio Grande and the
> Chama Rivers in Northern New Mexico"

New Mexico Department of Development
Tourist Division
113 Washington Avenue
Santa Fe, New Mexico   87501

> "Muscle Power"

NEW YORK

Delaware River Basin Commission
P.O. Box 360
Trenton, New Jersey   08603

"Delaware River Maps"

New York Department of Environmental Conservation
50 Wolf Road
Albany, New York   12205

"Adirondack Canoe Routes"
"Adirondack Canoe Routes--Lake Chains"
"Canoe Trips"

New York Department of Transportation
Albany, New York   12233

"Barge Canal System and Connecting Waterways"

NORTH CAROLINA

North Carolina Department of Natural and Economic Resources
Travel Development Section
P.O. Box 2768
Raleigh, North Carolina   27611

"North Carolina Outdoors"

NORTH DAKOTA

North Dakota Outdoor Recreation Agency
Route 2, Box 139
Mandan, North Dakota   58554

"North Dakota Canoeing Waters"
"Why Not Wakopa [Game Management Area]"

U.S. Department of the Army
Army Corps of Engineers
Garrison Dam
Riverdale, North Dakota   58565

"Lake Sakakawea"

U.S. Department of the Interior
Division of Wildlife Refuges
J. Clark Salyer National Refuge
Upham, North Dakota   58789

"Souris River Canoe Trail"

OHIO

Ohio Department of Natural Resources
Fountain Square
Columbus, Ohio   43224

"Canoe Liveries"
"Ohio's Natural Streams: the Scenic Rivers Program"

U.S. Department of the Army
Army Corps of Engineers
P.O. Box 1159
Cincinnati, Ohio 45201

"Ohio River and Tributaries Map"

OKLAHOMA

Grand Lake Association
P.O. Box 126
Grove, Oklahoma 74344

"Oklahoma's Grand Lake O' the Cherokees"

Kaw Lake Association
220 West Grand
Ponca City, Oklahoma 74601

"Oklahoma's Kaw Lake"

Keystone Lake Area Development Association
Saint Vir Lee Building
Cleveland, Oklahoma 74020

"Keystone Lake Guide"

Lake Eufaula Association
P.O. Box 822
Eufaula, Oklahoma 74432

"Oklahoma's Gentle Giant, Lake Eufaula"

Lake Tenkiller Association
P.O. Box 10 K
Cookson, Oklahoma 74427

"Oklahoma's Lake Tenkiller and the Illinois River"

Oklahoma Department of Tourism and Recreation
500 Will Rogers Building
Oklahoma City, Oklahoma 73105

"Oklahoma Campers Guide"
"Oklahoma Canoeing, River Floating"
"Oklahoma Lakes"

Oklahoma Department of Wildlife Conservation
1801 North Lincoln
Oklahoma City, Oklahoma 73105

"Floating the Illinois"

U.S. Department of the Army
Army Corps of Engineers
P.O. Box 61
Tulsa, Oklahoma 74102

"McClellan-Kerr Arkansas River Navigation System"
"Oologah Lake"

OREGON

Oregon Department of Transportation
Parks and Recreation Branch
300 State Highway Building
Salem, Oregon 97310

"Oregon's Willamette River Greenway"
"Willamette River Greenway Issues and Answers"
"Willamette River Recreation Guide Map"

Oregon Department of Transportation
Travel Information Division
140 Highway Building
Salem, Oregon 97310

"Oregon Boating Guide"

U.S. Department of Agriculture
Forest Service
1504 Northwest 6th Street
Grants Pass, Oregon 97526

"Siskiyou National Forest"

U.S. Department of the Interior
Bureau of Land Management
310 West 6th Street
Medford, Oregon 97501

"The Rogue River Wild and Scenic Map"

PENNSYLVANIA

American Youth Hostels
Pittsburgh Council
6300 5th Avenue
Pittsburgh, Pennsylvania 15232

"Canoeing in the Pittsburgh Area"
"Map of Canoeable Waters of Western Pennsylvania and Northern
    West Virginia"
"Watersheds of Pennsylvania"

Boy Scouts of America
Bucktail Council
49 East Long Avenue
Du Bois, Pennsylvania 15801

> "Eighty Miles of Wilderness Adventure on the West Branch of
> the Susquehanna River"

Gray, Thomas L.
11121 Dewey Road
Kensington, Maryland 20795

> "Canoeing Streams of the Upper Ohio Basin"

Penn State Outing Club
Recreation Building, Room 60
Pennsylvania State University
University Park, Pennsylvania 16802

> "Select Rivers of Central Pennsylvania"

Pennsylvania Department of Environmental Resources
202 Evangelical Press Building
Harrisburg, Pennsylvania 17105

> "Canoe Country Pennsylvania Style Map"

Pennsylvania State University
College of Agriculture
Agriculture Experiment Station
University Park, Pennsylvania 16802

> "Stream Map of Pennsylvania"

Western Pennsylvania Conservancy
204 5th Avenue
Pittsburgh, Pennsylvania 15222

> "Allegheny River Boat Trail"

RHODE ISLAND

Rhode Island Department of Economic Development
Tourism Division
1 Weybosset Hill
Providence, Rhode Island 02903

> "Boating in Rhode Island"
> "Camping in Rhode Island"

Rhode Island Department of Natural Resources
83 Park Street
Providence, Rhode Island 02903

"Rhode Island Recreation Map"

Rhode Island Fish and Wildlife Division
83 Park Street
Providence, Rhode Island 02903

"Pawcatuck River and Wood River"

SOUTH CAROLINA

South Carolina Department of Parks, Recreation, and Tourism
1205 Pendleton Street, Box 113
Columbia, South Carolina 29201

"South Carolina's Up Country"

South Carolina Wildlife and Marine Resources Department
P.O. Box 167, Dutch Plaza Building D
Columbia, South Carolina 29202

"South Carolina Float Trips" (Edisto, Little Pee Dee, Saluda, Savannah, and Black rivers)

U.S. Department of Agriculture
Forest Service
1801 Assembly Street, second floor
Columbia, South Carolina 29201

"Canoeing on the Chattooga" (S.C. Highway 28 to Earl's Ford)
"Canoeing on the Chattooga" (Earl's Ford to U.S. Highway 76)
"Gateway to the Mountains, Sumpter National Forest Map"

SOUTH DAKOTA

Boy Scouts of America
Sioux Council
P.O. Box 837
Sioux Falls, South Dakota 57100

"B.S.A. Lewis and Clark Historical Canoe Trail"

South Dakota Department of Game, Fish, and Parks
Division of Parks and Recreation
State Office Building 1
Pierre, South Dakota 57501

"Study Proposal of Big Sioux River Canoe Trail"

U.S. Department of the Army
Army Corps of Engineers
P.O. Box 103, Downtown Station
Omaha, Nebraska 68101

"Lake Francis Case"
"Lake Oahe"
"Lake Sharpe Reservoir"

TENNESSEE

Bluff City Canoe Club
P.O. Box 4523
Memphis, Tennessee   38104

"Mid-South River Guide"

Boy Scouts of America
Cherokee Area Council
P.O. Box 21226
Chattanooga, Tennessee   37421

"Chief John Ross Canoe Trek"

Chattanooga Convention and Visitors Bureau
399 McCallie Avenue
Chattanooga, Tennessee   37402

"North Chickamauga Creek Canoe Trail"

Tennessee Scenic Rivers Association
P.O. Box 3104
Nashville, Tennessee   37219

"Obed-Emory Canoe Trails Map"

Tennessee Valley Authority
TVA Canoe Trails
301 West Cumberland Avenue
Knoxville, Tennessee   37902

"Little Tennessee Valley Canoe Trails"
"Tennessee Valley Canoe Trails Map"

Tennessee Wildlife and Resource Agency
P.O. Box 40747
Nashville, Tennessee   37204

"Float Map Duck River Tennessee"
"Harpeth River Float Map"
"Little Tennessee River Float Waters"

TEXAS

Big Bend Natural History Association
Big Bend National Park, Texas   79834

"Guide to the Backcountry Roads and the River"

Texas Parks and Wildlife Department
4200 Smith School Road
Austin, Texas 78744

>   "Canoe, Kayak, and Raft Rentals in Texas"
>   "Waterways in Texas"

U.S. Department of the Interior
National Park Service
Big Bend National Park, Texas 79834

>   "Big Bend"

UTAH

U.S. Department of Agriculture
Forest Service
Flaming Gorge National Recreation Area
P.O. Box 157
Dutch John, Utah 84023

>   "Flaming Gorge National Recreation Area"

U.S. Department of the Interior
Bureau of Land Management
8239 Federal Building
Salt Lake City, Utah 84111

>   "Running the Green River"

U.S. Department of the Interior
Bureau of Reclamation
P.O. Box 11568
Salt Lake City, Utah 84111

>   "River Boating below Glen Canyon Dam"

U.S. Department of the Interior
National Park Service
Federal Building
Salt Lake City, Utah 84111

>   "Glen Canyon Dam and National Recreation Area"

Utah Division of Parks and Recreation
1586 West North Temple
Salt Lake City, Utah 84116

>   "Recreational Uses of Boating Waters in Utah"

Utah Travel Development
450 State Capitol
Salt Lake City, Utah 84114

"Lake Powell Recreational Facilities and Services"

VERMONT

Vermont Agency of Development and Community Affairs
109 State Street
Montpelier, Vermont   05602

"Vermont Boating and Water Sports"

Vermont Environmental Conservation Agency
Division of Recreation
5 Court Street
Montpelier, Vermont   05602

"Canoeing on the Connecticut River"
"Summer Canoe Trips in Vermont"

VIRGINIA

Virginia Game and Inland Fisheries Commission
4010 West Broad Street
Richmond, Virginia   23219

"Boating Access to Virginia Waters"
"Harwoods Mill Reservoir Map"
"Lake Cohoon Map"
"Lake Meade Map"
"Lake Prince Map"
"Lake Smith Map"

WASHINGTON

Angle Lake Cyclery
20840 Pacific Highway, S.
Seattle, Washington   98188

"Washington Rivers Map"

Washington Department of Fisheries
115 General Administration Building
Olympia, Washington   98504

"Grande Ronde River" (Oregon border to Snake River)

Washington Kayak Club
7724 211th Avenue, N.E.
Redmond, Washington   98052

"Map of Washington Rivers"

Booklets and Maps

WEST VIRGINIA

American Youth Hostels
Pittsburgh Chapter
6300 5th Avenue
Pittsburgh, Pennsylvania   15232

> "Map of Canoeable Waters of Western Pennsylvania and Northern
> West Virginia"

Gray, Thomas L.
11121 Dewey Road
Kensington, Maryland   20795

> "Canoeing Streams of the Potomac and Rappahannock Basins"
> "Canoeing Streams of the Upper Ohio Basin" (West Virginia,
> Maryland, New York, Ohio, Pennsylvania)

West Virginia Division of Wildlife Resources
State Office Building 3
Charleston, West Virginia   25305

> "West Virginia Stream Map"

WISCONSIN

Greater Area Chamber of Commerce
Black River Falls, Wisconsin   54615

> "River Floating on the Black River with Lake Arbutus Map"

U.S. Department of Agriculture
Forest Service
Chequamegon National Forest
Hayward, Wisconsin   54843

> "Chequamegon National Forest Map"

U.S. Department of Agriculture
Forest Service
Nicolet National Forest
Rhinelander, Wisconsin   54501

> "Nicolet National Forest Map"

U.S. Department of Agriculture
Forest Service
710 North 6th Street
Milwaukee, Wisconsin   53203

> "Superior National Forest and the Boundary Waters Canoe Area"

Vilas County Publicity Department
P.O. Box 71
Eagle River, Wisconsin 54521

"Vilas County Lake Region Map"

Wisconsin Division of Tourism
P.O Box 177
Madison, Wisconsin 53701

"Canoe the Kickapoo"

WYOMING

U.S. Department of Agriculture
Forest Service
Bridger National Forest
Kemmerer, Wyoming 83101

"Bridger National Forest Map" (Green River)

U.S. Department of Agriculture
Forest Service
Medicine Bow National Forest
P.O. Box 3355, University Station
Laramie, Wyoming 82070

"Medicine Bow National Forest Map" (North Platte River)

U.S. Department of Agriculture
Forest Service
Teton National Forest
Jackson, Wyoming 83001

"Teton Wilderness Map"

U.S. Department of the Interior
National Park Service
Grand Teton National Park
Moose, Wyoming 83012

"Floating the Snake River"
"Grand Teton National Park Map"

U.S. Department of the Interior
National Park Service
Yellowstone National Park, Wyoming 83020

"Wilderness Boating on Yellowstone Lakes"

Booklets and Maps

Wyoming Travel Commission
2320 Capitol Avenue
Cheyenne, Wyoming 82002

"Camping Big Wyoming Map"
"Family Water Sports Big Wyoming Map"

Part 3

ORGANIZATIONS AND GOVERNMENT AGENCIES

INTRODUCTION

Much of the information on wilderness waterways activities never is recorded in the standard bibliographies. This class of material is usually designated "ephemera" (brochures, maps, folders, mimeographed handouts). When a press run of brochures becomes exhausted, the supply is often not replenished. This is regrettable, since the material may provide the only information on a particular waterway or region. This loss may be compensated occasionally by replacement with updated material by the same or another issuing body. Thus, the approach to ephemeral materials is not only through their titles (many of which are cited in chapter 12), but directly to the issuing organization or agency.

These groups, from national organizations and federal agencies to local clubs and conservation societies, are listed in chapters 13 to 18. The chapters are arranged first by type of organization or agency, then alphabetically by nation, region, province, or state. The directories should also be useful to those seeking either geographically appropriate or concern-oriented groups to which specific inquiries may be addressed.

Chapter 18 lists hundreds of paddling clubs and affiliated groups. Such groups change addresses constantly--usually each time a new commodore, president, or secretary-treasurer is elected. Regardless, it is useful to have a fairly recent address, albeit stale, as the one currently in use can usually be learned through correspondence. It should be stated that, while the club directory is comprehensive, no effort was made to discover the addresses of paddling affiliates of college student unions, YMCA/YWCAs, or similar outdoor-oriented groups.

Chapter 13

NATIONAL CANOEING, KAYAKING, AND
RAFTING ORGANIZATIONS

CANADA

Boy Scouts of Canada
P.O. Box 5151, Station F
Ottawa, Ontario   K2C 3G7

> The Boy Scouts provides an educational, outdoor-oriented pro-
> gram for Canadian youth.   The national organization is divided
> into ten provincial councils:

> Alberta: 14205 109th Avenue, Edmonton T5N 1H5.
> British Columbia/Yukon Territory: 2188 West 12th Avenue,
>   Vancouver, British Columbia   V6K 2N2.
> Manitoba/Northwest Territories: 148 Colony Street, Winnipeg,
>   Manitoba R3C 1V9.
> New Brunswick: 151 King Street, E., St. John E2L 1G9.
> Newfoundland: P.O. Box 5334, St. John's A1C 5W2.
> Nova Scotia: P.O. Box 2003, Halifax B3J 3B2.
> Ontario: 9 Jackes Avenue, Toronto M4T 1E2.
> Prince Edward Island: 100 Upper Prince Street, Charlottetown
>   C1A 4S3.
> Quebec: 2001 Trans-Canada Highway, Dorval H9P 1J1.
> Saskatchewan: 14205 109th Avenue, Edmonton, Alberta T5N 1H5.

Canadian Camping Association
102 Eglinton Avenue, E., Suite 203
Toronto, Ontario M4P 1E1

> This organization is dedicated to promoting and enhancing the
> Canadian camping experience. It has a number of provincial
> affiliates (associations) among which are:

> Alberta: c/o YMCA, 332 6th Avenue, Calgary T2P 2G5.
> British Columbia: 4640 Clovelly Walk, West Vancouver V7W 1H4.
> Manitoba: 301 Vaughan Street, Winnipeg R3B 2N7.
> New Brunswick: P.O. Box 373, Fredericton E3B 4Z9.

Newfoundland/Labrador: P.O. Box 4188, St. John's, Newfoundland A1C 5Z7.
Nova Scotia: P.O. Box 3243 S, Halifax B3J 3E9.
Ontario: 102 Eglinton Avenue, E. Toronto M4P 1E1.
Quebec: 1415 est rue Jarry, Montreal H2E 2Z7.
Saskatchewan: P.O. Box 823, Regina S4P 3B1.

Canadian Canoe Association
333 River Road
Vanier City, Ontario K1L 8B9

The Canadian Canoe Association is the governing body for canoe activity in Canada; its interests include all aspects of paddling. The association organizes racing and the selection of Canadian teams for international competition. It publishes an official magazine, CANOE, and maintains a file of reports of specific canoe routes which are furnished to members on request. There are six divisions:

Atlantic: 35 Clearview Crescent, Dartmouth, Nova Scotia B3A 2M9.
Ontario (eastern): Rural Route 4, Odessa KOH 2HO.
Ontario (western): Rural Route 1, West Hill M1E 4R2.
Pacific: 1133 Pipeline Road, No. 33, Port Coquitlam, British Columbia V3B 4R8.
Prairie: 775 Willamette Drive, S.E., Calgary, Alberta T2J 2A3.
Quebec: 2200 St. Catherine, E., Montreal H2K 2J1.

Canadian Recreational Canoeing Association
441 Ridout Street, N.
London, Ontario N6A 2P6

This group is supported by Recreation Canada and is affiliated with the Canadian Canoe Association, Canadian Camping Association, and Canadian White Water Affiliation. The group promotes canoeing as an educational, cultural, historical, and constructive recreational experience. It provides the following services: standards, national canoe school for instructors, maps and codes, canoe history, safety equipment and specifications, canoe routes and information, outfitters, and canoeing ethics.

Canadian Red Cross Society
95 Wellesley Street, E.
Toronto, Ontario M4Y 1H6

The society, in addition to providing humanitarian and relief services, has an extensive water-safety program. Provincial offices will provide additional information:

Alberta: 1504 1st Street, S.E., Calgary T2G 2J5.
British Columbia: 4750 Oak Street, Vancouver V6H 2N9.

Manitoba: 226 Osborne Street, N., Winnipeg R3C 1V4.
New Brunswick: 1 Bayard Drive, Saint John E21 3X3.
Newfoundland: 55 Duckworth Street, St. John's A1C 1E6.
Nova Scotia: 1940 Gottingen Street, Halifax B3J 2H2.
Ontario: 460 Jarvis Street, Toronto M4Y 2H5.
Prince Edward Island: 62 Prince Street, Charlottetown C1A 4R2.
Quebec: 2170 Dorchester Boulevard, W., Montreal H3H 1R6.
Saskatchewan: 2571 Broad Street, Regina S4P 2N9.

Canadian White Water Affiliation
436 Stinson Avenue
Burlington, Ontario L7R 2W9

This organization is affiliated with the Canadian Canoe Association. Its functions include exploration, enjoyment, and preservation of Canadian waterways; safety; and distribution of paddling information. There are affiliation representatives for each
province in which there is an interest in whitewater paddling:

Alberta: (provincial directorship open).
British Columbia: Edna Hobbs, 340 Seymour River Place, Van-
couver V7H 1S8.
Manitoba: Manitoba Kayaking Association, 256 St. Annes Road,
Winnipeg R2M 3A4.
Maritimes: Jack Smith, Herring Cove Post Office, Herring
Cove, Nova Scotia B0J 1S0.
Ontario: Bud McVicar, 15 Vanity Court, Don Mills M3A 1W9.
Quebec: Bruce Jack, Terrasse St. Denis, Montreal H2X 1E7.
Saskatchewan: Eric Sprigings, Faculty of Physical Education,
University of Saskatchewan, Saskatoon S7N OWO.
Yukon Territory: Mentyn Williams, 150 Dalton Trail, White-
horse Y1A 3G2.

Canadian Youth Hostels Association
333 River Road
Vanier City, Ontario K1L 8B9

The association sponsors trips by canoe, foot, bike, and ski as
well as foreign travel. It maintains six regional offices:

Great Lakes: 86 Scollard Street, Toronto, Ontario M5R 1G3.
Maritime: 6260 Quinpool Road, Halifax, Nova Scotia B3L 1A3.
Mountain: 455 12th Street, N.W., Calgary, Alberta T2N 1Y9.
Northwest: 10922 88th Avenue, Edmonton, Alberta T6G OY9.
Pacific: 1406 West Broadway, Vancouver, British Columbia
V6H 1H4.
St. Lawrence: 1324 ouest rue Sherbrooke, Montreal, Province
of Quebec H3G 1H9.

Girl Guides of Canada
50 Merton Street
Toronto, Ontario M4S 1A3

The Girl Guides have eleven provincial-territorial councils:

Alberta: 10120 Jasper Avenue, Edmonton T5J 1W6.
British Columbia: 553 Granville Street, Vancouver V6C 1Y6.
Manitoba: 267 Edmonton Street, Winnipeg R3C 1S2.
New Brunswick: 28 Germain Street, Saint John E2L 2E5.
Newfoundland: Building 566, St. John's Place, Pleasantville,
    St. John's A1A 1S3.
Nova Scotia: 1871 Granville Street, Halifax B3J 1Y1.
Ontario: 50 Merton Street, Toronto M4S 1A3.
Prince Edward Island: 100 Upper Prince Street, Charlottetown
    C1A 4S3.
Quebec: 1939 de Maisonneuve Boulevard, W., Montreal
    H3H 1K3.
Saskatchewan: 3501 Dewney Avenue, Regina S4T OZ4.
Yukon Territory-Northwest Territories: 50 Merton Street, To-
    ronto, Ontario M4S 1A3.

North American Canoe Racing Association
c/o Canadian Canoe Association
333 River Road
Vanier City, Ontario K1L 8B9

The race venue and administration of this association alternates
between Canada and the United States. Inquiries may be addressed to the Canadian Canoe Association.

Wilderness Canoe Association
P.O. Box 75, Postal Station "U"
Toronto, Ontario M8Z 5M4

This is a new association active in wilderness preservation.
Membership is centered in eastern Canada, but the group wel-
comes all from Canada and the United States. Backcountry
trips are sponsored.

UNITED STATES

American Alliance for Health, Physical Education, and Recreation
1201 16th Street, N.W.
Washington, D.C. 20036

The professional fields of physical education, dance, health,
athletics, safety education, recreation, and outdoor education
are represented by this organization. It administers the awards
for the President's Council on Physical Fitness and Sports as
well as publishing several periodicals, including JOURNAL OF
PHYSICAL EDUCATION AND RECREATION and RESEARCH
QUARTERLY.

American Canoe Association
4260 East Evans Avenue
Denver, Colorado 80222

> The American Canoe Association is the governing body for ca-
> noe activity in the United States, with an interest in all as-
> pects of canoeing and in saving rivers and lakes. The associa-
> tion has committees on canoe poling, long distance, (marathon
> and open canoe) racing, Olympic (flatwater) paddling, rafting,
> slalom and wildwater racing. It publishes the bimonthly maga-
> zine CANOE.

American Guides Association
P.O. Box "B"
Woodland, California 95695

> This association trains, certifies, and otherwise improves ethical
> standards of professional guiding. It conducts courses in para-
> medics, rock climbing, river guiding, and more. The group
> maintains a small library of relevant materials and publishes a
> master schedule of chapter expeditions and area handbooks.

American National Red Cross
17th and D Streets, N.W.
Washington, D.C. 20006

> The activities of the Red Cross, other than the disaster relief
> for which it is best known, include small craft schools, basic
> canoeing courses, instructor-training rescue operations, and
> first aid. For information about these activities, contact the
> national office for the address of one of the more than 13,000
> local participating groups.

American Whitewater Affiliation
P.O. Box 321
Concord, New Hampshire 03301

> The American Whitewater Affiliation promotes river-running by
> canoe, kayak, and raft as well as having boating safety, tech-
> nique, equipment, and conservation programs. It performs a
> national service by evaluating rivers for boating and assisting
> in the protection of river ecology. The affiliation publishes
> the bimonthly AMERICAN WHITEWATER JOURNAL.

American Youth Hostels
National Campus
Delaplane, Virginia 22025

> The Youth Hostels is a nonprofit organization devoted to estab-
> lishing and maintaining low-cost accommodations in scenic,
> historical, and cultural areas. It presently has more than one

hundred facilities in thirty-two states. There are thirty councils across the country:

Arizona: 8026 North 15th Street, Phoenix 85020.
California: 625 Polk Street, Room 201, San Francisco 94102.
  7603 Beverly Boulevard, Los Angeles 90036.
  P.O. Box 13907, Sacramento 95813.
  1031 India Street, San Diego 92101.
Colorado: 1107 12th Street, Boulder 80302.
Connecticut: P.O. Box 1618, Bridgeport 06601.
  1007 Farmington Avenue, Room 15, W., Hartford 06107.
District of Columbia: 1520 16th Street, N.W., Washington, D.C. 20036.
Illinois: 3712 North Clark Street, Chicago 60613.
Indiana: 10611 Baker Place, Crown Point 46307.
Iowa: P.O. Box 10, Postville 52162.
Massachusetts: 251 Harvard Street, Brookline 02146.
Michigan: 14335 West McNichols, Detroit 48235.
  6045 Station "C", Grand Rapids 49506.
Minnesota: P.O. Box 9511, Minneapolis 55440.
Missouri: 2605 South Big Bend Boulevard, St. Louis 63143.
Nebraska: 333 North 14th Street, Lincoln 68508.
New York: 132 Spring Street, New York 10012.
  735 South Beech Street, Syracuse 13210.
Ohio: 815 Greenridge Road, Worthington 43085.
  304 North Church Street, Bowling Green 43402.
  P.O. Box 173, Lima 45802.
  P.O. Box 24069, Dayton 45424.
  2002 Birchwood, Toledo 43614.
  5400 Lanius Lane, Cincinnati 45224.
Pennsylvania: 4714 York Road, Philadelphia 19141.
  6300 Fifth Avenue, Pittsburgh 15232.
Washington: P.O. Box U-5373, Seattle 98105.
Wisconsin: 7218 West North Avenue, Wauwatosa 53213.

Boy Scouts of America
North Brunswick, New Jersey 08902

> The Boy Scouts provides an educational program for the develop-
> ment, citizenship training, and mental and physical fitness of
> youth. It has almost six million members and a staff of some
> forty-six hundred. It publishes the monthly BOY'S LIFE, the
> bimonthly, EXPLORING MAGAZINE, and SCOUTING MAGA-
> ZINE.

Camp Fire Girls
4601 Madison Avenue
Kansas City, Missouri 64112

> This organization has a membership of 500,000 and a staff of
> 750. It is for girls from age six through high school, and is

organized in four age levels: Blue Birds (ages 6 to 8), Camp
Fire Adventurers (ages 9 to 11), Discovery Club (ages 12 to
13), and Horizon Club (ages 14 to high school). Camp Fire
Girls publishes a quarterly entitled CAMP FIRE LEADERSHIP.

Girl Scouts of the United States of America
830 Third Avenue
New York, New York 10022

The Girl Scouts has about three million-three-hundred-thousand
members and a staff of 3,000. They attempt, with various
activities, to encourage personal development through a wide
variety of projects in social action, environmental action, youth
leadership, career exploration, coed groups, and community
service. There are four levels: Brownie Girl Scouts (ages 6
to 8), Junior Girl Scouts (9 to 11), Cadettes (12 to 13), and
Senior Girl Scouts (14 to 17). There are three publications:
AMERICAN GIRL (monthly), DAISY (9 times yearly), and GIRL
SCOUT LEADER (7 times yearly).

Intercollegiate Outing Club Association
c/o 3410-D. Paul Avenue
Bronx, New York 10468

This organization is composed of present members, or graduates,
of college outing clubs who are interested in enjoying and preserving the wilderness. The group sponsors caving, canoeing,
rock climbing, and backpacking trips with experienced leaders.
It publishes the IOCA NEWS (monthly) and the IOCA BULLETIN
(quarterly).

Outward Bound
165 West Putnam Avenue
Greenwich, Connecticut 06830

Outward Bound operates seven schools (21- to 26-day courses) in
the United States which are oriented to their sea, mountain,
and water-wilderness environments. They are located in Colorado, Minnesota, Maine, Oregon, North Carolina, New Hampshire, and New Mexico. The method of instruction employed
is to confront the student with a series of anxiety situations.
One Outward Bound school (330 Walker Avenue, S., Wayzata,
Minnesota 55391) specializes in wilderness canoeing and features an eleven-day expedition into the Superior-Quetico region.

United States Canoe Association
606 Ross Street
Middletown, Ohio 45042

The United States Canoe Association is involved in the promotion of all types of paddling activities, with a special focus on organizing downriver marathon races. It is subdivided by interest group: safety, competition, cruising, conservation, sailing, camaraderie, and camping. The bimonthly CANOE NEWS is their official publication.

Chapter 14

FEDERAL GOVERNMENT AGENCIES

CANADA

Department of Energy, Mines, and Resources
580 Booth Street
Ottawa, Ontario K1A OE4

> Earth Physics Branch
> 588 Booth Street
> Ottawa, Ontario K1A OE4
>
> Geological Survey of Canada
> 601 Booth Street
> Ottawa, Ontario K1A OE8
>
> Surveys and Mapping Branch
> 615 Booth Street
> Ottawa, Ontario K1A OE9

Department of Indian Affairs and Northern Development
400 Laurier Avenue, W.
Ottawa, Ontario K1A OH4

> Northern Natural Resources and Environment Branch
> 400 Laurier Avenue, W., Room 380 B
> Ottawa, Ontario K1A OH4
>
> Parks Canada
> 400 Laurier Avenue, W., Room 380 B
> Ottawa, Ontario K1A OH4

Department of Industry, Trade, and Commerce
112 Kent Street, Tower B
Ottawa, Ontario K1A OH5

> Canadian Government Office of Tourism
> 150 Kent Street
> Ottawa, Ontario K1A OH6

Department of National Health and Welfare
Brooke Claxton Building
Ottawa, Ontario K1A OK9

> Recreation Canada
> 365 Laurier Avenue, W.
> Ottawa, Ontario K1A OX6

> Sport Canada
> 365 Laurier Avenue, W.
> Ottawa, Ontario K1A OX6

Department of Transport
Ottawa, Ontario K1A ON5

> Arctic Transportation Administration
> Ottawa, Ontario K1A ON5

Environment Canada
580 Booth Street
Ottawa, Ontario K1A OH3

> Atmospheric Environment Service
> 4905 Dufferin Street
> Downsview, Ontario M3H 5T4

> Environmental Management Service (headquarters)
> Ottawa, Ontario K1A OH3

> Environmental Management Service
> Forestry Service
> Ottawa, Ontario K1A OH3

> Environmental Management Service
> Inland Waters Directorate
> Ottawa, Ontario K1A OH3

> Environmental Management Service
> Lands Directorate
> Ottawa, Ontario K1A OH3

> Environmental Protection Service
> Ottawa, Ontario K1A OH3

> Fisheries and Marine Service
> Ottawa, Ontario K1A OH3

> Hydrographic Service
> Marine Chart and Publications Sales
> 615 Booth Street
> Ottawa, Ontario K1A OE6

> Wildlife Service
> Ottawa, Ontario K1A OH3

Northern Canada Power Commission
Federal Crown Corp.
7909 51st Avenue
Edmonton, Alberta   T6C 4J8

Northern Transportation Co.
Federal Crown Corp.
9945 108th Street
Edmonton, Alberta   T5K 2G9

UNITED STATES

Interagency Whitewater Committee
c/o Marv Jensen
Grand Canyon National Park
Grand Canyon, Arizona   86023

> Member Agency:
>
> Bureau of Land Management (see U.S. Department of the Interior, below)
> Forest Service (see U.S. Department of Agriculture, below)
> National Park Service (see U.S. Department of the Interior, below)

U.S. Department of Agriculture
12th Street and Independence Avenue, S.W.
Washington, D.C.   20250

> Forest Service
> 12th Street and Independence Avenue, S.W.
> South Agriculture Building, Room 3225
> Washington, D.C.   20250
>
> Soil Conservation Service
> 12th Street and Independence Avenue, S.W.
> Washington, D.C.   20250

U.S. Department of Commerce
National Weather Service
8060 13th Street
Silver Spring, Maryland   20910

> Regional Offices:
>
> Alaska
> 632 6th Avenue
> Anchorage, Alaska   99501
>
> Central
> 585 Stewart Avenue
> Garden City, New York   11530

Pacific
1149 Bethel Street
Honolulu, Hawaii   96813

Southern
819 Taylor Street
Fort Worth, Texas   76102

Western
125 South State Street
Salt Lake City, Utah   84111

U.S. Department of the Army
Army Corps of Engineers
1000 Independence Avenue, S.W.
Washington, D.C.   20314

Division Offices:

Lower Mississippi Valley
P.O. Box 80
Vicksburg, Mississippi   39180

Missouri River
P.O. Box 103
Omaha, Nebraska   68101

New England
434 Trapelo Road
Waltham, Massachusetts   02154

North Atlantic
90 Church Street
New York, New York   10007

North Central
536 South Clark Street
Chicago, Illinois   60605

North Pacific
210 Custom House
Portland, Oregon   97209

Ohio River
P.O. Box 1159
Cincinnati, Ohio   45201

South Atlantic
30 Pryor Street, S.W.
Atlanta, Georgia   30303

South Pacific
630 Sansome Street
San Francisco, California   94111

Southwestern
1114 Commerce Street
Dallas, Texas 75202

U.S. Department of the Interior
Interior Building
Washington, D.C. 20240

Bureau of Land Management

Field Offices:

Alaska
555 Cordova Street
Anchorage, Alaska 99501

Arizona
Federal Building
Phoenix, Arizona 85025

California
Federal Building
Sacramento, California 95825

Colorado
Colorado State Bank Building
Denver, Colorado 80202

Eastern States
7981 Eastern Avenue
Silver Spring, Maryland 20910

Idaho
Federal Building
Boise, Idaho 83724

Montana, North Dakota, South Dakota
Federal Building
Billings, Montana 59101

Nevada
Federal Building
Reno, Nevada 89502

New Mexico, Oklahoma
Federal Building
Santa Fe, New Mexico 87501

Oregon, Washington
729 Northeast Oregon Street
Portland, Oregon 97208

Utah
Federal Building
Salt Lake City, Utah 84111

Wyoming, Kansas, Nebraska
Federal Building
Cheyenne, Wyoming 82001

Bureau of Outdoor Recreation

Regional Offices:

Lake Central
3853 Research Park Drive
Ann Arbor, Michigan 48104

Mid-Continent
Denver Federal Center, Building 41
P.O. Box 25387
Denver, Colorado 80225

Northeast
600 Arch Street
Philadelphia, Pennsylvania 19106

Northwest
915 3nd Avenue
Seattle, Washington 98104

Pacific Southwest
450 Golden Gate Avenue
San Francisco, California 94102

South Central
5000 Marble Avenue, N.E.
Albuquerque, New Mexico 87110

Southeast
148 Cain Street
Atlanta, Georgia 30303

Bureau of Reclamation

Regional Offices:

Lower Colorado Region
P.O. Box 427
Boulder City, Nevada 89005

Lower Missouri Region
Box 25247
Denver Federal Center, Building 20
Denver, Colorado 80225

Mid-Pacific Region
2800 Cottage Way
Sacramento, California 95825

Pacific Northwest Region
550 W. Fort Street
Boise, Idaho 83707

Southwest Region
Herring Plaza, Box H-4377
Amarillo, Texas 79101

Upper Colorado Region
P.O. Box 11568
Salt Lake City, Utah 84147

Upper Missouri Region
P.O. Box 2553
Billings, Montana 59103

Bureau of Sport Fisheries and Wildlife

Regional Offices:

Midwest
Federal Building
Fort Snelling, Twin Cities, Minnesota 55111

Northeast
U.S. Post Office and Court House, Room 821
Boston, Massachusetts 02109

Northwest
P.O. Box 3737
Portland, Oregon 97208

Southeast
17 Executive Park Drive, N.E.
Atlanta, Georgia 30329

Southwest
P.O. Box 1306
Albuquerque, New Mexico 87103

Bureau of Sport Fisheries and Wildlife
Division of Wildlife Refuges

Regional Offices:

Alaska
813 D Street
Anchorage, Alaska 99501

Colorado
10597 West 6th Avenue
Denver, Colorado 80215

Georgia
17 Executive Park Drive, N.E.
Atlanta, Georgia 30329

Massachusetts
John A. McCormack Courthouse
Boston, Massachusetts 02109

Minnesota
Federal Building
Twin Cities, Minnesota 55111

New Mexico
P.O. Box 1306
Albuquerque, New Mexico 87103

Oregon
1500 Plaza Building
Portland, Oregon 97208

Geological Survey
12201 Sunrise Valley Drive
Reston, Virginia 22092

National Park Service

Regional Offices:

Mid-Atlantic
143 South 3rd Street
Philadelphia, Pennsylvania 19106

Midwest
1709 Jackson Street
Omaha, Nebraska 68102

National Capitol Parks
1100 Ohio Drive, S.W.
Washington, D.C. 20242

North Atlantic
150 Causeway Street
Boston, Massachusetts 02114

Pacific Northwest
1424 4th Avenue
Seattle, Washington 98101

Rocky Mountain
645-655 Parfet Avenue
Denver, Colorado 80215

Southeast
3401 Whipple Street
Atlanta, Georgia 30344

Southwest
P.O. Box 728
Santa Fe, New Mexico 87501

Western
450 Golden Gate Avenue
San Francisco, California 94102

U.S. Department of Transportation

U.S. Coast Guard
400 Seventh Street, S.W.
Washington, D.C. 20590

District Commands:

1st District
John F. Kennedy Building, Government Center
Boston, Massachusetts 02203

2d District
1520 Market Street
St. Louis, Missouri 63103

3d District
Governors Island
New York, New York 10004

5th District
431 Crawford Street
Portsmouth, Virginia 23750

7th District
51 Southwest First Avenue
Miami, Florida 33130

8th District
Customhouse
New Orleans, Louisiana 70130

9th District
1240 East 9th Street
Cleveland, Ohio 44199

11th District
19 Pine Avenue
Long Beach, California 90802

12th District
630 Sansome Street
San Francisco, California 94126

13th District
618 Second Avenue
Seattle, Washington 98104

14th District
677 Ala Moana Boulevard
Honolulu, Hawaii 96813

17th District
P.O. Box 3-5000
Juneau, Alaska 99801

Chapter 15
PROVINCIAL AND STATE AGENCIES

CANADA

ALBERTA

Environmental Protection

Department of the Environment
10040 104th Street
Edmonton, Alberta   T5J OZ6

Fish and Game

Fish and Wildlife Division
Department of Lands and Forests
109th Street and 99th Avenue
Edmonton, Alberta   T5K 2E1

Natural Resources

Public Affairs Bureau
Department of Lands and Forests
9945 108th Street
Edmonton, Alberta   T5K 2B6

Parks and Recreation

Department of Recreation, Parks, and Wildlife
10004 104th Avenue
Edmonton, Alberta   T5J OK5

Publicity, Information, and Development

Travel Alberta
10255 104th Street
Edmonton, Alberta   T5J 1B1

BRITISH COLUMBIA

Environmental Protection

Department of Environment
Parliament Buildings
Victoria, British Columbia   V8V 2M3

Fish and Game

Fish and Wildlife Branch
Department of Recreation and Conservation
Parliament Buildings
Victoria, British Columbia   V8V 1X4

Natural Resources

Department of Lands, Forests, and Water Resources
Parliament Buildings
Victoria, British Columbia   V8V 1X5

Parks and Recreation

Parks Branch
Department of Recreation and Travel Industry
Parliament Buildings
Victoria, British Columbia   V8W 2Y9

Publicity, Information, and Development

Department of Travel Industry
1019 Wharf Street
Victoria, British Columbia   V8W 2Z2

LABRADOR (see NEWFOUNDLAND)

MANITOBA

Environmental Protection

Department of Mines, Resources, and Environmental Management
139 Tuxedo Boulevard, Box 7
Winnipeg, Manitoba   R3N 8H6

Fish and Game

Wildlife Branch
139 Tuxedo Boulevard, Box 11
Winnipeg, Manitoba   R3C OV8

Natural Resources

Department of Mines, Resources, and Environmental Management
139 Tuxedo Boulevard, Box 11
Winnipeg, Manitoba   R3C OV8

Parks and Recreation

Department of Tourism, Recreation, and Cultural Affairs
Parks Branch
200 Vaughan Street
Winnipeg, Manitoba   R3C OP8

Publicity, Information, and Development

Manitoba Government Travel
408-401 York Avenue
Winnipeg, Manitoba   R3C 1T5

NEW BRUNSWICK

Environmental Protection

Environmental Services Branch
Department of Fisheries and Environment
P.O. Box 6000
Fredericton, New Brunswick   E3B 5H1

Fish and Game

Fish and Wildlife Branch
349 King Street
Fredericton, New Brunswick   E3B 5H1

Natural Resources

Department of Natural Resources
575 Centennial Building
Fredericton, New Brunswick   E3B 5H1

Parks and Recreation

Parks Operations Branch
Department of Tourism
P.O. Box 6000
Fredericton, New Brunswick   E3B 5H1

Publicity, Information, and Development

Department of Tourism
Departmental Building
Fredericton, New Brunswick   E3B 5C3

NEWFOUNDLAND and LABRADOR

Environmental Protection

Clean Air, Water, and Soil Authority
Department of Consumer Affairs and Environment
Elizabeth Towers, Elizabeth Avenue
St. John's, Newfoundland   A1C 5T7

Fish and Game

Department of Fisheries
Viking Building, Crosbie Road
St. John's, Newfoundland   A1B 3K4

Natural Resources

Department of Forestry and Agriculture
P.O. Box 4750
St. John's, Newfoundland   A1C 5T7

Parks and Recreation

Department of Tourism
Parks Division
P.O. Box 9340, Postal Station "B"
St. John's, Newfoundland   A1A 2Y3

Publicity, Information, and Development

Department of Tourism
Confederation Building
St. John's, Newfoundland   A1A 1P9

NORTHWEST TERRITORIES

Environmental Protection

Chief Environment Protection Officer
Yellowknife, Northwest Territories   X0E 1H0

Fish and Game

Regional Director of Fisheries
501 University Crescent
Winnipeg, Manitoba   R3T 3N6

Publicity, Information, and Development

TravelArctic
Division of Tourism
Yellowknife, Northwest Territories   X1A 2L9

NOVA SCOTIA

Environmental Protection

Department of the Environment
P.O. Box 2107
Halifax, Nova Scotia   B3J 3C7

Fish and Game

Department of Fisheries
P.O. Box 2223
Halifax, Nova Scotia   B3J 3C4

Natural Resources

Department of Lands and Forests
P.O. Box 68
Truro, Nova Scotia   B2N 5B8

Parks and Recreation

Department of Recreation
P.O. Box 864
Halifax, Nova Scotia   B3J 2V2

Publicity, Information, and Development

Department of Tourism
P.O. Box 456
Halifax, Nova Scotia   B3J 2R5

ONTARIO

Environmental Protection

Ministry of the Environment
135 St. Clair Avenue, W.
Toronto, Ontario   M4V 1P5

Fish and Game

Division of Fish and Wildlife
Whitney Block, Queen's Park
Toronto, Ontario   M7A 1W3

Natural Resources

Information Branch
Ministry of Natural Resources
Whitney Block, Queen's Park, Room 5314
Toronto, Ontario   M7A 1W3

Parks and Recreation

Division of Parks
Ministry of Natural Resources
Whitney Block, Queen's Park
Toronto, Ontario   M7A 1W3

Publicity, Information, and Development

Ministry of Industry and Tourism
900 Bay Street
Toronto, Ontario   M7A 1S6

PRINCE EDWARD ISLAND

Environmental Protection

Environmental Control Commission
P.O. Box 2000
Charlottetown, Prince Edward Island   C1A 7N8

Fish and Game

Department of Fisheries
P.O. Box 2000
Charlottetown, Prince Edward Island   C1A 7N8

Natural Resources

Forestry Branch
Department of Agriculture and Forestry
P.O. Box 2000
Charlottetown, Prince Edward Island   C1A 7N8

Parks and Recreation

Parks and Resorts Branch
P.O. Box 2000
Charlottetown, Prince Edward Island   C1A 7N8

Publicity, Information, and Development

Tourist Information Centre
P.O. Box 940
Charlottetown, Prince Edward Island   C1A 7M5

QUEBEC

Environmental Protection

Environmental Protection Services
Building D, Cité Parlementaire
Quebec, Province of Quebec   G1A 1B7

Fish and Game

Fisheries Branch
Department of Industry and Commerce
Government Buildings
Quebec, Province of Quebec G1A 1L1

Natural Resources

Department of Natural Resources
1620 boulevard de l'Entente
Quebec, Province of Quebec G1S 4N6

Parks and Recreation

Parks Branch
Department of Tourism, Fish, and Game
Building G, Cité Parlementaire
Quebec, Province of Quebec G1A 1R4

Publicity, Information, and Development

Department of Tourism, Fish, and Game
150 est boulevard Saint-Cyrille
Quebec, Province of Quebec G1R 4Y3

SASKATCHEWAN

Environmental Protection

Department of the Environment
Saskatchewan Power Building, 11th Floor
Regina, Saskatchewan S4P OR9

Fish and Game

Fisheries and Wildlife Branch
Department of Tourism and Renewable Resources
Provincial Office Building
Prince Albert, Saskatchewan S6V 1B5

Natural Resources

Department of Natural Resources
Provincial Office Building
Prince Albert, Saskatchewan S6V 1B5

Parks and Recreation

Parks and Recreation Branch
Department of Tourism and Renewable Resources
P.O. Box 7105
Regina, Saskatchewan S4P 3N2

Publicity, Information, and Development

Tourist Branch
Department of Tourism and Renewable Resources
P.O. Box 7105
Regina, Saskatchewan   S4P 3N2

YUKON TERRITORY

Fish and Game

Game Branch
P.O. Box 2703
Whitehorse, Yukon Territory   Y1A 2C6

Parks and Recreation

Recreation Branch
Department of Education
P.O. Box 2703
Whitehorse, Yukon Territory   Y1A 2C6

Publicity, Information, and Development

Tourism and Information Branch
Department of Travel and Information
P.O. Box 2703
Whitehorse, Yukon Territory   Y1A 2C6

UNITED STATES

ALABAMA

Environmental Protection

Environmental Health Administration
Department of Public Health
State Office Building
Montgomery, Alabama   36104

Fish and Game

Division of Game and Fish
Department of Conservation and Natural Resources
Administration Building
Montgomery, Alabama   36104

Natural Resources

Department of Conservation and Natural Resources
Administration Building
Montgomery, Alabama   36104

Parks and Recreation

Division of Parks
Department of Conservation and Natural Resources
Administration Building
Montgomery, Alabama 36104

Publicity, Information, and Development

Bureau of Publicity and Information
State Capitol
Montgomery, Alabama 36104

ALASKA

Environmental Protection

Department of Environmental Conservation
Pouch O
Juneau, Alaska 99801

Fish and Game

Department of Fish and Game
Subport Building
Juneau, Alaska 99801

Natural Resources

Department of Natural Resources
Pouch M
Juneau, Alaska 99801

Parks and Recreation

Division of Parks
Department of Natural Resources
323 East 4th Street
Anchorage, Alaska 99501

Publicity, Information, and Development

Tourism Division
Department of Commerce and Economic Development
Pouch E
Juneau, Alaska 99801

ARIZONA

Environmental Protection

Bureau of Water Quality Control
Department of Health Services
State Capitol
Phoenix, Arizona 85007

Fish and Game

Game and Fish Department
2222 West Greenway Road
Phoenix, Arizona 85023

Natural Resources

Land Department
1624 West Adams Street
Phoenix, Arizona 85007

Parks and Recreation

State Parks Board
1688 West Adams Street
Phoenix, Arizona 85007

Publicity, Information, and Development

Office of Tourism
State Capitol
Phoenix, Arizona 85007

ARKANSAS

Environmental Protection

Environmental Health Services
Department of Health
State Capitol
Little Rock, Arkansas 72205

Fish and Game

Game and Fish Commission
Game and Fish Building
Little Rock, Arkansas 72201

Natural Resources

Geological Commission
3819 West Roosevelt Road
Little Rock, Arkansas 72204

Parks and Recreation

Department of Parks and Tourism
149 State Capitol
Little Rock, Arkansas 72201

Publicity, Information, and Development

Department of Parks and Tourism
149 State Capitol
Little Rock, Arkansas 72201

CALIFORNIA

Environmental Protection

Water Resources Control Board
1416 Ninth Street
Sacramento, California 95814

Fish and Game

Department of Fish and Game
1416 Ninth Street
Sacramento, California 95814

Natural Resources

Department of Conservation
1416 Ninth Street
Sacramento, California 95814

Parks and Recreation

Department of Parks and Recreation
P.O. Box 2390
Sacramento, California 95811

Publicity, Information, and Development

Commission for Economic Development
1400 Tenth Street
Sacramento, California 95814

COLORADO

Environmental Protection

Office of the Governor
136 State Capitol Building
Denver, Colorado 80203

Fish and Game

Division of Wildlife
Department of Natural Resources
6060 Broadway
Denver, Colorado 80216

Natural Resources

Department of Natural Resources
1845 Sherman
Denver, Colorado 80203

Parks and Recreation

Division of Parks and Outdoor Recreation
Department of Natural Resources
1845 Sherman
Denver, Colorado 80203

Publicity, Information, and Development

Division of Commerce and Development
Department of Local Affairs
600 Capitol Annex
Denver, Colorado 80203

CONNECTICUT

Environmental Protection

Department of Environmental Protection
State Office Building
Hartford, Connecticut 06115

Fish and Game

Department of Environmental Protection
State Office Building
Hartford, Connecticut 06115

Natural Resources

Department of Environmental Protection
State Office Building
Hartford, Connecticut 06115

Parks and Recreation

State Park Division
Department of Environmental Protection
State Office Building
Hartford, Connecticut 06115

Publicity, Information, and Development

Department of Commerce
210 Washington Street
Hartford, Connecticut 06115

DELAWARE

Environmental Protection

Division of Environmental Control
Department of Natural Resources and Environmental Control
Tatnall Building
Dover, Delaware 19901

Fish and Game

Division of Fish and Wildlife
Department of Natural Resources and Environmental Control
Natural Resources Building
Dover, Delaware 19901

Natural Resources

Department of Natural Resources and Environmental Control
Tatnall Building
Dover, Delaware 19901

Parks and Recreation

Division of Parks, Recreation, and Forestry
Department of Natural Resources and Environmental Control
Natural Resources Building
Dover, Delaware 19901

Publicity, Information, and Development

Bureau of Travel Development
45 The Green
Dover, Delaware 19901

DISTRICT OF COLUMBIA

Parks and Recreation

National Park Service
National Capitol Region
1100 Ohio Drive, S.W.
Washington, D.C. 20242

Publicity, Information, and Development

Washington Area Convention and Visitors Bureau
1129 29th Street, N.W.
Washington, D.C. 20036

FLORIDA

Environmental Protection

Division of Environmental Research and Protection
Department of Natural Resources
Crown Building
Tallahassee, Florida 32304

Fish and Game

Division of Game and Fresh Water Fish
Department of Natural Resources
Bryant Building
Tallahassee, Florida 32304

Natural Resources

Department of Natural Resources
Crown Building
Tallahassee, Florida 32304

Parks and Recreation

Division of Recreation and Parks
Department of Natural Resources
Crown Building
Tallahassee, Florida 32304

Publicity, Information, and Development

Division of Tourism
Department of Commerce
Collins Building
Tallahassee, Florida 32304

GEORGIA

Environmental Protection

Division of Environmental Protection
Department of Natural Resources
19 Hunter Street, S.W.
Atlanta, Georgia 30334

Fish and Game

Game and Fish Division
Department of Natural Resources
270 Washington, S.W.
Atlanta, Georgia   30334

Natural Resources

Department of Natural Resources
270 Washington Street, S.W.
Atlanta, Georgia   30334

Parks and Recreation

Division of Parks and Historic Sites
Department of Natural Resources
270 Washington Street, S.W.
Atlanta, Georgia   30334

Publicity, Information, and Development

Industry and Trade Division
Department of Community Development
P.O. Box 38097
Atlanta, Georgia   30334

HAWAII

Environmental Protection

Office of Environmental Quality Control
Department of Land and Natural Resources
State Office Building
Honolulu, Hawaii   96809

Fish and Game

Fish and Game Division
Department of Land and Natural Resources
1179 Punchbowl Street
Honolulu, Hawaii   96813

Natural Resources

Department of Land and Natural Resources
State Office Building
Honolulu, Hawaii   96809

Parks and Recreation

Outdoor Recreation and Historic Sites Division
Department of Land and Natural Resources
State Office Building
Honolulu, Hawaii   96809

Publicity, Information, and Development

Hawaii Visitors Bureau
2270 Kalakaua Avenue
Honolulu, Hawaii 96815

IDAHO

Environmental Protection

Environmental Services
Department of Health and Welfare
Len B. Jordan Building
Boise, Idaho 83720

Fish and Game

Department of Fish and Game
600 South Walnut Street, Box 25
Boise, Idaho 83707

Natural Resources

Department of Water Resources
4th and Fort Streets
Boise, Idaho 83720

Parks and Recreation

Department of Parks and Recreation
2263 Warm Springs Avenue
Boise, Idaho 83720

Publicity, Information, and Development

Division of Tourism and Industrial Development
Capitol Building, Room 108
Boise, Idaho 83720

ILLINOIS

Environmental Protection

Environmental Protection Agency
2200 Churchill Road
Springfield, Illinois 62706

Fish and Game

Department of Conservation
602 State Office Building
Springfield, Illinois 62706

Natural Resources

Department of Conservation
602 State Office Building
Springfield, Illinois 62706

Parks and Recreation

Division of Lands and Historic Sites
Department of Conservation
901 1/2 South Spring Street
Springfield, Illinois 62706

Publicity, Information, and Development

Office of Tourism
Department of Business and Development
205 West Wacker Drive
Chicago, Illinois 60606

INDIANA

Environmental Protection

Environmental Health Division
Board of Health
1330 West Michigan Street
Indianapolis, Indiana 46206

Fish and Game

Fish and Wildlife Division
Department of Natural Resources
607 State Office Building
Indianapolis, Indiana 46204

Natural Resources

Department of Natural Resources
State Office Building
Indianapolis, Indiana 46204

Parks and Recreation

Department of Natural Resources
Division of Outdoor Recreation
612 State Office Building
Indianapolis, Indiana 46204

Publicity, Information, and Development

Tourism Division
Department of Commerce
336 State House
Indianapolis, Indiana 46204

IOWA

Environmental Protection

Department of Environmental Quality
3920 Delaware Avenue
Des Moines, Iowa 50319

Fish and Game

Fish and Wildlife Division
Conservation Commission
300 4th Street
Des Moines, Iowa 50319

Natural Resources

Natural Resources Council
Grimes Building
Des Moines, Iowa 50319

Parks and Recreation

Conservation Commission
300 4th Street
Des Moines, Iowa 50319

Publicity, Information, and Development

Travel Development
Development Commission
250 Jewett Building
Des Moines, Iowa 50319

KANSAS

Environmental Protection

Division of Environment
Department of Health and Environment
10th and Topeka Avenues
Topeka, Kansas 66612

Fish and Game

Forestry, Fish, and Game Commission
P.O. Box 1028
Pratt, Kansas 67124

Parks and Recreation

Park Resources Authority
801 Harrison Street
Topeka, Kansas 66612

Publicity, Information, and Development

Travel Division
Department of Economic Development
State Office Building
Topeka, Kansas 66612

KENTUCKY

Environmental Protection

Bureau of Environmental Quality
Department for Natural Resources and Environmental Protection
Capitol Plaza Tower
Frankfort, Kentucky 40601

Fish and Game

Department of Fish and Wildlife Resources
Capitol Plaza Tower
Frankfort, Kentucky 40601

Natural Resources

Department for Natural Resources and Environmental Protection
Capitol Plaza Tower
Frankfort, Kentucky 40601

Parks and Recreation

Parks Department
Capitol Plaza Tower
Frankfort, Kentucky 40601

Publicity, Information, and Development

Department of Public Information
Capitol Annex
Frankfort, Kentucky 40601

LOUISIANA

Environmental Protection

Council on Environmental Quality
State Capitol
Baton Rouge, Louisiana 70804

Fish and Game

Wildlife and Fisheries Commission
400 Royal Street
New Orleans, Louisiana 70160

Natural Resources

Department of Conservation
Land and Natural Resources Building
Baton Rouge, Louisiana 70804

Parks and Recreation

Parks and Recreation Commission
P.O. Drawer 1111
Baton Rouge, Louisiana 70821

Publicity, Information, and Development

Tourist Development Commission
Pentagon Courts
Baton Rouge, Louisiana 70804

MAINE

Environmental Protection

Department of Environmental Protection
State House
Augusta, Maine 04330

Fish and Game

Department of Inland Fisheries and Wildlife
State Office Building
Augusta, Maine 04330

Natural Resources

Department of Conservation
State Office Building
Augusta, Maine 04330

Parks and Recreation

Bureau of Parks and Recreation
Department of Conservation
State Office Building
Augusta, Maine 04330

Publicity, Information, and Development

Development Office
Executive Department
State House
Augusta, Maine 04333

MARYLAND

Environmental Protection

Environmental Services
Department of Natural Resources
Tawes State Office Building
Annapolis, Maryland 21401

Fish and Game

Fisheries Administration
Department of Natural Resources
Tawes State Office Building
Annapolis, Maryland 21401

Natural Resources

Department of Natural Resources
Tawes State Office Building
Annapolis, Maryland 21401

Parks and Recreation

Park Service
Department of Natural Resources
Tawes State Office Building
Annapolis, Maryland 21401

Publicity, Information, and Development

Division of Tourist Development
Department of Economic and Community Development
2525 Riva Road
Annapolis, Maryland 21401

MASSACHUSETTS

Environmental Protection

Executive Office of Environmental Affairs
18 Tremont Street
Boston, Massachusetts 02108

Fish and Game

Division of Fisheries and Game
Department of Natural Resources
State Office Building
Boston, Massachusetts 02202

Natural Resources

Department of Natural Resources
State Office Building
Boston, Massachusetts 02202

Parks and Recreation

Division of Forests and Parks
Department of Natural Resources
State Office Building
Boston, Massachusetts 02202

Publicity, Information, and Development

Department of Commerce and Development
State Office Building
Boston, Massachusetts 02202

MICHIGAN

Environmental Protection

Environmental Protection Branch
Department of Natural Resources
Stevens T. Mason Building
Lansing, Michigan 48926

Fish and Game

Wildlife Division
Department of Natural Resources
Stevens T. Mason Building
Lansing, Michigan 48926

Natural Resources

Department of Natural Resources
Stevens T. Mason Building
Lansing, Michigan 48926

Parks and Recreation

Parks Division
Department of Natural Resources
Stevens T. Mason Building
Lansing, Michigan 48926

Publicity, Information, and Development

Tourist Council
Department of Commerce
300 South Capitol
Lansing, Michigan 48913

MINNESOTA

Environmental Protection

Environmental Planning Division
State Planning Agency
100 Capitol Square Building
St. Paul, Minnesota 55101

Fish and Game

Fish and Wildlife Division
Department of Natural Resources
Centennial Building
St. Paul, Minnesota 55155

Natural Resources

Department of Natural Resources
Centennial Building
St. Paul, Minnesota 55155

Parks and Recreation

Parks and Recreation Division
Department of Natural Resources
Centennial Building
St. Paul, Minnesota 55155

Publicity, Information, and Development

Tourism Division
Department of Economic Development
Hanover Building
St. Paul, Minnesota 55101

MISSISSIPPI

Environmental Protection

Air and Water Pollution Control Commission
Robert E. Lee Building
Jackson, Mississippi 39205

Fish and Game

Game and Fish Commission
Robert E. Lee Building
Jackson, Mississippi 39205

Parks and Recreation

Park Commission
717 Robert E. Lee Building
Jackson, Mississippi 39205

Publicity, Information, and Development

Travel and Tourism Department
2000 Sillers Building
Jackson, Mississippi 39205

MISSOURI

Environmental Protection

Division of Environmental Quality
Department of Natural Resources
P.O. Box 176
Jefferson City, Missouri 65101

Fish and Game

Department of Conservation
P.O. Box 180
Jefferson City, Missouri 65101

Natural Resources

Department of Natural Resources
P.O. Box 176
Jefferson City, Missouri 65101

Parks and Recreation

Division of Parks and Recreation
Department of Natural Resources
State Office Building
Jefferson City, Missouri 65101

Publicity, Information, and Development

Division of Tourism
P.O. Box 1055
Jefferson City, Missouri 65101

MONTANA

Environmental Protection

Environmental Sciences Division
Department of Health and Environmental Sciences
Cogswell Building
Helena, Montana 59601

Fish and Game

Fish and Game Department
Sam W. Mitchell Building
Helena, Montana 59601

Natural Resources

Department of Natural Resources and Conservation
32 South Ewing Street
Helena, Montana 59601

Parks and Recreation

Recreation and Parks Division
Department of Fish and Game
Sam W. Mitchell Building
Helena, Montana 59601

Publicity, Information, and Development

Travel Promotion Unit
Department of Highways
1315 8th Avenue
Helena, Montana 59601

NEBRASKA

Environmental Protection

Department of Environmental Control
P.O. Box 94653
Lincoln, Nebraska 68509

Fish and Game

Game and Parks Commission
P.O. Box 30370
Lincoln, Nebraska 68503

Natural Resources

Natural Resources Commission
Terminal Building
Lincoln, Nebraska 68508

Parks and Recreation

Games and Parks Commission
P.O. Box 30370
Lincoln, Nebraska 68503

Publicity, Information, and Development

Division of Travel and Tourism
Department of Economic Development
State Capitol
Lincoln, Nebraska 68508

NEVADA

Environmental Protection

Environmental Protection Commission
213 Nye Building
Carson City, Nevada 89701

Fish and Game

Department of Fish and Game
P.O. Box 10678
Reno, Nevada 89510

Natural Resources

Department of Conservation and Natural Resources
213 Nye Building
Carson City, Nevada 89701

Parks and Recreation

Division of State Parks
Department of Conservation and Natural Resources
221 Nye Building
Carson City, Nevada 89701

Publicity, Information, and Development

Department of Economic Development
State Capitol
Carson City, Nevada 89701

NEW HAMPSHIRE

Environmental Protection

Water Supply and Pollution Control Commission
105 Loudon Road
Concord, New Hampshire 03301

Fish and Game

Fish and Game Department
34 Bridge Street
Concord, New Hampshire 03301

Natural Resources

Department of Resources and Economic Development
State House Annex
Concord, New Hampshire 03301

Parks and Recreation

Division of Parks
Department of Resources and Economic Development
State House Annex
Concord, New Hampshire 03301

Publicity, Information, and Development

Division of Economic Development
Department of Resources and Economic Development
State House Annex
Concord, New Hampshire 03301

NEW JERSEY

Environmental Protection

Division of Environmental Quality
Department of Environmental Protection
John Fitch Plaza
Trenton, New Jersey 08625

Fish and Game

Division of Fish, Game, and Shell Fisheries
Department of Environmental Protection
John Fitch Plaza
Trenton, New Jersey 08625

Natural Resources

Department of Environmental Protection
John Fitch Plaza
Trenton, New Jersey 08625

Parks and Recreation

Bureau of Parks
Department of Environmental Protection
P.O. Box 1420
Trenton, New Jersey 08625

Publicity, Information, and Development

Tourism and Promotion
Department of Labor and Industry
John Fitch Plaza
Trenton, New Jersey 08625

NEW MEXICO

Environmental Protection

Environmental Improvement Agency
Pera Building
Santa Fe, New Mexico 87501

Fish and Game

Department of Game and Fish
Villagra Building
Santa Fe, New Mexico 87501

Natural Resources

Natural Resources Conservation Commission
321 West San Francisco
Santa Fe, New Mexico 87501

Parks and Recreation

Park and Recreation Commission
141 East DeVargas
Santa Fe, New Mexico 87501

Publicity, Information, and Development

Tourist Division
Department of Development
113 Washington Avenue
Santa Fe, New Mexico 87501

NEW YORK

Environmental Protection

Department of Environmental Conservation
50 Wolf Road
Albany, New York 12205

Fish and Game

Division of Fish and Wildlife
Department of Environmental Conservation
50 Wolf Road
Albany, New York 12205

Natural Resources

Department of Environmental Conservation
50 Wolf Road
Albany, New York 12205

Parks and Recreation

Office of Parks and Recreation
Empire State Plaza
Albany, New York   12226

Publicity, Information, and Development

Bureau of Travel
Department of Commerce
99 Washington Avenue
Albany, New York   12210

NORTH CAROLINA

Environmental Protection

Environmental Management
Department of Natural and Economic Resources
Old Health Building
Raleigh, North Carolina 27611

Fish and Game

Wildlife Resources Commission
Department of Natural and Economic Resources
Albemarle Building
Raleigh, North Carolina 27611

Natural Resources

Department of Natural and Economic Resources
Administration Building
Raleigh, North Carolina 27611

Parks and Recreation

Division of Parks and Recreation
Department of Natural and Economic Resources
Administration Building
Raleigh, North Carolina 27611

Publicity, Information, and Development

Travel Development Section
Department of Natural and Economic Resources
P.O. Box 2768
Raleigh, North Carolina 27611

NORTH DAKOTA

Environmental Protection

Environmental Engineering Division
Department of Health
State Capitol
Bismarck, North Dakota 58505

Fish and Game

Game and Fish Department
2121 Lovett Avenue
Bismarck, North Dakota 58501

Natural Resources

Natural Resources Council
State Capitol
Bismarck, North Dakota 58505

Parks and Recreation

Outdoor Recreation Agency
Route 2, Box 139
Mandan, North Dakota 58554

Publicity, Information, and Development

Travel Division
Highway Department
Highway Building
Bismarck, North Dakota 58505

OHIO

Environmental Protection

Environmental Protection Agency
361 East Broad Street
Columbus, Ohio 43215

Fish and Game

Wildlife Division
Department of Natural Resources
Fountain Square
Columbus, Ohio 43224

Natural Resources

Department of Natural Resources
Fountain Square
Columbus, Ohio 43224

Parks and Recreation

Division of Parks and Recreation
Department of Natural Resources
Fountain Square
Columbus, Ohio   43224

Publicity, Information, and Development

Travel and Tourism
Department of Economic and Community Development
30 Broad Street
Columbus, Ohio   43215

OKLAHOMA

Environmental Protection

Environmental Health Services
Department of Health
10th and Stonewall
Oklahoma City, Oklahoma   73105

Fish and Game

Department of Wildlife Conservation
1801 North Lincoln
Oklahoma City, Oklahoma   73105

Parks and Recreation

Division of State Parks
Tourism and Recreation Department
500 Will Rogers Building
Oklahoma City, Oklahoma   73105

Publicity, Information, and Development

Tourism and Recreation Department
500 Will Rogers Building
Oklahoma City, Oklahoma   73105

OREGON

Environmental Protection

Department of Environmental Quality
1234 Southwest Morrison Street
Portland, Oregon   97205

Fish and Game

Wildlife Commission
1634 Southwest Alder Street
Portland, Oregon   97208

Natural Resources

Department of Natural Resources
207 State Capitol
Salem, Oregon 97310

Parks and Recreation

Parks and Recreation Branch
Department of Transportation
300 State Highway Building
Salem, Oregon 97310

Publicity, Information, and Development

Travel Information Division
Department of Transportation
140 Highway Building
Salem, Oregon 97310

PENNSYLVANIA

Environmental Protection

Department of Environmental Resources
202 Evangelical Press Building
Harrisburg, Pennsylvania 17105

Fish and Game

Fish Commission
3532 Walnut Street
Harrisburg, Pennsylvania 17120

Natural Resources

Department of Environmental Resources
202 Evangelical Press Building
Harrisburg, Pennsylvania 17105

Parks and Recreation

Bureau of State Parks
Department of Environmental Resources
Evangelical Press Building
Harrisburg, Pennsylvania 17105

Publicity, Information, and Development

Bureau of Travel Development
Department of Commerce
432 South Office Building
Harrisburg, Pennsylvania 17120

RHODE ISLAND

Environmental Protection

Governor's Task Force on Environment
State House
Providence, Rhode Island   02903

Fish and Game

Fish and Wildlife Division
Department of Natural Resources
83 Park Street
Providence, Rhode Island   02903

Natural Resources

Department of Natural Resources
83 Park Street
Providence, Rhode Island   02903

Parks and Recreation

Division of Parks and Recreation
Department of Natural Resources
83 Park Street
Providence, Rhode Island   02903

Publicity, Information, and Development

Tourism Division
Department of Economic Development
1 Weybosset Hill
Providence, Rhode Island   02903

SOUTH CAROLINA

Environmental Protection

Environmental Health and Safety
Department of Health and Environmental Control
2600 Bull Street
Columbia, South Carolina   29201

Fish and Game

Wildlife and Marine Resources Department
P.O. Box 167
Dutch Plaza, Building D
Columbia, South Carolina   29202

Natural Resources

Development Board
1301 Gervais Street
Columbia, South Carolina 29201

Parks and Recreation

Department of Parks, Recreation, and Tourism
1205 Pendleton Street, Box 113
Columbia, South Carolina 29201

Publicity, Information, and Development

Department of Parks, Recreation, and Tourism
1205 Pendleton Street, Box 113
Columbia, South Carolina 29201

SOUTH DAKOTA

Environmental Protection

Department of Environmental Protection
State Office Building 2
Pierre, South Dakota 57501

Fish and Game

Division of Game and Fish
Department of Game, Fish, and Parks
Anderson Building
Pierre, South Dakota 57501

Natural Resources

Department of Natural Resources Development
State Office Building 2
Pierre, South Dakota 57501

Parks and Recreation

Division of Parks and Recreation
Department of Game, Fish, and Parks
State Office Building 1
Pierre, South Dakota 57501

Publicity, Information, and Development

Division of Tourism
Department of Economic and Tourism Development
State Office Building 2
Pierre, South Dakota 57501

TENNESSEE

Environmental Protection

Bureau of Environmental Health
Department of Public Health
349 Cordell Hull Building
Nashville, Tennessee 37219

Fish and Game

Wildlife and Resource Agency
P.O. Box 40747
Nashville, Tennessee 37204

Natural Resources

Department of Conservation
2611 West End Avenue
Nashville, Tennessee 37203

Parks and Recreation

State Parks
Department of Conservation
2611 West End Avenue
Nashville, Tennessee 37203

Publicity, Information, and Development

Tourist Development Division
Department of Economic and Community Development
1028 Andrew Jackson Building
Nashville, Tennessee 37219

TEXAS

Fish and Game

Parks and Wildlife Department
4200 Smith School Road
Austin, Texas 78744

Parks and Recreation

Parks and Wildlife Department
4200 Smith School Road
Austin, Texas 78744

Publicity, Information, and Development

Tourist Development Agency
500 John H. Reagan Building
Austin, Texas 78701

UTAH

Environmental Protection

Bureau of Environmental Health
Department of Social Services
State Capitol
Salt Lake City, Utah 84114

Fish and Game

Division of Wildlife Resources
1596 West North Temple
Salt Lake City, Utah 84116

Natural Resources

Department of Natural Resources
438 State Capitol
Salt Lake City, Utah 84114

Parks and Recreation

Division of Parks and Recreation
Department of Natural Resources
1586 West North Temple
Salt Lake City, Utah 84116

Publicity, Information, and Development

Travel Development
Department of Development Services
450 State Capitol
Salt Lake City, Utah 84114

VERMONT

Environmental Protection

Environmental Conservation Agency
5 Court Street
Montpelier, Vermont 05602

Fish and Game

Department of Fish and Game
Environmental Conservation Agency
5 Court Street
Montpelier, Vermont 05602

Natural Resources

Natural Resources Conservation Council
Environmental Conservation Agency
5 Court Street
Montpelier, Vermont   05602

Parks and Recreation

Department of Forests and Parks
Environmental Conservation Agency
5 Court Street
Montpelier, Vermont   05602

Publicity, Information, and Development

Information and Travel Division
Agency of Development and Community Affairs
109 State Street
Montpelier, Vermont   05602

VIRGINIA

Environmental Protection

Council on the Environment
9th Street Office Building
Richmond, Virginia   23219

Fish and Game

Game and Inland Fisheries Commission
4010 West Broad Street
Richmond, Virginia   23219

Natural Resources

Department of Conservation and Economic Development
1100 State Office Building
Richmond, Virginia   23219

Parks and Recreation

Division of Parks
Department of Conservation and Economic Development
1201 State Office Building
Richmond, Virginia   23219

Publicity, Information, and Development

Travel Services
Department of Conservation and Economic Development
6 North 6th Street
Richmond, Virginia   23219

WASHINGTON

Environmental Protection

Department of Ecology
Lacey, Washington 98504

Fish and Game

Department of Fisheries
115 General Administration Building
Olympia, Washington 98504

Natural Resources

Department of Natural Resources
Public Lands Building
Olympia, Washington 98504

Parks and Recreation

Parks and Recreation Commission
P.O. Box 1128
Olympia, Washington 98504

Publicity, Information, and Development

Tourist Promotion Division
Department of Commerce and Economic Development
101 General Administration Building
Olympia, Washington 98504

WEST VIRGINIA

Environmental Protection

Department of Natural Resources
State Office Building 3
Charleston, West Virginia 25305

Fish and Game

Division of Wildlife Resources
Department of Natural Resources
State Office Building 3
Charleston, West Virginia 25305

Natural Resources

Department of Natural Resources
State Office Building 3
Charleston, West Virginia 25305

Parks and Recreation

Division of Parks and Recreation
Department of Natural Resources
State Office Building 3
Charleston, West Virginia 25305

Publicity, Information, and Development

Department of Commerce
Travel Development
1900 Washington Street, E.
Building B
Charleston, West Virginia 25305

WISCONSIN

Environmental Protection

Division of Environmental Standards
Department of Natural Resources
Pyare Square Building
Madison, Wisconsin 53701

Fish and Game

Bureau of Fish and Wildlife Management
Department of Natural Resources
4610 University Avenue
Madison, Wisconsin 53701

Natural Resources

Department of Natural Resources
4610 University Avenue
Madison, Wisconsin 53701

Parks and Recreation

Bureau of Parks and Recreation
Department of Natural Resources
4610 University Avenue
Madison, Wisconsin 53701

Publicity, Information, and Development

Division of Tourism
P.O. Box 177
Madison, Wisconsin 53701

WYOMING

Environmental Protection

Department of Environmental Quality
State Office Building
Cheyenne, Wyoming 82002

Fish and Game

Game and Fish Commission
5400 Bishop Boulevard
Cheyenne, Wyoming 82001

Natural Resources

Department of Economic Planning and Development
720 West 18th Street
Cheyenne, Wyoming 82001

Parks and Recreation

Recreation Commission
604 East 25th Street
Cheyenne, Wyoming 82001

Publicity, Information, and Development

Travel Commission
2320 Capitol Avenue
Cheyenne, Wyoming 82002

Chapter 16
NATIONAL CONSERVATION
AND ENVIRONMENTAL ORGANIZATIONS

CANADA

Arctic Resources Committee
46 Elgin Street, Room 11
Ottawa, Ontario   K1P 5K6

Canadian Environmental Law Association
1 Spadina Crescent, Suite 303
Toronto, Ontario   M5S 2J5

Canadian Environmental Law Research
Foundation
1 Spadina Crescent, Suite 303
Toronto, Ontario   M5S 2J5

Canadian Forestry Association
185 Somerset Street, W.   Suite 303
Ottawa, Ontario   K2P OJ2

Canadian Nature Federation
46 Elgin Street, Suite 40
Ottawa, Ontario   K1P 5K6

Canadian Water Resources Association
P.O. Box 1322
Regina, Saskatchewan   S4P 3B8

Canadian Wildlife Federation
1419 Carling Avenue
Ottawa, Ontario   K1Z 7L7

Citizens' Committee for Pollution
Control
P.O. Box 38
Burlington, Ontario   L7R 3X8

Committee of a Thousand
P.O. Box 185
Niagara Falls, Ontario   L2E 6T3

Committee of the International Association on Water Pollution Research
c/o Dr. C.P. Fisher
Canada Centre for Inland Waters
Burlington, Ontario

Council Organized to Protect the
Environment
22 Tarlton Road
Toronto, Ontario   M5P 2M4

Ducks Unlimited
1495 Pembina Highway
Winnipeg, Manitoba   R3T 2E2

National and Provincial Parks Association of Canada
47 Colborne Street, Suite 308
Toronto, Ontario   M5C 2A2

Conservation & Environmental Organizations

UNITED STATES

American Rivers Conservation Council
317 Pennsylvania Avenue, S.E.
Washington, D.C. 20003

American Shore and Beach Preservation
Association
412 O'Brien Hall
University of California
Berkeley, California 94720

Conservation Foundation
1717 Massachusetts Avenue, N.W.
Washington, D.C. 20036

Ducks Unlimited
P.O. Box 66300
Chicago, Illinois 60666

Environmental Action
1346 Connecticut Avenue, N.W.
Suite 731
Washington, D.C. 20036

Environmental Action Foundation
1346 Connecticut Avenue, N.W.
Suite 731
Washington, D.C. 20036

Environmental Defense Fund
162 Old Town Road
East Setauket, New York 11733

Environmental Law Institute
1346 Connecticut Avenue, N.W.
Suite 620
Washington, D.C. 20036

Friends of the Earth
124 Spear Street
San Francisco, California 94105

Institute for Environmental Awareness
113 Beacon Street
Greenfield, Massachusetts 01301

Izaak Walton League of America
1800 North Kent Street
Suite 806
Arlington, Virginia 22209

Jackson Hole Preserve
30 Rockefeller Plaza
New York, New York 10020

League of Conservation Voters
317 Pennsylvania Avenue, S.E.
Washington, D.C. 20003

National Audubon Society
950 Third Avenue
New York, New York 10022

National Parks and Conservation
Association
1701 18th Street, N.W.
Washington, D.C. 20009

National Watershed Congress
1025 Vermont Avenue, N.W.
Washington, D.C. 20005

National Wildlife Federation
1412 Sixteenth Street, N.W.
Washington, D.C. 20036

River Rights Action Committee
4260 East Evans Avenue
Denver, Colorado 80222

Sierra Club
530 Bush Street
San Francisco, California 94108

Sierra Club Legal Defense Fund
311 California Street
Suite 311
San Francisco, California   94104

Trout Unlimited
4260 East Evans
Denver, Colorado   80222

Water Pollution Control Federation
2626 Pennsylvania Avenue, N.W.
Washington, D.C.   20037

Wilderness Public Rights Fund
P.O. Box 308
Orinda, California   94563

Wilderness Society
1901 Pennsylvania Avenue, N.W.
Washington, D.C.   20006

Chapter 17

PROVINCIAL, STATE, AND REGIONAL ORGANIZATIONS

CANADA

ALBERTA

Alberta Recreational Canoeing Association
Department of Culture, Youth, and Recreation
10004 104th Avenue
Edmonton, Alberta   T5J OK5

Alberta Whitewater Association
P.O. Box 6624, Postal Station D
Calgary, Alberta   T2P 2V8

Alberta Wilderness Association
P.O. Box 6398, Postal Station D
Calgary, Alberta T2P 2E1

Foothills Recreation Association
400 Lancaster Building
Calgary, Alberta

Sierra Club
Alberta Chapter
3019 Beil Avenue, N.W.
Calgary, Alberta   T2L 1K6

Sport Alberta
P.O. Box 37
Edmonton, Alberta T5J 2H2

BRITISH COLUMBIA

British Columbia Recreation Association
1606 West Broadway
Vancouver, British Columbia   V6J 1X7

Canoe Sport British Columbia
1606 West Broadway
Vancouver, British Columbia V6J 1X7

Citizens Association to Save the
Environment
6002 West Saanich Road, Rural Rte. 7
Victoria, British Columbia   V8X 3X3

Northwest Wilderness Society
949 West 49th Avenue
Vancouver, British Columbia V5Z 2T1

Powell River Anti-Pollution Association
5878 Taku Street
Powell River, British Columbia
V8A 4V7

Sierra Club
Western Canada Chapter
P.O. Box 35520, Postal Station E
Vancouver, British Columbia
V6M 4G8

Wander Paddlers Guild
724 Poplar Street
Coquitlam, British Columbia
V3J 3S3

Western Guides and Outfitters
Association
1717 3rd Avenue, Room 213
Prince George, British Columbia
V2L 3G7

MANITOBA

Manitoba Paddling Association
Sports Administrative Center
379 Cumberland Avenue
Winnipeg, Manitoba   R3B 1T5

NEW BRUNSWICK

Conservation Council of New Brunswick
P.O. Box 541
Fredericton, New Brunswick E3B 5A6

New Brunswick Federation of Sports,
Recreation, and Physical Education
Centennial Building, Room 315
Fredericton, New Brunswick E3B 5H1

NEWFOUNDLAND

The Working Group on Environment
P.O. Box 9425
St. John's, Newfoundland A1A 2Y3

NORTHWEST TERRITORIES

Ecology North
P.O. Box 2888
Yellowknife, Northwest Territories
X0E 1H0

NOVA SCOTIA

Atlantic Provinces Health, Physical
Education, Recreation Association
Dalhousie University
School of Physical Education
Halifax, Nova Scotia B3H 4H8

Ecology Action Center
Dalhousie University
Forest Building, Room 20-A
Halifax, Nova Scotia B3H 4H8

Sport Nova Scotia
P.O. Box 982
Halifax, Nova Scotia B3L 4K9

ONTARIO

Algonquin Wildlands League
1430 Yonge Street
Toronto, Ontario   M4T 1Y6

Canoe Ontario
c/o Sport Ontario
559 Jarvis Street
Toronto, Ontario M4Y 2J1

Ecological Society
P.O. Box 325
Port Credit, Ontario L5G 4L8

Federation of Ontario Naturalists
1262 Don Mills Road
Don Mills, Ontario M3B 2W7

Ontario Recreation Society
559 Jarvis Street
Toronto, Ontario M4Y 2J1

Quetico Foundation
224 1/2 Simcoe Street
Toronto, Ontario M5T 1T4

Save the Lakeshore Association
P.O. Box 711
Burlington, Ontario L7R 3Y5

Sierra Club
Ontario Chapter
47 Colborne Street
Toronto, Ontario M5E 1E3

Sport Ontario
559 Jarvis Street
Toronto, Ontario M4Y 2J1

Wildwater Affiliation (Ontario)
c/o Bud McVicar
21 Vanity Court
Don Mills, Ontario M3A 1W9

QUEBEC

Association de la Vallee de la Rouge
St. Jovite County
Case Postale 970
Terrebonne, Province of Quebec
J6W 3L5

Confederation des Loisirs du Quebec
1135 chemin St. Louis
Quebec, Province of Quebec G1S 1E7

Confederation des Sports du Quebec
881 est boulevard de Maisonneuve
Montreal, Province of Quebec H2L 1Y8

Federation Quebecoise de Canot-Kayak
1415 est rue Jarry
Montreal, Province of Quebec H2E 2Z7

James Bay Committee
2050 ouest boulevard de Maisonneuve
Suite 202
Montreal, Province of Quebec H3H 1K7

Pollution Action Committee
1080 Beaver Hall Hill
Montreal, Province of Quebec H2Z 1S8

Quebec Camping Association
2233 Belgrave Avenue
Montreal, Province of Quebec H4A 2L9

SASKATCHEWAN

Saskatoon Environmental Society
P.O. Box 1372
Saskatoon, Saskatchewan S7K 3N9

Sask Sport
1950 Broad Street
Regina, Saskatchewan S4P 1X9

YUKON TERRITORY

Yukon Conservation Society
P.O. Box 4163
Whitehorse, Yukon Territory
Y1A 3S9

UNITED STATES

ALABAMA

Alabama Mountain Lakes Association
P.O. Box 2222
Decatur, Alabama 35601

North Alabama River Runners Association
8120 Hickory Hill Lane
Huntsville, Alabama 35802

Tallacoosa Highland Lakes Association
P.O. Box 277
Talladega, Alabama 35160

ALASKA

Alaska Conservation Society
P.O. Box 80192
College, Alaska 99701

Alaska Whitewater Association
Glenallen, Alaska 99588

Friends of the Earth
P.O. Box 1977
Anchorage, Alaska 99501

Sierra Club
Alaska Chapter
P.O. Box 2025
Anchorage, Alaska 99501

ARIZONA

Sierra Club
Grand Canyon Chapter
2950 North 7th Street
Phoenix, Arizona 85014

ARKANSAS

Ozark Society
P.O. Box 2914
Little Rock, Arkansas 72203

Upper Eleven Point River Association
P.O. Box 343
Pocahontas, Arkansas 72455

CALIFORNIA

American River Touring Association
1016 Jackson Street
Oakland, California 94607

Anti Marysville Dam Committee
P.O. Box 254
Forbestown, California 95941

California Tomorrow
681 Market Street
San Francisco, California 94105

Committee of Two Million
760 Market Street
San Francisco, California 94102

Committee to Save the Kings River
P.O. Box 4471
Fresno, California 93744

Environmental Defense Fund
2728 Durant Avenue
Berkeley, California 94704

League to Save Lake Tahoe
695 North Lake
Tahoe City, California 95730

Natural Resources Defense Council
664 Hamilton Avenue
Palo Alto, California 94301

Planning Conservation League
1225 8th Street, Suite 310
Sacramento, California 95814

Protect the American River Canyons
Association
P.O. Box 1978
Meadow Vista, California 95722

Sierra Club
Angeles Chapter
2410 Beverly Boulevard, Suite 2
Los Angeles, California 90057

Sierra Club
Kern Kaweah Chapter
P.O. Box 3295
Bakersfield, California 93305

Sierra Club
Loma Prieta Chapter
190 California Avenue
Palo Alto, California 94306

Sierra Club
Los Padres Chapter
P.O. Box 30222
Santa Barbara, California 93105

Sierra Club
Mother Lode Chapter
P.O. Box 1335
Sacramento, California 95806

Sierra Club
Redwood Chapter
3144 Valley Green Lane
Napa, California 94558

Sierra Club
San Diego Chapter
1549 El Prado
San Diego, California 92101

Sierra Club
San Francisco Bay Chapter
5608 College Avenue
Oakland, California 94618

Sierra Club
San Gorgonio Chapter
P.O. Box 1023
Riverside, California 92502

Sierra Club
Santa Lucia Chapter
765 Highland Drive
Los Osos, California 93401

Sierra Club
Tehipite Chapter
P.O. Box 5396
Fresno, California 93755

Sierra Club
Ventana Chapter
P.O. Box 5667
Carmel, California 93921

Southern California Canoe Association
3906 South Menlo Avenue
Los Angeles, California 90037

Stanislaus River Group
Sierra Club
1176 Emerson Street
Palo Alto, California 94301

COLORADO

Colorado Whitewater Association
4260 East Evans Avenue
Denver, Colorado 80222

Sierra Club
Rocky Mountain Chapter
P.O. Box 6312, Cherry Creek Station
Denver, Colorado 80206

Wilderness Society
Western Region
4260 East Evans Avenue
Denver, Colorado 80222

CONNECTICUT

Appalachian Mountain Club
Connecticut Chapter
37 Play Street
Thompsonville, Connecticut 06082

Farmington River Watershed Association
195 East Main Street
Avon, Connecticut 06001

Sierra Club
Connecticut Chapter
P.O. Box 153
Storrs, Connecticut 06268

DISTRICT OF COLUMBIA

Friends of the Earth
917 15th Street, N.W.
Washington, D.C. 20005

Interstate Commission on the Potomac
River Basin
203 Transportation Building
Washington, D.C. 20006

Sierra Club
Potomac Chapter
324 "C" Street, S.E.
Washington, D.C. 20003

FLORIDA

Florida Trail Association
4410 Northwest 18th Place
Gainesville, Florida 32605

Sierra Club
Florida Chapter
2405 Delgado Drive
Tallahassee, Florida 32304

GEORGIA

American Rafting Association
76 Third Street, N.W.
Atlanta, Georgia 30308

Georgia Canoeing Association
P.O. Box 7023
Atlanta, Georgia 30309

Sierra Club
Chattahoochee Chapter
P.O. Box 19574, Station N
Atlanta, Georgia 30325

HAWAII

Friends of the Earth
1372 Kapiolani Boulevard
Honolulu, Hawaii 96814

International Hawaiian Canoe
Association
1638 Kona, Suite A
Honolulu, Hawaii 96814

Sierra Club
Hawaii Chapter
P.O. Box 6037
Honolulu, Hawaii 96818

IDAHO

Hells Canyon Preservation Council
P.O. Box 2317
Idaho Falls, Idaho 83401

Idaho Environmental Council
P.O. Box 3371, University Station
Moscow, Idaho 83843

River of No Return Wilderness Council
P.O. Box 844
Boise, Idaho 83701

Sierra Club
Northern Rockies Chapter
7717 Ustick Road
Boise, Idaho 83704

ILLINOIS

Chicago Portage Heritage Committee
8800 Harlen, No. 108
Bridgeview, Illinois 60455

Chicago Whitewater Association
98040 Lake Drive, Apt. 104
Clarendon Hills, Illinois 60514

Coalition on American Rivers
P.O. Box 2667, Station A
Champaign, Illinois 61820

Illinois Paddling Council
2316 Prospect Avenue
Evanston, Illinois 60201

Lake Michigan Federation
53 West Jackson
Chicago, Illinois 60604

Mid-America Paddling Association
1224 North Berkeley Avenue
Peoria, Illinois 61603

Sierra Club
Great Lakes Chapter
616 Delles
Wheaton, Illinois 60187

Upper Mississippi River Conservation
Committee
1504 Third Avenue
Rock Island, Illinois 61201

IOWA

Iowa Canoe Association
211 South Olive
Maquoketa, Iowa 52060

Sierra Club
Iowa Chapter
P.O. Box 171
Des Moines, Iowa 50301

KANSAS

Kansas Canoe Association
71 Cody Road
Manhattan, Kansas 66205

Kansas Trails Council
P.O. Box 3162
Shawnee Mission, Kansas 66203

KENTUCKY

Kentucky Canoe Association
2006 Marilee Drive
Louisville, Kentucky 40272

Sierra Club
Cumberland Chapter
320 Mariemont Drive
Lexington, Kentucky 40505

LOUISIANA

Ecology Center of Louisiana
P.O. Box 19344
New Orleans, Louisiana 70179

Ozark Society
Bayou Chapter
203 Pennsylvania
Shreveport, Louisiana 71105

Sierra Club
Delta Chapter
1006 National Bank of Commerce
Building
New Orleans, Louisiana 70112

MAINE

Appalachian Mountain Club
Maine Chapter
55 Belton Avenue
Watertown, Maine 02171

Friends of Nature
Brooksville, Maine 04617

MASSACHUSETTS

Appalachian Mountain Club
(Headquarters)
5 Joy Street
Boston, Massachusetts 02108

Appalachian Mountain Club
Berkshire Chapter
61 Manchester Terrace
Springfield, Massachusetts 01108

Appalachian Mountain Club
Worcester Chapter
c/o John Dryden
Grafton Road
Milbury, Massachusetts 05127

Charles River Watershed Association
2391 Commonwealth Avenue
Auburndale, Massachusetts 02166

Connecticut River Watershed Council
125 Combs Road
Easthampton, Massachusetts 01027

New England Camping Association
29 Commonwealth Avenue
Boston, Massachusetts 02116

New England Trail Conference
P.O. Box 153
Ashfield, Massachusetts 01330

Northeast Sports and Recreation
Association
2 Fairmont Terrace
Wakefield, Massachusetts 01880

Sierra Club
New England Chapter
14 Beacon Street, Room 719
Boston, Massachusetts 02108

MICHIGAN

American Canoe Association
Michigan Division
1402 Henry
Ann Arbor, Michigan 48104

Lower Michigan Paddling Council
8266 Patton
Detroit, Michigan 48228

Michigan Canoe Association
9763 Beard Road
Byron, Michigan 48418

Michigan Canoe Race Association
2081 Grange Hall Road
Fenton, Michigan 48430

Recreational Canoeing Association
P.O. Box 265
Baldwin, Michigan 49304

Sierra Club
Mackinac Chapter
409 Seymour Street
Lansing, Michigan 48933

Upper Michigan Canoe Association
c/o Gil Grinsteiner
Menominee County Journal
Stephenson, Michigan 49887

MINNESOTA

Friends of the Wilderness
3515 East Fourth Street
Duluth, Minnesota 55804

Minnesota Canoe Association
9th and Cedar Streets
St. Paul, Minnesota 55108

Northwest Guides Association
6043 Thomas Avenue, S.
Minneapolis, Minnesota 55410

Sierra Club
North Star Chapter
P.O. Box 80004
St. Paul, Minnesota 55108

MISSOURI

Ozark National Scenic Riverways
P.O. Box 448
Van Buren, Missouri 63965

Ozark Wilderness Waterways Club
P.O. Box 8165
Kansas City, Missouri 64112

Sierra Club
Ozark Chapter
P.O. Box 12424
Olivette, Missouri 63122

MONTANA

Montana Wilderness Association
P.O. Box 548
Bozeman, Montana 59715

NEBRASKA

Midwest Canoe Association
3150 South 58th Street
Lincoln, Nebraska 68505

NEVADA

Sierra Club
Toiyabe Chapter
P.O. Box 8096, University Station
Reno, Nevada 89507

NEW HAMPSHIRE

Appalachian Mountain Club
New Hampshire Chapter
167 Berkdale Road
Bedford, New Hampshire 03102

NEW JERSEY

Delaware River Basin Commission
P.O. Box 360
Trenton, New Jersey 08603

Delaware River Watershed Association
P.O. Box 44
Far Hills, New Jersey 07931

New York-New Jersey River Conference
52 West Union Avenue
Bound Brook, New Jersey 08805

Sierra Club
New Jersey Chapter
360 Nassau Street
Princeton, New Jersey 08540

NEW MEXICO

Sierra Club
Rio Grande Chapter
P.O. Box 351
Los Alamos, New Mexico 87544

NEW YORK

Adirondack Mountain Club (Headquarters)
172 Ridge Street
Glens Falls, New York 12801

Adirondack Mountain Club
Brooklyn Chapter
c/o Arthur Wickborn
315 Wyckoff Avenue
Brooklyn, New York 11227

Adirondack Mountain Club
Genesee Valley Chapter
581 Lake Road
Webster, New York 14580

Adirondack Mountain Club
Schenectady Chapter
c/o Betty Lou Bailey
Schuyler 16, Netherlands Village
Schnectady, New York 12308

Appalachian Mountain Club
New York Chapter
190 Columbia Heights
Brooklyn, New York 11201

New York Canoe Racing Association
Route 1, Box 132
Otego, New York 13825

Scenic Hudson Preservation
Conference
545 Madison Avenue
New York, New York 10022

Sierra Club
Atlantic Chapter
50 West 40th Street
New York, New York 10018

NORTH CAROLINA

Conservation Council of North
Carolina
P.O. Box 553
Carrboro, North Carolina 27510

OHIO

Ohio River Basin Commission
36 East 4th Street, Suite 208-20
Cincinnati, Ohio 45202

Rivers Unlimited
3012 Section Road
Cincinnati, Ohio 45237

Sierra Club
Ohio Chapter
9900 Grass Creek Court
Cincinnati, Ohio 45231

OKLAHOMA

Sierra Club
Oklahoma Chapter
P.O. Box 53401
Oklahoma City, Oklahoma 73105

OREGON

The Mazamas
909 Northwest 19th Avenue
Portland, Oregon 97220

Rogue River Guides Association
P.O. Box 792
Medford, Oregon 97501

PENNSYLVANIA

Adirondack Mountain Club
Delaware Valley Chapter
306 Crestview Circle
Media, Pennsylvania 19063

American Nessmuk Society
109 Furnace Street
Birdsboro, Pennsylvania 19508

Eastern Professional River Outfitters
Association
P.O. Box 252
Hot Springs, North Carolina 28743

Neshaminy Valley Watershed Association
8 West Oakland Avenue
Doylestown, Pennsylvania 18901

Pennsylvania Association of Canoeing
and Kayaking
Rural Delivery 1, Woodland Oaks
Tunkhannock, Pennsylvania 18657

Sierra Club
Pennsylvania Chapter
2015 Land Title Building
Philadelphia, Pennsylvania 19110

Western Pennsylvania Conservancy
204 Fifth Avenue
Pittsburgh, Pennsylvania 15222

Wissahickon Valley Watershed
Association
473 Bethlehem Pike
Fort Washington, Pennsylvania 15222

SOUTH CAROLINA

Carolina Whitewater Canoeing
Association
3142 Harvard Avenue
Columbia, South Carolina 29205

Sierra Club
Joseph LeConte Chapter
26 Tranquil Avenue
Greenville, South Carolina 29607

TENNESSEE

Sierra Club
Tennessee Chapter
708 Georgetown Drive
Nashville, Tennessee 37205

Tennessee Scenic Rivers Association
P.O. Box 3104
Nashville, Tennessee 37219

TEXAS

American Canoe Association
Central Division
1900 Aden Road
Fort Worth, Texas 76116

River Recreation Association of Texas
P.O. Box 12734
Austin, Texas 78711

Sierra Club
Lone Star Chapter
27190 Lana Lane
Conroe, Texas 77301

Texas Canoe Racing Association
Route 2, Box 43-G
San Marcos, Texas 78666

Texas Whitewater Association
P.O. Box 5264
Austin, Texas 78763

United States Canoe Association
Texas Division
4430 Nina Lee Lane
Houston, Texas 77092

UTAH

Sierra Club
Uinta Chapter
P.O. Box 8393, Foothill Station
Salt Lake City, Utah 84108

Western River Guides Association
994 Denver Street
Salt Lake City, Utah 84111

WASHINGTON

American Canoe Association
Northwest Division
4702 Edgewater Lane, N.E.
Seattle, Washington 98155

Columbia River Conservation League
1234 Gowen
Richland, Washington 99352

Federation of Western Outdoor Clubs
16603 53rd Avenue, S.
Seattle, Washington 98188

The Mountaineers
719 Pike Street
Seattle, Washington 98111

Sierra Club
Pacific Northwest Chapter
4534 1/2 University Way, N.E.
Seattle, Washington 98105

WEST VIRGINIA

Appalachian Trail Conference
P.O. Box 236
Harpers Ferry, West Virginia 25425

West Virginia Wildwater Association
2737 Daniels Avenue
South Charleston, West Virginia
25303

WISCONSIN

Minnesota-Wisconsin Boundary Area
Commission
619 2nd Street
Hudson, Wisconsin 54016

Northern Environmental Council
P.O. Box 89
Ashland, Wisconsin 54806

Sierra Club
John Muir Chapter
2604 North Murray Avenue, No. 107
Milwaukee, Wisconsin 53211

Wisconsin Canoe Association
10915 North Sherwood Drive
Mequon, Wisconsin 53092

Chapter 18

CLUBS AND AFFILIATED GROUPS

CANADA

ALBERTA

Alberta Recreational Canoe Association
13 Mission Avenue, Box 205
St. Albert, Alberta T8N 1H6

Alberta Whitewater Association
P.O. Box 6624
Calgary, Alberta T2P 2V8

Blue Lake School Canoe Club
Hinton, Alberta TOE 1BO

Bow Waters Canoe Club
2119 45th Street, S.E.
Calgary, Alberta T2B 1K1

Calgary Canoe Club
93 Gainsborough Drive, S.W.
Calgary, Alberta T3E 4W6

Calgary Whitewater Club
85 Hartford Road, N.W.
Calgary, Alberta T2K 2A4

Canadian Canoe Association
Alberta Division
13 Mission Avenue, Box 205
St. Albert, Alberta T8N 1H6

Edmonton Canoe Club
39 Northwoods Village
Edmonton, Alberta T5X 1T2

Edmonton Whitewater Paddlers
10974 70th Avenue
Edmonton, Alberta T6H 2G8

Edson Canoe Club
c/o Jim Froggett
Edson, Alberta TOE OPO

Grande Prairie Canoe Club
9926 80th Avenue
Grande Prairie, Alberta T8V 3S7

Lacombe Canoe Club
c/o Howard Fredeen
Lacombe, Alberta TOC 1SO

Lethbridge Canoe Club
P.O. Box 655
Lethbridge, Alberta T1J 3Z4

Medicine Hat Canoe Club
P.O. Box 605, 607
Medicine Hat, Alberta T1A 7G5

North West Voyageurs
10922 88th Avenue
Edmonton, Alberta T6G OZ1

Red Deer Canoe and Kayak Club
4522 45th Street
Red Deer, Alberta T4N 1K1

Sundre Canoe Club
c/o Ross Dawnes
Sundre, Alberta TOM 1XO

Whitewater Strathcona-Tweedsmuir
Club
c/o Strathcona Tweedsmuir School
Rural Route 2
Okotoks, Alberta TOL 1TO

Clubs and Affiliated Groups

BRITISH COLUMBIA

B.C. Kayak and Canoe Club
2041 Trafalgar
Vancouver, British Columbia V6K 3S5

Burnaby Aquatic Club
636 Tyndall Street
Coquitlam, British Columbia V3J 3S3

Burquitlam Canoe Club
636 Tyndall Street
Coquitlam, British Columbia V3J 3S3

Canoe Sport British Columbia
1606 West Broadway
Vancouver, British Columbia V6J 1X7

Port Moody Canoe Club
634 Bently Road
Port Moody, British Columbia V3H 3A3

Simon Fraser University Outdoors Club
Simon Fraser University
Department of Recreation
Burnaby, British Columbia V5A 1S6

University of British Columbia Kayak
and Canoe Club
University of British Columbia
A.M.S. Building
Vancouver, British Columbia V6T 1W5

Vernon Canoe Club
c/o Les Holmes
Rural Route 1, Angus Drive
Westbank, British Columbia VOH 2AO

Victoria Whitewater Club
593 John Street, No. 2
Victoria, British Columbia V8T 1T7

Wander Paddlers Guild
724 Poplar Street
Coquitlam, British Columbia V3J 3S3

MANITOBA

Winnipeg Canoe Club
Lot 13, Fraser Road
St. Germain, Manitoba ROG 2AO

NOVA SCOTIA

Abenaki Aquatic Club
26 Swanton Drive
Dartmouth, Nova Scotia B2W 2C4

Banook Canoe Club
60 Pleasant Street
Dartmouth, Nova Scotia B2Y 3P5

Beaver Canoe Club
P.O. Box 14
Sheet Harbour, Nova Scotia B3J 2L7

Cheema Aquatic Club
c/o Orville Murray
Waverly Post Office
Halifax County, Nova Scotia
BON 2SO

Chignecto Canoe Club
1058 Tower Road
Halifax, Nova Scotia B3H 2Y5

Maskwa Aquatic Club
14 Hamshaw Drive
Halifax, Nova Scotia B3M 2G8

Mic Mac Amateur Aquatic Club
84 Fenwick Street
Dartmouth, Nova Scotia B2Y 2J6

Milo Aquatic Club
c/o Richie Hubbard
Court House
Yarmouth, Nova Scotia B5A 1A2

Pisiquid Aquatic Club
Lakeview Drive
Windsor, Nova Scotia BON 2TO

Senobe Aquatic Club
68 Celtic Drive
Dartmouth, Nova Scotia B2Y 3G6

ONTARIO

Ak-O-Mak Canoe Club
56 Amberdale Drive
Scarborough, Ontario M1P 4C2

Balmy Beach Canoe Club
84 Willow Avenue, Apt. 27
Toronto, Ontario M4E 3K2

Brownsea Base Boy Scouts
P.O. Box 742
Peterborough, Ontario K9J 6Z6

Canoe Ontario
c/o Sport Ontario
559 Jarvis Street
Toronto, Ontario M4Y 2J1

Carleton Place Canoe Club
P.O. Box 1829
Carleton Place, Ontario KOA 1JO

Cataraqui Canoe Club
c/o Fred Johnston
Rural Route 4
Odessa, Ontario KOH 2HO

Fourth Etobicoke Central Venturers
75 Thicket Road
Etobicoke, Ontario M9C 2T4

Gananoque Canoe Club
P.O. Box 519
Gananoque, Ontario KOH 1RO

Guelph Canoeing and Outing Club
33 Dawson Road
Guelph, Ontario N1H 5V2

Hamilton Whitewater Paddlers
c/o Glenn Barnett
Trinity Side Road
Ancaster, Ontario L96 3L2

Lakefield College School Canoe Club
Lakefield College School
c/o Dave Hodkins
Lakefield, Ontario KOL 2HO

London Canoe Club
429 Averill Crescent
London, Ontario N6C 2R8

Mississauga Canoe Club
871 Parkland Avenue
Mississauga, Ontario L5H 3G9

Mohawk Canoe Club
P.O. Box 212
Burlington, Ontario L7R 3Y1

Mohawk Rod and Gun Club
15 Langside Drive
Weston, Ontario M9N 3E2

Morrisburg Canoe Club
47 Meikle Street
Morrisburg, Ontario KOC 1XO

Newmarket Whitewater Club
751 Botany Hills Crescent
Newmarket, Ontario L3Y 3A7

North Bay Canoe Club
c/o Charles Olmstead
Rural Route 3, Anita Avenue
North Bay, Ontario P1B 8G4

Oakville Racing Canoe Club
581 Exbury Crescent
Mississauga, Ontario L5G 2P4

Ona Lac Canoe Club
P.O. Box 232
Onaping, Ontario POM 2RO

Ontario Canoe Cruisers
P.O. Box 225
Etobicoke, Ontario M9C 4V3

Ontario Voyageurs Kayak Club
2121 Calstock Drive
Rexdale, Ontario M9V 1H1

Ontario Wild Water Affiliation
21 Vanity Court
Don Mills, Ontario M3A 1W9

Ottawa River Runners
2308 Hillary Avenue
Ottawa, Ontario K1H 7J3

Queen's University Wild Water Club
21 Lakeshore Boulevard
Kingston, Ontario K7M 4J8

Rideau Canoe Club
13 Phillip Drive
Ottawa, Ontario K2E 6R6

Sudbury Canoe Club
61 St. Lawrence Street
Sudbury, Ontario P3C 2X3

University of Guelph Canoe Club
University of Guelph
Box A451
Guelph, Ontario N1G 2W2

Victoria Park Kayak Club
4 Cave Hill Crescent
Scarborough, Ontario M1R 4P9

West Rouge Canoe Club
368 Rouge Hill Drive
West Hill, Ontario M1C 2Z4

Clubs and Affiliated Groups

QUEBEC

Arpikayak
C.P. 215 boulevard du Lac
Lac Beauport, Province of Quebec
G0A 2C0

Association Canot-Kayak-Camping de
l'Outaouais
23 rue du Parc
Limbour, Province of Quebec

Les Cageux de Vaudreuil Soulanges
356 Boul Roche
Vaudreuil, Province of Quebec

Canot-Kayak-Camping l'Aval
1600 rue St. Denis Ste. Foy
Quebec, Province of Quebec H2X 3K2

Cartierville Boating Club
12280 Jasmin Street
Montreal, Province of Quebec H4K 1V8

Cegep de Shawinigan
1472 Frontenac, No. 2
Shawinigan, Province of Quebec
G9N 2R2

Cepal
425 chemin St. Dominique
Jonquiere, Province of Quebec
G7X 6P9

Chateauguay Canoe Club
253 Cedar Avenue
Chateauguay, Province of Quebec
J6J 3S7

Club de Canotage de Quebec
135 Laurier Avenue
Quebec, Province of Quebec G1R 2K8

Club de Canotage du Cap de la Madeleine
304 St. Georges Street
Cap de la Madeleine, Province of Quebec
G8T 5E8

Echohamok
199 rue Lachance
Beaupre, Province of Quebec G0A 1E0

Ecole de Canot-Kayak de Mont Tremblay
881 est boulevard de Maisonneuve
Montreal, Province of Quebec H2L 1Y8

Federation Quebecoise de Canot-
Kayak
1415 est rue Jarry
Montreal, Province of Quebec
H2E 2Z7

Huntingdon Paddling Club
Ste. Agnes de Dundee
Huntingdon, Province of Quebec
J0S 1H0

Kayakogak
67 Desjardins, Apt. 1
Levis, Province of Quebec G6V 5V3

Keno
58-A St. Laurent
Valleyfield, Province of Quebec
J6S 2M4

Lachine Racing Canoe Club
228 Darwin, Apt. 208
Montreal, Province of Quebec
H3E 1C6

Onake Paddling Club
P.O. Box 326
Caughnawaga, Province of Quebec
J0L 1B0

Otterburn Boating Club
604 Dublin Street
Beloeil, Province of Quebec
J3H 1N6

Les Portageurs
348 Avenue Lippens
Montreal, Province of Quebec
A2M 1H6

Rabaska
776 Dalquier-Ste. Foy
Quebec, Province of Quebec
G1V 3H9

Rivyak
6020 Esplanade
Montreal, Province of Quebec
H2T 3A3

Universite Laval
1416 St. Georges
Ancienne-Lorette, Province of Quebec
G2E 1J2

Les Voyageurs
2290 Pincourt
Duvernay, Ville de Laval, Province of
Quebec H7E 2H7

SASKATCHEWAN

Historic Trails Canoe Club
24 Pleasantview Bay
Regina, Saskatchewan S4R 5H3

Regina Canoe Club
2058 Lorne Street
Regina, Saskatchewan S4P 2M2

Saskatoon Canoe Club
Sub Post Office 6, Box 363
Saskatoon, Saskatchewan S7K 3L3

YUKON TERRITORIES

Yukon Voyageurs Canoe Club
P.O. Box 4478
Whitehorse, Yukon Territory

UNITED STATES

ALABAMA

Birmingham Canoe Club
P.O. Box 3831
Birmingham, Alabama 35208

North Alabama River Runners Association
8120 Hickory Hill Lane
Huntsville, Alabama 35802

ALASKA

Alaska Whitewater Association
Glenallen, Alaska 99588

Knik Kanoers and Kayakers
3014 Columbia
Anchorage, Alaska 99504

ARIZONA

Dry Wash Canoe and Kayak Club
Arizona State University
MPE Building INTRAM
Tempe, Arizona 85281

ARKANSAS

Arkansas Canoe Club
1595 Woodbrook
Fayetteville, Arkansas 72701

Bow and Stern
440 Mission Boulevard
Fayetteville, Arkansas 72701

Ozark Mountain Canoe Club
c/o Les Long
Star Route 1
Russellville, Arkansas 72801

CALIFORNIA

American Youth Hostels
Santa Clara Valley Club
5493 Blossom Wood Avenue
San Jose, California 95124

Anhinga Boating Club
727 South 3rd Street
Richmond, California 94804

Antioch Whitewater Club
44 North Lake Drive
Antioch, California 94509

Ballona Creek Paddling Club of Los
Angeles
933 North Orlando Drive
Los Angeles, California 90069

Cakara
675 Overhill Drive
Redding, California 96001

Chasm Outing Club
P.O. Box 5622
Orange, California 92667

Clubs and Affiliated Groups

Echo Wilderness Club
2424 Russell Street
Berkeley, California 94705

Feather River Kayak Club
1773 Broadway
Marysville, California 95901

Haystackers Whitewater Canoe Club
P.O. Box 675
Kernville, California 93238

Humboldt River Touring Club
650 10th Street
Arcata, California 95521

Idlewild Yacht Club
800 Market Street
San Francisco, California 94102

Lera Canoe Club
200 Almond Avenue
Los Altos, California 94022

Lerc Voyageurs Canoe and Kayak Club
12814 Arminta Street
North Hollywood, California 91605

Loma Prieta Paddlers
1374 Colinton Way
Sunnyvale, California 94087

Lorien Canoe Club
P.O. Box 1238
Vista, California 92083

Marin Canoe Club
P.O. Box 3023
San Rafael, California 94902

Mother Lode Outdoor School
581 Continental Drive
San Jose, California 95111

National Friends of the River
1964 Menalto Avenue
Menlo Park, California 94025

Pacific Paddlers
22406 DeKalb Drive
Woodland Hills, California 91364

Powell Boating Club of University
of California–Berkeley
5499 Claremont Avenue
Oakland, California 94618

Sierra Club
Mother Lode Chapter
914 Stanford Avenue
Modesto, California 95350

Sierra Club
River Touring Bay Chapter
1455 Union Street, No. 10
San Francisco, California 94109

Sierra Club
River Touring Section
1760 Walnut Street
Berkeley, California 94709

Sierra Club
San Francisco Chapter
River Touring Section
94 El Toyonal
Orinda, California 94563

Sierra Club
Yokut River Touring Section
914 Stanford
Modesto, California 95350

Sierra Club River Conservation
Committee
2750 Shasta Road
Berkeley, California 94708

Southern California Canoe Association
3906 South Menlo Avenue
Los Angeles, California 90037

Tomales Bay Kayak Club
P.O. Box 468
Point Reyes Station, California 94956

Truckee River Kayaks
P.O. Box 1592
Tahoe City, California 95730

Valley Canoe Club
10363 Calvin Avenue
Los Angeles, California 90025

Vander Meer Voyageurs
19027 Mayberry Drive
Castro Valley, California 94546

Westlake Canoe Club
3427 Gloria
Newbury Park, California 91320

YMCA Whitewater Club of San Joaquin
County
640 North Center Street
Stockton, California 95202

Yokeet Wilderness Group
914 Stanford Avenue
Modesto, California 95350

COLORADO

Colorado Whitewater Association
4260 East Evans Avenue
Denver, Colorado 80222

Colorado State University Whitewater
Club
Colorado State University
Activities Center, Box 411
Fort Collins, Colorado 80523

Rocky Mountain Canoe Club
P.O. Box 4490
Boulder, Colorado 80302

Whitewater Expeditions
Box A-122
Ent Air Force Base, Colorado 80912

CONNECTICUT

Amston Lake Canoe Club
c/o Robert Dickinson
Deepwood Drive
Amston, Connecticut 06231

Appalachian Mountain Club
Connecticut Chapter
20 Dyer Avenue
Collinsville, Connecticut 06059

Columbia Canoe Club
c/o Mrs. William Murphy
Lake Road
Columbia, Connecticut 06237

Greenwich High School Kayak Club
10 Hillside Road
Greenwich, Connecticut 06830

OGRCC Family Paddlers
20 Arcadia Road
Old Greenwich, Connecticut 06870

University of Connecticut Outing
Club
Holcom Hall, Box 110
Storrs, Connecticut 06268

Waterford Canoe Club
P.O. Box 111
Waterford, Connecticut 06385

DELAWARE

Brandywine Canoe Club
3212 Romilly Road
Wilmington, Delaware 19810

Brandywine Valley Outing Club
P.O. Box 7033
Wilmington, Delaware 19803

Buck Ridge Ski Club
Route 1, Box 426 E
Hockessin, Delaware 19707

Wilmington Trail Club
Inverness Circle, Apt. M-9
Newcastle, Delaware 19720

DISTRICT OF COLUMBIA

Canoe Cruisers Association of
Greater Washington
6400 MacArthur Boulevard
Washington, D.C. 20016

Potomac Boat Club
3530 Water Street, N.W.
Washington, D.C. 20007

Washington Canoe Club
3700 K Street, N.W.
Washington, D.C. 20007

FLORIDA

Citrus County Kayak Club
Route 1, Box 415
Floral City, Florida 32636

Everglades Canoe Club
239 Northeast 20th Street
Delray Beach, Florida 33440

Florida Sport Paddling Club
133 Hickory Lane
Seffner, Florida 33584

Florida Trail Association
4410 Northwest 18th Place
Gainesville, Florida 32605

Seminole Canoe and Yacht Club
5653 Windermere Drive
Jacksonville, Florida 32211

GEORGIA

American Rafting Association
76 3rd Street, N.W.
Atlanta, Georgia 30308

Camp Merrie-Wood
3245 Nancy Creek Road, N.W.
Atlanta, Georgia 30327

Dean's Club
6277 Roswell Road, N.E.
Atlanta, Georgia 30328

Explorer Post 49
1506 Brawley Circle
Atlanta, Georgia 30313

Georgia Canoeing Association
P.O. Box 7023
Atlanta, Georgia 30309

YMCA
Gillionville Road
Albany, Georgia 31707

HAWAII

Hawaii Kayak Club
407 D Keariani Street
Kailea, Hawaii 96734

International Hawaiian Canoe
Association
1638 Kona, Suite A
Honolulu, Hawaii 96814

Outrigger Canoe Club
2909 Kalakaua Avenue
Honolulu, Hawaii 96815

IDAHO

American Indian Center Canoe Club
115 North Walnut
Boise, Idaho 83702

Idaho Alpine Club
P.O. Box 2885
Idaho Falls, Idaho 83401

Idaho State University Outdoor
Program
Idaho State University
P.O. Box 9024
Pocatello, Idaho 83209

Sawtooth Wildwater Club
1255 Elm Street
Mountain Home, Idaho 83647

University of Idaho Outdoor Program
Student Union Building
Moscow, Idaho 83843

ILLINOIS

American Indian Center Canoe Club
1630 North Wilson
Chicago, Illinois 60640

Belleville Whitewater Club
3 Oakwood Street
Belleville, Illinois 62223

Boy Scouts of America, Troop 54
408 Springcrest Road
East Dundee, Illinois 60632

Caterpillar Canoe Club
344 West Arnold Road
Sandwich, Illinois 60548

Chicago Whitewater Association
98040 Lake Drive, Apt. 104
Clarendon Hills, Illinois 60514

Illini Downstreamers
4702 Stonewall Avenue
Downers Grove, Illinois 60515

Illinois Paddling Council
2316 Prospect Avenue
Evanston, Illinois 60201

Le Brigade Illinois
451 South Saint Marys Road
Libertyville, Illinois 60048

Lincoln Park Boat Club
2737 North Hampden Court
Chicago, Illinois 60614

Mackinaw Canoe Club
120 Circle Drive
East Peoria, Illinois 61611

Mid-America Paddling Association
1224 North Berkeley Avenue
Peoria, Illinois 61603

Prairie Club Canoeists
517 Miller Road
Barrington, Illinois 60010

Prairie State Canoeists
5055 North Kildare Avenue
Chicago, Illinois 60630

Saint Charles Canoe Club
240 East Schick Road
Bloomingdale, Illinois 60108

Sauk Valley Canoe Club
c/o John Whitver
Rural Route 2
Morrison, Illinois 61270

Sierra Club Canoeists
625 West Barry
Chicago, Illinois 60657

Tippee Canoe Club
1630 East Wood Street
Decatur, Illinois 62521

University of Chicago Whitewater Club
933 East 56th Street
Chicago, Illinois 60637

YMCA Camping Office
178 East 155th Street
Harvey, Illinois 60426

INDIANA

Bloomington Canoe and Kayak Club
1201 West Allen, No. 29
Bloomington, Indiana 47401

Boy Scouts of America
Pioneer Trails Council
P.O. Box 1328
Elkhart, Indiana 46514

Connersville Canoe Club
c/o Arlington Hudson
Rural Route 3
Connersville, Indiana 47331

Culver Military Academy Canoe Club
c/o Phillip Mallory
Culver, Indiana 46511

Elkhart YMCA Canoe Club
229 West Franklin Street
Elkhart, Indiana 46514

Girl Scout Troop 10
3012 Wilshire Drive
West Lafayette, Indiana 47906

Hoosier Canoe Club
5815 Critenden Drive
Indianapolis, Indiana 46224

Kekionga Voyageurs
3727 Meda Pass
Ft. Wayne, Indiana 46809

Lafayette Canoe Club
60 Cardinal Court
Lafayette, Indiana 47905

L and M Explorer Post 60
c/o A.K. Olson
Rural Route 1
Lyons, Indiana 47443

Northwest Paddle Pushers
8145 Lake Shore Drive
Cedar Lake, Indiana 46303

Paddle Pushers Canoe Club
2506 Rainbow Drive
Lafayette, Indiana 47904

Prairie Club Canoeists
364 Rose Ellen Drive
Crown Point, Indiana 46307

St. Joe Valley Canoe and Kayak Club
200 East Jackson
Elkhart, Indiana 46514

South Lake YMCA
Court Street
Crown Point, Indiana 46307

Sugar Creek Paddlers
c/o Faye Swisher
2206 Country Club Road
Crawfordsville, Indiana 47933

Tippecanoe Voyageurs Canoe Club
Route 1, Box 8-A
Winamac, Indiana 46996

Tukunu Club
952 Riverside Drive
South Bend, Indiana 46616

Whitewater Valley Canoe Club
1032 Cliff Street
Brookville, Indiana 47012

Wild American Paddlers
Route 7, Box 66D
Greenfield, Indiana 46140

Wildcat Canoe Club
1116 South Hay Street
Kokomo, Indiana 46901

IOWA

Decorah Canoe Club
Luther College
c/o George Knudson
Decorah, Iowa 52101

Iowa Canoe Association
211 South Olive
Maquoketa, Iowa 52060

Port of Sioux City Rivercade
P.O. Box 1318
Sioux City, Iowa 51100

KANSAS

American Red Cross
Midway Kansas Chapter
321 North Topeka
Wichita, Kansas 67202

Johnson County Canoe Club
7832 Rosewood Lane
Prairie Village, Kansas 66208

Kansas Canoe Association
71 Cody Road
Manhattan, Kansas 66502

Ozark Wilderness Waterways Club
3305 West 50th Terrace
Shawnee Mission, Kansas 66205

Prairie Voyageurs Canoe Club
4722 East 11th Street
Wichita, Kansas 67212

Wichita Camp Fire Council
1607 South Broadway
Wichita, Kansas 67211

Wichita Girl Scouts Council
2009 North Woodlawn
Wichita, Kansas 67208

YMCA
8025 East Douglas
Wichita, Kansas 67207

KENTUCKY

Blue Grass Pack and Paddle Club
216 Inverness Drive
Lexington, Kentucky 40503

Blue Grass Wildwater Association
3489 Lansdowne, Apt. 72
Lexington, Kentucky 40502

Four Rivers Canoe Club
523 Alben Barkley Drive
Paducah, Kentucky 42001

Kentucky Canoe Association
2006 Marilee Drive
Louisville, Kentucky 40272

Kentucky Rivers Canoe Club
P.O. Box 986
Bowling Green, Kentucky 42101

Louisville Paddle Club
2006 Marilee Drive
Louisville, Kentucky 40272

Viking Canoe Club
622 Maryhill Lane
Louisville, Kentucky 40207

LOUISIANA

Bayou Haystackers
624 Moss Street
New Orleans, Louisiana 70119

MAINE

Bates Outing Club
Bates College
Lewiston, Maine 04240

Penobscot Paddle and Chowder Society
P.O. Box 121
Stillwater, Maine 04489

Saco Bound Canoe and Kayak Club
c/o Ned McSherry
Fryeburg, Maine 04037

MARYLAND

Appalachian River Runners Federation
P.O. Box 107
McHenry, Maryland 21541

Baltimore Kayak Club
1099 Tollgate Road
Belair, Maryland 21014

Canoe Cruisers Association
384 North Summit Avenue
Gaithersburg, Maryland 20760

Canoe Cruisers of Greater
Washington, D.C.
6827 Red Top Road, No. 1-B
Takoma Park, Maryland 20012

Explorer Post 757
203 Longwood Road
Baltimore, Maryland 21210

Frederick Canoe Club
Shookstown Road
Frederick, Maryland 21701

Greater Baltimore Canoe Club
3012 Abel Avenue
Baltimore, Maryland 21218

Mason-Dixon Canoe Cruisers
222 Pheasant Terrace
Hagerstown, Maryland 21740

Mattapony Canoe Club
2109 Ellamont Street
Baltimore, Maryland 21216

Monocacy Canoe Club
P.O. Box 1083
Frederick, Maryland 21701

Potomac River Paddlers
18505 Kingshill Road
Germantown, Maryland 20767

St. Mary's College of Maryland
Canoe Club
c/o John Spangler
St. Mary's City, Maryland 20686

Terrapin Trail Club
University of Maryland
Student Union Building, Box 18
College Park, Maryland 20742

MASSACHUSETTS

Cochituate Canoe Club
99 Dudley Road
Cochituate, Massachusetts 01760

Foxboro Canoe Club
32 Taunton Street
Bellingham, Massachusetts 02019

Hampshire College Outdoors Program
Hampshire College
Amherst, Massachusetts 01002

Holyoke Canoe Club
Holyoke College
Holyoke, Massachusetts 01040

Kayak and Canoe Club of Boston
156 High Street
Medford, Massachusetts 02155

Lake Chaogg Canoe Club
P.O. Box 512
Webster, Massachusetts 01570

MIT Whitewater Club
Massachusetts Institute of Technology
Box R 6432
Cambridge, Massachusetts 02139

Nor'east Voyageurs
c/o R.A. Paulson
West Street
Kingston, Massachusetts 02360

Northeast Sports and Recreation
Association
2 Fairmont Terrace
Wakefield, Massachusetts 01880

Phillips Academy Outing Club
Phillips Academy
Andover, Massachusetts 01810

Rat Pack Paddlers
P.O. Box 372
Athol, Massachusetts 01331

Waupanoag Paddlers
13 Borden Street
North Scituate, Massachusetts 02060

Westfield River Whitewater Canoe Club
90 West Silver Street
Westfield, Massachusetts 01085

MICHIGAN

American Canoe Association
Michigan Division
1402 Henry
Ann Arbor, Michigan 48104

Canadian Canoe Adventurers
106 Church Street
Highland Park, Michigan 48203

Kalamazoo Down Streamers
6820 Evergreen
Kalamazoo, Michigan 49002

Lansing Canoe Club
6101 Norburn Way
Lansing, Michigan 48910

Lower Michigan Paddling Council
8266 Patton
Detroit, Michigan 48228

Michigan Canoe Association
9763 Beard Road
Byron, Michigan 48418

Michigan Canoe Race Association
2081 Grange Hall Road
Fenton, Michigan 48430

Michigan Trailfinders Club
2630 Rockhill, N.E.
Grand Rapids, Michigan 49505

Niles Kayak Club
Route 1, Box 83
Buchanan, Michigan 49107

Raw Strength and Courage Kayakers
2185 Mershon Drive
Ann Arbor, Michigan 48103

Recreational Canoeing Association
P.O. Box 265
Baldwin, Michigan 49304

Upper Michigan Canoe Association
c/o Gil Grinsteiner
Menominee County Journal
Stephenson, Michigan 49887

MINNESOTA

Cascaders Canoe and Kayak Club
3128 West Calhoun Boulevard
Minneapolis, Minnesota 55416

Minnesota Canoe Association
9th and Cedar Streets
St. Paul, Minnesota 55108

MISSISSIPPI

Bayou Haystackers
112 Grosvenor
Waveland, Mississippi 39576

MSUBEE Canoe Club
3 Prospect Place
Starkville, Mississippi 39759

MISSOURI

Arnold Whitewater Association
4805 Theiss Road
St. Louis, Missouri 63128

Central Missouri State College Outing
Club
Central Missouri State College
c/o Dr. O. Hawksley, Biology Department
Warrensburg, Missouri 64093

Explorer Post 29
266 Iowa Street
Camdenton, Missouri 65020

Kamikaze Canoe and Kayak Club
P.O. Box 1261
Jefferson City, Missouri 65101

Meramec River Canoe Club
26 Lake Road
Fenton, Missouri 63026

Ozark Cruisers
1 Blue Acres Trailer Court
Columbia, Missouri 65201

Ozark Wilderness Waterways Club
P.O. Box 8165
Kansas City, Missouri 64112

Student Life Wilderness Adventures
University of Missouri
18 Read Hall
Columbia, Missouri 65201

University of Missouri Recreation
Committee
University of Missouri
212 Read Hall
Columbia, Missouri 65201

MONTANA

Montana Kayak Club
P.O. Box 213
Brady, Montana 59416

NEBRASKA

Explorer Post 136
2623 Avenue D
Kearney, Nebraska 68847

Fort Kearney Canoeists
2623 Avenue D
Kearney, Nebraska 68847

Great Missouri River Raft Regatta
3000 Farnam
Omaha, Nebraska 68131

Midwest Canoe Association
3150 South 58th Street
Lincoln, Nebraska 68505

Platte River Raft Regatta
411 East 11th Street
Schuyler, Nebraska 68661

NEVADA

Basic High School Canoe Club
751 Palo Verde Drive
Henderson, Nevada 89015

NEW HAMPSHIRE

Androscoggin Canoe and Kayak Club
c/o John Wilson
Lancaster, New Hampshire 03584

Ledyard Canoe Club
Dartmouth College
Robinson Hall
Hanover, New Hampshire 03755

Mad Pemi Canoe Club
93 Realty
Campton, New Hampshire 03223

Mt. Washington Valley Canoe and
Kayak Club
P.O. Box 675
North Conway, New Hampshire
03860

NEW JERSEY

Kayak and Canoe Club of New York
6 Winslow Avenue
East Brunswick, New Jersey 08816

Knickerbocker Canoe Club
1263 River Road
Edgewater, New Jersey 07020

Mohawk Canoe Club
455 West State Street
Trenton, New Jersey 08618

Murray Hill Canoe Club
c/o Carol Maclennan
Bell Laboratory, Room 1E-436
Murray Hill, New Jersey 07974

Neversink Sailing Society
c/o William Reed
Oak Tree Lane
Rumson, New Jersey 07760

New York-New Jersey River Conference
Canoe and Kayak Council
52 West Union Avenue
Bound Brook, New Jersey 08805

Red Dragon Canoe Club
221 Edgewater Avenue
Edgewater Park, New Jersey 08010

Rutgers University Outdoor Club
Rutgers University
P.O. Box 2913
New Brunswick, New Jersey 08903

Wanda Canoe Club
47 Summit Street
Ridgefield Park, New Jersey 07660

NEW MEXICO

Albuquerque Whitewater Club
804 Warm Sands Drive, S.E.
Albuquerque, New Mexico 87123

Explorer Post 20
4091 Trinity Drive
Los Alamos, New Mexico 87544

Rio Grande River Runners
2210 Central Avenue, S.E.
Albuquerque, New Mexico 87106

NEW YORK

Appalachian Mountain Club
New York Canoe Commission
P.O. Box 1956
Syosset, New York 11791

Boulder Bashers Canoe Club
353 Seneca Road
Hornell, New York 14843

Canoe and Kayak Club
257 Dutchess Turnpike
Poughkeepsie, New York 12603

Colgate Outing Club
Colgate University
Recreation Office
Hamilton, New York 13346

Cornell Outing Club
937 1/2 East State Street
Ithaca, New York 14850

Fulton County Canoe Club
40 North Main Street
Gloversville, New York 12078

Genesee Down River Paddlers
Route 2, Proctor Road
Wellsville, New York 14895

Inwood Canoe Club
509 West 212 Street
New York, New York 10036

Ka-Na-Wa-Ke Canoe Club
407 Beattie Street
Syracuse, New York 13224

Kayak and Canoe Club--Cooperstown
c/o Agnes Jones
Riverbrink
Cooperstown, New York 13326

New York Canoe Racing Association
Route 1, Box 132
Otego, New York 13825

Niagara Gorge Kayak Club
41 17th Street
Buffalo, New York 14213

Otterkill Canoe Club
5 Yankee Main Lane
Goshen, New York 10924

Sebago Canoe Club
9622 Avenue M
Brooklyn, New York 11236

Sierra Club--Canoe Commission
5 Lakeview Avenue
North Tarrytown, New York 10591

TASCA
P.O. Box 41
Oakland Gardens, New York 11364

Trail North Paddlers
960-A Troy-Schenectady Road
Letham, New York 12110

Wellsville Downriver Paddlers
c/o Leroy Dodson
Proctor Road
Wellsville, New York 14895

Yonkers Canoe Club
360 Edward Place
Yonkers, New York 10701

NORTH CAROLINA

Alamance Rafting Association
P.O. Box 51
Graham, North Carolina 27253

Atlantic Surf Kayak Club
P.O. Box 2228
Greensboro, North Carolina 27402

Blue Ridge Canoe Club
P.O. Box 828
Morganton, North Carolina 28655

Boy Scouts of America, Troop 822
622 Starmont Drive
Durham, North Carolina 27705

Carolina Canoe Club
P.O. Box 9011
Greensboro, North Carolina 27408

University of North Carolina-Charlotte
Venture Program
Cone University Center
Charlotte, North Carolina 28223

Watauga Whitewater Club
c/o Richard Furman

State Farm Road
Boone, North Carolina 28607

YWCA
1201 Glade Street
Winston-Salem, North Carolina
27104

OHIO

American Red Cross
Canton Chapter
618 2nd Street, N.W.
Canton, Ohio 44703

American Red Cross
Dayton Area Chapter
370 West First Street
Dayton, Ohio 45402

American Red Cross (Small Craft)
1477 Elbur Avenue
Lakewood, Ohio 44107

Boy Scouts of America, Troop 35
7155 Frank Avenue, N.W.
North Carolina, Ohio 44720

CMAC Kayak and Canoe Club
35124 Euclid Avenue
Willoughby, Ohio 44094

Cuyahoga Canoe Cruising Club
10465 State Road 44
Box T
Mantua, Ohio 44255

Dayton Canoe Club
1020 Riverside Drive
Dayton, Ohio 45405

Keel-Haulers Canoe Club
1649 Allen Drive
Westlake, Ohio 44145

Madhatters Canoe Club
2647 Norway Drive
Perry, Ohio 44081

American Youth Hostels
Miami Valley Council-AYH
1813 Shady Lane
Dayton, Ohio 45432

Oh-Penn Paddlers Canoe Club, Conneaut,
Ohio
c/o William Porter
4231 Springfield Road
East Springfield, Pennsylvania 16411

St. Joe Paddlers Canoe Club
104 Empire Street
Montpelier, Ohio 43543

Springfield Water Sports Club
728 Cedar Street
Springfield, Ohio 45504

Toledo Area Canoe and Kayak Enthusiasts
c/o W. McKnight
Route 1, River Road
Grand Rapids, Ohio 43522

Valley Voyageurs
5848 Montgomery Road, Apt. 3
Cincinnati, Ohio 45212

Warner and Swasey Canoe Club
406 Mill Avenue, S.W.
New Philadelphia, Ohio 44663

OKLAHOMA

OK Canoers
3112 Chaucer Drive
Village, Oklahoma 73120

Tulsa Canoe and Camping Club
5810 East 30th Place
Tulsa, Oklahoma 74114

OREGON

Crag Rats
Route 1, Box 505
Hood River, Oregon 97031

Eugene Kayak and Canoe Association
874 Sunnyside Drive
Eugene, Oregon 97404

Lower Columbia Canoe Club
Route 1, Box 134E
Scappoose, Oregon 97056

Mary Kayak Club
830 Northwest 23rd, No. 17
Corvallis, Oregon 97330

Oregon Kayak and Canoe Club
P.O. Box 692
Portland, Oregon 97207

Oregon Rafting Club
Route 1, Box 300
Hubbard, Oregon 97032

Willamette Kayak and Canoe Club
P.O. Box 1062
Corvallis, Oregon 97330

PENNSYLVANIA

Allegheny Canoe Club
755 West Spring Street
Titusville, Pennsylvania 16354

Allegheny Outing Club
Allegheny College
P.O. Box 1796
Meadville, Pennsylvania 16335

Allentown Hiking Club
124 South 16th Street
Allentown, Pennsylvania 18102

American Red Cross
701 Centre Avenue
Reading, Pennsylvania 19601

Benscreek Canoe Club
Route 5, Box 256
Johnstown, Pennsylvania 15905

Boat Technology Club
310 Curtin Avenue
Pittsburgh, Pennsylvania 15210

Boy Scouts of America, Post 42
Route 2
Palmerton, Pennsylvania 19053

Boy Scouts of America, Post 101
Lock Drawer 179
Bellefonte, Pennsylvania 16823

Bucknell Outing Club
Bucknell University
Box C-1610
Lewisburg, Pennsylvania 17837

Buck Ridge Ski Club
1728 Earlington Road
Havertown, Pennsylvania 19083

Canoe and Camping Club
Gettysburg College
P.O. Box 679
Gettysburg, Pennsylvania 17325

Central Ski Club of Philadelphia
345 South 18th Street
Philadelphia, Pennsylvania 19103

Columbia-Montour Council Boy Scouts
212 West 5th Street
Bloomsburg, Pennsylvania 17815

Conewago Canoe Club
2267 Willow Road
York, Pennsylvania 17404

Delaware Canoe Club
14 South 14th Street
Easton, Pennsylvania 18042

Endless Mountain Voyageurs
285 Shorthill Road
Clarks Green, Pennsylvania 18411

Exchange Club of Oil City Canoe Club
448 Colbert Avenue
Oil City, Pennsylvania 16301

Explorer Post 65
22 Catalpa Place
Pittsburgh, Pennsylvania 15228

Fox Chapel Canoe Club
610 Squaw Run Road
Pittsburgh, Pennsylvania 15328

Clubs and Affiliated Groups

Gettysburg College Recreation Committee
Gettysburg College
Student Union
Gettysburg, Pennsylvania 17325

Indiana University Outing Club
c/o David Cox
Chemistry Department
Indiana, Pennsylvania 15701

Kishacoquillas Canoe and Rafting Club
P.O. Box 97
Ohiopyle, Pennsylvania 15470

Mohawk Canoe Club
6 Canary Road
Levittown, Pennsylvania 19057

North Allegheny River Rats
1130 Sandalwood Lane
Pittsburgh, Pennsylvania 15237

North End Wanderers Canoe Club
308 Woodlawn Avenue
Bethlehem, Pennsylvania 18016

North Hills YMCA Whitewater Club
1130 Sandalwood Lane
Pittsburgh, Pennsylvania 15237

Oil Creek Valley Canoe Club
214 North 1st Street
Titusville, Pennsylvania 16354

Paoli Troop 1
Boy Scouts of America
432 Strafford Avenue
Wayne, Pennsylvania 19087

Penn Hills Whitewater Canoe Club
12200 Garland Drive
Pittsburgh, Pennsylvania 15235

Penn State Outing Club
118 South Buckhout Street
State College, Pennsylvania 16801

Pennsylvania Association of Canoeing
and Kayaking
Rural Delivery 1, Woodland Oaks
Tunkhannock, Pennsylvania 18657

Philadelphia Canoe Club
4900 Ridge Avenue
Philadelphia, Pennsylvania 19128

Puddle Jumpers Canoe Club
225 Oakhaven Drive
Corapolis, Pennsylvania 15108

River Runners
Post 772
Boy Scouts of America
605 George Street
Greensburg, Pennsylvania 15601

Scudder Falls Whitewater Club
795 River Road
Yardley, Pennsylvania 19067

Shenango Valley Canoe Club
863 Bechtal Avenue
Sharon, Pennsylvania 16146

Sierra Club
Allegheny River Group
Pennsylvania Chapter
P.O. Box 7404
Pittsburgh, Pennsylvania 15213

Slippery Rock State College
c/o L.H. Heddleston, Director
Student Activities and Recreation Program
Slippery Rock, Pennsylvania 16057

Sylvan Canoe Club
132 Arch Street
Verona, Pennsylvania 15147

Wildwater Boating Club
Lock Drawer 179
Bellefonte, Pennsylvania 16823

Williamsport YMCA Canoe Club
343 West 4th Street
Williamsport, Pennsylvania 17701

RHODE ISLAND

Brown University Outing Club
Brown University
Providence, Rhode Island 02912

Rhode Island River Rats
53 Maplewood Avenue
Misquamicut, Rhode Island 02891

Rhode Island Whitewater Club
10 Pond Street
Wakefield, Rhode Island 02879

SOUTH CAROLINA

Carolina Paddlers
3912 Edmond Drive
Columbia, South Carolina 29205

Carolina Whitewater Canoeing Association
3142 Harvard Avenue
Columbia, South Carolina 29205

Palmetto Kayakers
210 Irene Street
North Augusta, South Carolina 29381

Savannah River Paddlers
Explorer Ship 121 and Sea Scout 404
1211 Woodbine Road
Aiken, South Carolina 29801

Sierra Club
Canoe Section
Route 12, Saluda Lake Road
Greenville, South Carolina 29611

USC Whitewater Club
University of South Carolina
Box 80090
Columbia, South Carolina 29033

SOUTH DAKOTA

Boy Scouts of America
Sioux Council
P.O. Box 837
Sioux Falls, South Dakota 57100

TENNESSEE

Baylor School Canoe Club
Baylor School
Chattanooga, Tennessee 37401

Bluff City Canoe Club
P.O. Box 4523
Memphis, Tennessee 38104

Carbide Canoe Club
104 Ulena Lane
Oak Ridge, Tennessee 37830

Chota Canoe Club
University Station
P.O. Box 8270
Knoxville, Tennessee 37916

East Tennessee Whitewater Club
c/o Richard Gammage
P.O. Box 3074
Oak Ridge, Tennessee 37830

Footsloggers
2220 North Roan Street
Johnson City, Tennessee 37601

Sewanee Skiing and Outing Club
University of the South
Sewanee, Tennessee 37375

Tennessee Valley Canoe Club
P.O. Box 11125
Chattanooga, Tennessee 37401

Tenn-Tucky Lake Canoe-Camping Club
Route 1, Box 23A
Tennessee Ridge, Tennessee 37178

University of Tennessee
Hiking and Canoe Club
c/o William Krueger
Route 6
Concord, Tennessee 37730

TEXAS

American Canoe Association
Central Division
1900 Aden Road
Fort Worth, Texas 76116

Austin Canoe and Kayak Club
5213 Avenue G
Austin, Texas 78751

Boy Scouts of America, Sam Houston
Council
1911 Bagby
Houston, Texas 77002

Boy Scouts of America, Troop 51
2008 Bedford Street
Midland, Texas 79701

Corpus Christi Canoe Club
2409 Retta
Corpus Christi, Texas 78418

Dallas Canoe Club
12200 Coit Road
Dallas, Texas 75320

Down River Club–Dallas
1412 Oak Lea
Irving, Texas 75061

Explorer Post 151
2008 Bedford Street
Midland, Texas 79701

Explorer Post 425
708 Mercedes
Fort Worth, Texas 76126

Greater Fort Worth Sierra Club
River Touring Section
P.O. Box 1057
Fort Worth, Texas 76101

Heart of Texas Canoe Club
P.O. Box 844
Temple, Texas 76501

Houston Canoe Club
1003 West Shoreacres
La Porte, Texas 77574

River Recreation Association of Texas
P.O. Box 12734
Austin, Texas 78711

San Antonio Canoe Club
6202 Rain Cloud
San Antonio, Texas 78238

San Marcos Canoe Club
Route 2, Box 43G
San Marcos, Texas 78666

Seadrift Canoe Club
P.O. Box 736
Seadrift, Texas 77983

Texas Canoe Racing Association
Route 2, Box 43G
San Marcos, Texas 78666

Texas Explorers Club
P.O. Box 844
Temple, Texas 76501

Texas Instruments Canoe Club
P.O. Box 2909
c/o Mail Station 2016
Austin, Texas 78769

Texas Whitewater Association
P.O. Box 5264
Austin, Texas 78763

TMI Canoe Club
800 College Boulevard
San Antonio, Texas 78209

Trinity University Canoe Club
715 Stadium Drive
Box 180
San Antonio, Texas 78284

United States Canoe Association
Texas Division
4430 Nina Lee Lane
Houston, Texas 77092

Victoria Canoe Club
Route 1, Box 143A
Victoria, Texas 77901

UTAH

Wasatch Mountain Club
1425 Perry Avenue
Salt Lake City, Utah 84108

Wasatch Whitewater Association
161 South 11, E.
Salt Lake City, Utah 84102

VERMONT

Brattleboro Outing Club
1 Dracon Place
Brattleboro, Vermont 05301

Johnson State Outing Club
Johnson State College
Johnson, Vermont 05656

Johnson Whitewater Club
P.O. Box 649
Johnson, Vermont 05656

Marlboro College Outdoor Program
Marlboro College
c/o Malcolm Moore
Marlboro, Vermont 05344

Northern Vermont Canoe Cruisers
P.O. Box 254
Shelburne, Vermont 05482

Norwich University Outing Club
Norwich University
c/o L.J. Hurley
Northfield, Vermont 05663

Clubs and Affiliated Groups

VIRGINIA

American Red Cross
Hampton Roads Chapter
4915 West Mercury Boulevard
Newport News, Virginia 23605

American Red Cross
Richmond Chapter
409 East Main Street
Richmond, Virginia 23219

American Red Cross
Tidewater Chapter
414 West Bute Street
Norfolk, Virginia 23510

Appalachian Transit Authority
11453 Washington Plaza
Reston, Virginia 22070

Blue Ridge Voyagers
8119 Hillcrest
Manassas, Virginia 22110

Canoe Cruisers Association
1515 North Buchanan Street
Arlington, Virginia 22205

Coastal Canoeists
319 65th Street
Newport News, Virginia 23607

Explorer Post 999
3509 North Colonial Drive
Hopewell, Virginia 23860

Shenandoah River Canoe Club
P.O. Box 1423
Front Royal, Virginia 22630

University of Virginia Outing Club
Newcomb Hall Station
Box 101X
Charlottesville, Virginia 22903

WASHINGTON

American Canoe Association
Northwest Division
18028 187th Avenue, S.E.
Renton, Washington 98055

Cascade Canoe Club
111 Somerset Street
Richland, Washington 99352

Desert Kayak and Canoe Club
450 Mateo Court
Richland, Washington 99352

Evergreen River Rats
Evergreen State College
c/o Nancy Jones
Olympia, Washington 98505

Mountaineers Canoe and Kayak Committee
2835 60th Street, S.E.
Mercer Island, Washington 98040

Paddle Trails Canoe Club
5638 59th Street, N.E.
Seattle, Washington 98105

Seattle Canoe Club
6019 51st, N.E.
Seattle, Washington 98115

Spokane Canoe Club
North 10804 Nelson
Spokane, Washington 99218

Tacoma Mountaineers
Kayak and Canoe Committee
3512 Crystal Springs
Tacoma, Washington 98466

Tri-C Camping Association
17404 8th Avenue
Seattle, Washington 98155

University of Washington Canoe Club
University of Washington
IMA Building
Seattle, Washington 98105

Washington Foldboat Club
5622 Seaview Avenue
Seattle, Washington 98107

Washington Kayak Club
7724 211th Avenue, N.E.
Redmond, Washington 98052

Washington State University
Outdoor Activities Program
Compton Union Building
Pullman, Washington 99164

Whitewater Northwest Kayak Club
P.O. Box 1081
Spokane, Washington 99201

Yakima Canoe Group
724 North 34th Avenue
Yakima, Washington 98901

WEST VIRGINIA

West Virginia Wildwater Association
2737 Daniels Avenue
South Charleston, West Virginia 25303

Whitewater Canoe Club
West Virginia University
Mountain Lair Recreation Center
Morgantown, West Virginia 26506

WISCONSIN

Fond du Lac Voyageurs Canoe Club
P.O. Box 1752
Fond du Lac, Wisconsin 54935

Nicolet College Outing Club
P.O. Box 518
Rhinelander, Wisconsin 54501

Rock River Canoe Association
P.O. Box 263
Janesville, Wisconsin 53545

Sierra Club
John Muir Chapter
2604 North Murray Avenue, No. 107
Milwaukee, Wisconsin 53211

Wild Rivers Club
4901 36th Avenue, Apt. 206
Kenosha, Wisconsin 53140

Wisconsin Canoe Association
10915 North Sherwood Drive
Mequin, Wisconsin 53092

Wisconsin Hoofers Outing Club
University of Wisconsin Union
800 Langdon Street
Madison, Wisconsin 53706

Wolf River Canoe Club
c/o R.C. Steed
Wolf River Lodge
White Lake, Wisconsin 54491

WYOMING

Croaking Toad Boat Works
Game Hill Ranch
Bondurant, Wyoming 82922

Western Wyoming Kayak Club
c/o Donald Hahn
General Delivery
Wilson, Wyoming 83014

Part 4

PUBLISHERS, BOOK DEALERS, LIBRARIES,

AND OTHER SOURCES

INTRODUCTION

An information guide would be deficient if it did not list the publishers and booksellers in its field. This particularly holds for a subject such as wilderness waterways touring, about which there are many worthwhile books published and sold by very small companies, or perhaps even individuals. This guide lists many books by small publishers; since their addresses are often not found in the general directories, chapter 19 lists them and their larger counterparts. Only those publishers whose works are listed in the bibliographic sections of this guide have been included. The second section of chapter 19 is a directory of book dealers, most of whom specialize in general outdoor books and a few of whom sell only canoe-, kayak-, and raft-related works. Those dealers retailing current books on paddle sports are indicated by an asterisk.

Maps are certainly as indispensable as matches to the paddle tourer. Chapter 20 presents a listing of major governmental map sources. Although commercial map publishers have not been listed, a sampling of map bibliographies which list their offerings comprises the first section of the chapter.

There are no museums or libraries which were identified as being exclusively committed to the collection of materials on canoeing, kayaking, and rafting, or closely allied subjects. Just one museum, the Kandalore International Museum of Canoes and Kayaks, has a specialized focus. Chapter 21, then, is primarily a list of institutions with more generalized collections, but which indicate fair holdings in some aspect of wilderness waterways touring.

Chapter 19

PUBLISHERS AND BOOK DEALERS

PUBLISHERS

Canada

Canadiana House
P.O. Box 306, Station F
Toronto, Ontario   M4Y 2L7

Canadian Camping Association
102 Eglinton Avenue, E., Suite 203
Toronto, Ontario   M4P 1C2

CanoeCanada
P.O. Box 479
Lakefield, Ontario   KOL 2HO

Canoe Sport British Columbia
1606 West Broadway
Vancouver, British Columbia   V6J 1X7

Clarke, Irwin and Co.
791 St. Clair Avenue, W.
Toronto, Ontario   M6C 1B8

Coles Publishing Co.
90 Ronson Drive
Rexdale, Ontario   M9W 1C1

Gray's Publishing
P.O. Box 2160
Sidney, British Columbia   V8L 3S6

Greey de Pencier Publications
59 Front Street, E.
Toronto, Ontario   M5E 1B3

Hancock House Publishers
3215 Island View Road
Saanichton, British Columbia
VOS 1MO

McClelland and Stewart
25 Hollinger Road
Toronto, Ontario   M4B 3G2

McGill-Queen's University Press
1020 Pine Avenue, W.
Montreal, Province of Quebec
H3A 1A2

McGraw-Hill Ryerson
330 Progress Avenue
Scarborough, Ontario   M1P 2Z7

MacMillan of Canada
70 Bond Street
Toronto, Ontario   M5B 1X3

Publishers and Book Dealers

Messageries du Jour
8253 rue Durocher
Montreal, Province of Quebec
H3N 2A8

New Press
30 Lesmill Road
Don Mills, Ontario   M3B 2T6

Nova Scotia Camping Association
P.O. Box 3243 S
Halifax, Nova Scotia B3J 3E9

Nunaga Publishing Co.
P.O. Box 157
New Westminster, British Columbia
V3L 4Y4

Oxford University Press (Canadian Office)
70 Wynford Drive
Don Mills, Ontario   M3C 1J9

Pagurian Press
335 Bay Street, Suite 1106
Toronto, Ontario   M5H 2R3

Queen's Printer, Ontario
Parliament Buildings
3B7 Macdonald Block
Ottawa, Ontario

Quetico Foundation of Ontario
224 1/2 Simcoe Street
Toronto, Ontario M5T 1T4

Star Printing
111 Strickland Street
Whitehorse, Yukon Territory Y1A 2J6

University of Toronto Press
University of Toronto
St. George Campus
Toronto, Ontario   M5S 1A6

G.R. Welch Co.
310 Judson Street
Toronto, Ontario   M8Z 1J9

United States

Abelard-Schuman
(See T.Y. Crowell Co.)

Adirondack Mountain Club
172 Ridge Street
Glens Falls, New York   12801

Adirondack Museum and Library
Blue Mountain Lake, New York 12812

Adventure Guides
35 East 57th Street
New York, New York 10022

Alaska Northwest Publishing Co.
130 Second Avenue, S.
Edmonds, Washington   98020

American Camping Association
Bradford Woods
Martinsville, Indiana   46151

American Canoe Association
4260 East Evans Avenue
Denver, Colorado   80222

American River Touring Association
1016 Jackson Street
Oakland, California   94607

American West Publishing Co.
599 College Avenue
Palo Alto, California   94306

American Whitewater Association
P.O. Box 1584
San Bruno, California 94066

American Youth Hostels
Pittsburgh Council
6300 Fifth Avenue
Pittsburgh, Pennsylvania 15232

AMS Press
56 East 13th Street
New York, New York 10003

Appalachian Books
P.O. Box 248
Oakton, Virginia 22124

Appalachian Mountain Club
5 Joy Street
Boston, Massachusetts 02108

Arizona Historical Foundation
Arizona State University
Tempe, Arizona 85281

Arizona State University Press
Arizona State University
Tempe, Arizona 85281

Association Press
291 Broadway
New York, New York 10007

Ballantine Books
201 East 50th Street
New York, New York 10022

A.S. Barnes and Co.
Forsgate Drive
Cranbury, New Jersey 08512

Berkshire Traveller Press
Stockbridge, Massachusetts 01262

Big Bend Natural History Association
Big Bend National Park, Texas 79834

Binford and Mort
2536 Southeast 11th
Portland, Oregon 97202

Bobbs-Merrill
4 West 58th Street
New York, New York 10019

Boy Scouts of America
National Council
North Brunswick, New Jersey 08902

Boy Scouts of America
Sam Houston Council
1911 Bagby
Houston, Texas 77002

Brigham Young University Press
209 University Press Building
Provo, Utah 84602

William C. Brown
2460 Kerper Boulevard
Dubuque, Iowa 52001

Burgess Publishing Co.
7108 Ohms Lane
Minneapolis, Minnesota 55435

Caxton Printers
Caldwell, Idaho 83605

Chronicle Books
870 Market Street
San Francisco, California 94102

Colorado Outward Bound School
P.O. Box 7247, Park Hill Station
Denver, Colorado 80207

Columbia Publishing Co.
Frenchtown, New Jersey 08825

Connecticut River Watershed Council
497 Main Street
Greenfield, Massachusetts 01301

Clyde C. Council
5632 Bronx Avenue
Sarasota, Florida 33511

Country Beautiful Corporation
24198 West Bluemound Road
Waukesha, Wisconsin 53186

Courier-Gazette
1 Park Drive
Rockland, Maine 04841

Creative Holiday Guides
P.O. Box 7097
Charleston, South Carolina 29405

T.Y. Crowell Co.
Abelard-Schuman Division
666 Fifth Avenue
New York, New York 10019

Da Capo Press
227 West 17th Street
New York, New York 10011

Dell Publishing Co.
245 East 47th Street
New York, New York 10017

Directions Simplified
529 North State Road
Briarcliff Manor, New York 10510

Dodd, Mead and Co.
79 Madison Avenue
New York, New York 10016

Doubleday and Co.
245 Park Avenue
New York, New York 10017

Drake Publishers
381 Park Avenue, S.
New York, New York 10016

E.P. Dutton and Co.
201 Park Avenue, S.
New York, New York 10003

Eastwoods Press
421 Hudson Street
New York, New York 10014

Evergreen Paddleways
1416 21st Street
Two Rivers, Wisconsin 54241

Fairleigh Dickinson University Press
Rutherford, New Jersey 07070

Farmington River Watershed
Association
195 East Main Street
Avon, Connecticut 06001

Farrar, Straus and Giroux
19 Union Square, W.
New York, New York 10003

Ferro Corporation
Fiberglass Division
Fiber Glass Road
Nashville, Tennessee 37211

Fiddleneck Press
P.O. Box 114
Sunnyvale, California 94088

W.A. Fisher Co.
123 Chestnut Street
Virginia, Minnesota 55792

Follett Publishing Co.
1010 West Washington Boulevard
Chicago, Illinois 60607

Burt Franklin and Co.
235 East 44th Street
New York, New York 10017

Funk and Wagnalls Book Publishing
666 5th Avenue
New York, New York 10019

Gardner Printing and Mailing Co.
(See Georgie's Royal River Rats)

GBH Press
125 Upland
Kentfield, California 94904

Georgie's Royal River Rats
P.O. Box 12489
Las Vegas, Nevada 89112

Thomas L. Gray
11121 Dewey Road
Kensington, Maryland 20795

Great Lakes Living Press
435 North Michigan Avenue, Suite 2217
Chicago, Illinois 60611

Stephen Greene Press
P.O. Box 1000
Brattleboro, Vermont 05301

Grossman Publishers
625 Madison Avenue
New York, New York 10022

Grumman Boats
Marathon, New York 13803

Hallowell Printing Co.
145 Water Street
Hallowell, Maine 04347

Harper and Row, Publishers
10 East 53rd Street
New York, New York 10022

Bev Hartline
2714 94th Street
Seattle, Washington 98115

Herald-Review Co.
Grand Rapids, Minnesota 55744

Houghton Mifflin Co.
2 Park Street
Boston, Massachusetts 02107

Howell-North Books
1050 Parker Street
Berkeley, California 94710

Illinois Country Outdoor Guides
4400 North Merrimac Avenue
Chicago, Illinois 60630

Illinois Paddling Council
2316 Prospect Avenue
Evanston, Illinois 60201

Alfred A. Knopf
201 East 50th Street
New York, New York 10022

Lafayette Natural History Museum
and Planetarium
637 Girard Park Drive
Lafayette, Louisiana 70501

Lane Publishing Co.
Menlo Park, California 94025

La Siesta Press
P.O. Box 406
Glendale, California 91209

Ledyard Canoe Club
Dartmouth College
Hanover, New Hampshire 03755

Le Voyageur Publishing Co.
1319 Wentworth Drive
Irving, Texas 75061

Libraries Unlimited
P.O. Box 263
Littleton, Colorado 80120

J.B. Lippincott
521 Fifth Avenue
New York, New York 10017

Little, Brown and Co.
34 Beacon Street
Boston, Massachusetts 02106

Liveright
500 Fifth Avenue
New York, New York 10036

Lycoming County Planning Commission
Lycoming County Courthouse
Williamsport, Pennsylvania 17701

McClain Printing Co.
212 Main Street
Parsons, West Virginia 26287

McGraw-Hill Book Co.
1221 Avenue of the Americas
New York, New York 10020

David McKay Co.
750 Third Avenue
New York, New York 10017

A.C. Mackenzie Press
P.O. Box 9301, Richmond Heights
Station
St. Louis, Missouri 63117

Macmillan Co.
866 Third Avenue
New York, New York 10022

Louis J. Matacia
P.O. Box 32
Oakton, Virginia 22124

The Mazamas
909 Northwest 19th Avenue
Portland, Oregon 97209

Minnesota Historical Society
690 Cedar Street
St. Paul, Minnesota 55101

Montana State College
(See Montana State University)

Montana State University
Bozeman, Montana 59715

William Morrow and Co.
105 Madison Avenue
New York, New York 10016

Motorboating and Sailing Books
224 West 57th Street
New York, New York 10019

The Mountaineers
P.O. Box 122
Seattle, Washington 98111

New Hampshire Publishing Co.
P.O. Box 70
Somersworth, New Hampshire 03878

North-Central Canoe Trails
Ladysmith, Wisconsin 54848

W.W. Norton and Co.
500 Fifth Avenue
New York, New York 10036

Ozark Society Book Service
P.O. Box 725
Hot Springs, Arkansas 71901

Packsack Press
P.O. Box 177
Winton, Minnesota 55796

Pelican Publishing Co.
630 Burmaster Street
Gretna, Louisiana 70053

Pequot Press
Old Chester Road
Chester, Connecticut 06412

Powell Society
750 Vine Street
Denver, Colorado 80206

Princeton University Press
Princeton University
Princeton, New Jersey 08540

Pruett Publishing Co.
3235 Prairie Avenue
Boulder, Colorado 80301

Quadrangle/New York Times Book Co.
10 East 53rd Street
New York, New York 10022

Rand McNally and Co.
P.O. Box 7600
Chicago, Illinois 60680

Recreational Publications
P.O. Box 215
University, Mississippi 38677

Henry Regnery Co.
180 North Michigan Avenue
Chicago, Illinois 60601

Rich Designs
481 South Ashburton
Columbus, Ohio 43213

Ronald Press Co.
79 Madison Avenue
New York, New York 10016

Rutgers University Press
30 College Avenue
New Brunswick, New Jersey 08901

Saturday Review Press
(See E.P. Dutton and Co.)

Schocken Books
200 Madison Avenue
New York, New York 10016

Charles Scribner's Sons
597 Fifth Avenue
New York, New York 10017

Sheed Andrews and McMeel
6700 Squibb Road
Mission, Kansas 66202

Sheed and Ward
(See Sheed Andrews and McMeel)

Shorey Publications
815 Third Avenue
Seattle, Washington 98104

Sierra Club Books
1050 Mills Tower
San Francisco, California 94104

Signpost Publications
16812 36th Avenue, W.
Lynnwood, Washington 98036

Peter Smith
6 Lexington Avenue
Gloucester, Massachusetts 01930

Soccer Associates
P.O. Box 634
New Rochelle, New York   10802

Southern Press
301 Terry Hutchens Building
Huntsville, Alabama   35801

Specialty Press
P.O. Box 2187
Ocean, New Jersey   17712

Sportshelf
(See Soccer Associates)

Stackpole Books
Cameron and Kelker Streets
Harrisburg, Pennsylvania   17105

Strode Publishers
6802 Jones Valley Drive, S.E.
Huntsville, Alabama   35802

Survival Education Association
9035 Golden Given Road
Tacoma, Washington   98445

Syracuse University Press
1011 East Water Street
Syracuse, New York   13210

Tab Books
Blue Ridge Summit, Pennsylvania   17214

Tamal Vista Publications
547 Howard Street
San Francisco, California   94105

Texas Explorers Club
P.O. Box 844
Temple, Texas   76501

Texas Rivers and Rapids
P.O. Box 673
Humble, Texas   77338

Timber Press
P.O. Box 92
Forest Grove, Oregon   97116

Tobey Publishing Co.
(Dell Publishing Co.)
245 East 47th Street
New York, New York   10017

Touchstone Press
P.O. Box 81
Beaverton, Oregon   97005

Transatlantic Arts
North Village Green
Levittown, New York   11756

Tri-County Conservatory
Chadds Ford, Pennsylvania   19317

Charles E. Tuttle Co.
28 South Main Street
Rutland, Vermont   05701

United States Canoe Association
c/o Jim Mack
606 Ross Street
Middletown, Ohio   45042

University of Chicago Press
5801 Ellis Avenue
Chicago, Illinois   60637

University of Illinois Press
University of Illinois
Urbana, Illinois   61801

University of Miami Press
Drawer 9088
Coral Gables, Florida   33124

University of Minnesota Press
2037 University Avenue, S.E.
Minneapolis, Minnesota   55455

University of Missouri Press
107 Swallow Hall
Columbia, Missouri 65201

University of New Mexico Press
University of New Mexico
Albuquerque, New Mexico 87131

University of Oklahoma Press
1005 Asp Avenue
Norman, Oklahoma 73069

Vanguard Press
424 Madison Avenue
New York, New York 10017

Warner Books
75 Rockefeller Plaza
New York, New York 10019

Western Piedmont Community College
1001 Burkemont Avenue
Morganton, North Carolina 28655

West Virginia Wildwater Association
Route 1, Box 95
Ravenswood, West Virginia 26164

Westwater Books
P.O. Box 365
Boulder City, Nevada 89005

Wilderness Holidays Publications
P.O. Box 7097
Charleston, South Carolina 29405

Wildwater Designs
Penllyn Pike and Morris Road
Penllyn, Pennsylvania 19422

Winchester Press
205 East 42nd Street
New York, New York 10017

Wisconsin Indian Head Country
3015 East Clairemont Avenue
Eau Claire, Wisconsin 54701

Wisconsin Tales and Trails
517 North Segoe Road
Madison, Wisconsin 53705

Yale University Press
302 Temple Street
New Haven, Connecticut 06511

BOOK DEALERS: CURRENT, EARLY, RARE

Adco Sports Book Exchange
P.O. Box 48577, Briggs Station
Los Angeles, California 90048

Adventure Bookshelf
42-37 203 Street
Bayside, New York 11361

All-American Sports Books
P.O. Box 156
Laurel, Maryland 20810

American Canoe Association*
4260 East Evans Avenue
Denver, Colorado 80222

Appalachian Books*
P.O. Box 248
Oakton, Virginia 22124

Arctician Books
P.O. Box 194
Bangor, Maine 04401

ATC Books
321 East Superior Street
Duluth, Minnesota 55802

Beaver Books
P.O. Box 974
Daly City, California 94017

British Book Centre*
153 East 78th Street
New York, New York 10021

Chicagoland Canoe Base*
4019 North Narragansett
Chicago, Illinois 60634

Q.M. Dabney and Co.
P.O. Box 31061
Washington, D.C. 20031

James T. Elder
Route 2, Box 911
Odessa, Florida 33556

Freelance Writer
28 Clark Avenue
Cornwall-on-Hudson, New York
12520

Gene E. Fries Books
335 18th Street, S.E.
Cedar Rapids, Iowa 52403

Greenstone Books
P.O. Box 1801
Cullowhee, North Carolina 28723

Hoffman Research Service
124 Whitmore Road
Irwin, Pennsylvania 15642

J. McGovern
516 Washington Boulevard
Oak Park, Illinois 60302

Moor and Mountain*
63 Park Street
Andover, Massachusetts 01810

Northwest River Supplies*
214 North Main Street
Moscow, Indiana 83843

Ohio Canoe Adventures*
P.O. Box 2092
Sheffield, Ohio 44054

Harold Scammell Books
Route 152
Nottingham, New Hampshire 03290

Stamelman Books
48 Heron Road
Livingston, New Jersey   07039

Sullivan Sporting Books
3748 North Damen Avenue
Chicago, Illinois   60618

C.J. Tatro
60 Goff Road
Wethersfield, Connecticut   06109

Trackside Books
4940 Eleven Mile Road
Rockford, Michigan   49341

Waters*
111 East Sheridan Street
Ely, Minnesota   55731

Westwater Books*
P.O. Box 365
Boulder City, Nevada   89005

A.M. Weyand
11 Tangle Lane
Wantagh, New York   11793

World Publications*
P.O. Box 366
Mountain View, California   94042

Chapter 20

MAP SOURCES

MAP BIBLIOGRAPHIES AND CATALOGS

MAPS TO ANYWHERE. 4th ed. Hollywood, Calif.: Travel Centers of the
World, 1976. 190 p. Paperbound.

> This is a sales catalog, not a major reference work on maps.
> Information is presented in five columns: name of map, order
> number, publisher, wholesale price, and suggested retail price.
> There are 3,772 entries, of which about 75 percent represent
> road and topographic maps.

OFFICIAL EASTERN NORTH AMERICA MAP AND CHART INDEX CATALOG.
Neenah, Wis.: U.S.-Canadian Map Service Bureau, 1975. 186 p. Paperbound.

> See annotation directly below.

OFFICIAL WESTERN NORTH AMERICA MAP AND CHART INDEX CATALOG.
Neenah, Wis.: U.S.-Canadian Map Service Bureau, 1975. 226 p. Paperbound.

> The publisher is a commercial firm which sells the maps and
> charts listed in these two volumes. The books reproduce U.S.
> Geological Survey national and state topographic index maps,
> National Ocean Survey nautical chart indexes, and indexes for
> Canadian topographic maps and nautical charts. (This informa-
> tion is available without charge from the Canada Map Distribu-
> tion Office and the U.S. Geological Survey Map Information
> Office; see below under Principal Federal Government Map
> Sources.) The catalogs provide access to more than 200,000
> maps and charts. They are similar in arrangement and format.
> The geographical boundary which separates coverage in the two
> books is the Mississippi River north to Hudson Bay. Each cata-
> log is divided into ten sections: map scales, equivalents, symbols,
> U.S. special-interest maps, U.S. topographic maps on a one-
> to-250,000 scale, U.S. topographic maps on a one-to-24,000

to one-to-62,500 scale, U.S. raised relief maps, Canadian
special-interest maps, Canadian topographic maps up to a one-
to-50,000 scale, U.S. hydrographic charts and publications,
and Canadian hydrographic charts and publications.

Winch, Kenneth L., ed. INTERNATIONAL MAPS AND ATLASES IN PRINT.
2d ed., rev. New York: Bowker Publishing Co., 1976. 866 p.

This carto-bibliography provides information on more than 8,000
maps and atlases. The book attempts comprehensive assembly of
data on maps currently available from existing bibliographies,
publisher catalogs, library accession lists, and other sources.
Aeronautical and nautical navigation charts and those maps produced for advertising use have been excluded. Arrangement is
by world region and country. Within a country designation,
the publications are divided into map and atlas categories and
are further subdivided into twenty types. Cited information includes title, scale, publisher, year of publication, and general
description.

PRINCIPAL FEDERAL GOVERNMENT MAP SOURCES

Map Distribution Office
Federal Surveys and Mapping Branch
Department of Energy, Mines, and Resources
615 Booth Street
Ottawa, Ontario K1A OE9

The Federal Surveys and Mapping Branch publishes a booklet
listing index maps for the available topographic series: scales of
one-to-125,000; one-to-250,000; one-to-500,000; and one-to-
one million. Also included is a master index map to the regional
index maps in the one-to-50,000 series. For index maps and
the individual national topographic series maps, address orders
and payment to the Map Distribution Office.

Map Information Office
U.S. Geological Survey
12201 Sunrise Valley Drive
Reston, Virginia 22092

The U.S. Geological Survey publishes index maps for each state
showing maps available for ordering in three series: one-to-
24,000; one-to-62,500; and one-to-250,000. The index maps
also list the dealers and libraries in each state which stock topographic maps. There are two federal distribution centers. For
states east of the Mississippi contact the Distribution Section,
U.S. Geological Survey, 1200 South Eads Street, Arlington,
Virginia 22202. For index maps and orders for states west of

the Mississippi contact the Distribution Section, U.S. Geological Survey, Federal Center, Denver, Colorado 80225. Maps must be ordered by name, state, and series, and must be accompanied with exact payment in cash, check, or money order. Aerial photographs are often available, sometimes in stereo pairs, from various agencies. The U.S. Geological Survey supplies information on these photographs in its publication STATUS OF AERIAL PHOTOGRAPHY, which is available free upon request.

OTHER FEDERAL GOVERNMENT MAP SOURCES

Bureau of Land Management
U.S. Department of the Interior
Washington, D.C. 20240

Maps of the Bureau of Land Management lands are available by request from regional centers:

Alaska: 555 Cordova Street, Anchorage 99501.
Arizona: Federal Building, Phoenix 85025.
California: Federal Building, Sacramento 95825.
Colorado: Colorado State Bank Building, Denver 80202.
Eastern States: 7981 Eastern Avenue, Silver Spring, Maryland 20910.
Idaho: Federal Building, Boise 83724.
Montana, North Dakota, South Dakota: Federal Building,
  Billings, Montana 59101.
Nevada: Federal Building, Reno 89502.
New Mexico, Oklahoma: Federal Building, Santa Fe, New
  Mexico 87501.
Oregon, Washington: 729 Northeast Oregon Street, Portland,
  Oregon 97208.
Utah: Federal Building, Salt Lake City 84111.
Wyoming, Kansas, Nebraska: Federal Building, Cheyenne,
  Wyoming 82001.

Canada Hydrographic Service
Marine Chart and Publications Sales
615 Booth Street
Ottawa, Ontario K1A OE9

Charts for all the Great Lakes and Canadian coastal waters are sold through this office.

Defense Mapping Agency
Topographic Center
Washington, D.C. 20315

The Defense Mapping Agency (formerly the U.S. Army Map Service) has extensive inventories of maps from virtually every region in the world. Many of the larger libraries maintain a collection of these maps.

Map Sources

Earth Physics Branch
Department of Energy, Mines, and Resources
Ottawa, Ontario K1A OE4

> The Earth Physics Branch has an inventory of specialized maps:
> gravity, magnetic, and seismic.

Forest Service
U.S. Department of Agriculture
Washington, D.C. 20250

> For maps of waterways within national forest boundaries, inquire
> at the regional office nearest the area of interest:
>
> Alaska: Federal Office Building, Juneau 99801.
> California: 630 Sansome Street, San Francisco 94111.
> Eastern: 633 West Wisconsin Avenue, Milwaukee, Wisconsin
> 53203.
> Intermountain: 324 25th Street, Ogden, Utah 84401.
> Northern: Federal Building, Missoula, Montana 59801.
> Pacific Northwest: P.O. Box 36231, Portland, Oregon 97208.
> Rocky Mountain: 11177 West 8th Avenue, Lakewood, Colorado
> 80225.
> Southern: 1720 Peachtree Road, N.W., Atlanta, Georgia 30309.
> Southwestern: 517 Gold Avenue, S.W., Albuquerque, New
> Mexico 87102.

Library of Congress
Geography and Map Division
845 South Pickett Street
Alexandria, Virginia 22304

> The "Pickett Street Annex" contains one of the largest carto-
> graphic collections in the world. It houses 3,500,000 maps;
> 38,000 ctlases; and 400 globes.

Public Archives of Canada
395 Wellington Street
Ottawa, Ontario K1A ON3

> The Public Archives maintains a departmental library housing
> the national map collection. It is open to all, with no intro-
> duction needed for students beyond high school.

U.S. Army Corps of Engineers
Map Information Office
Fort Belvoir, Virginia 22060

> The U.S. Army Corps of Engineers has maps of the many river
> drainages and lakes where its developmental projects have taken
> place. The maps may be obtained by referral from the Map

Information Office at Fort Belvoir, or directly from the corps's regional office located nearest the area of interest:

Albuquerque: P.O. Box 1538, Albuquerque, New Mexico 87103.
Baltimore: P.O. Box 1715, Baltimore, Maryland 21203.
Buffalo: Foot of Bridge Street, Buffalo, New York 14207.
Charleston: P.O. Box 905, Charleston, South Carolina 29402.
Chicago: 219 Dearborn Street, Chicago, Illinois 60604.
Detroit: P.O. Box 1027, Detroit, Michigan 48231.
Fort Worth: P.O. Box 1600, Fort Worth, Texas 76101.
Huntington: P.O. Box 2127, Huntington, West Virginia 25701.
Jacksonville: P.O. Box 4970, Jacksonville, Florida 32201.
Kansas City: 1800 Federal Office Building, Kansas City, Missouri 64106.
Little Rock: P.O. Box 867, Little Rock, Arkansas 72203.
Los Angeles: P.O. Box 17277, Foy Station, Los Angeles, California 90017.
Louisville: P.O. Box 59, Louisville, Kentucky 40201.
Memphis: 668 Federal Building, Memphis, Tennessee 38103.
Mobile: P.O. Box 1169, Mobile, Alabama 36601.
Nashville: P.O. Box 1070, Nashville, Tennessee 37202.
New Orleans: P.O. Box 60267, New Orleans, Louisiana 70160.
New York: 111 East 16th Street, New York, New York 10003.
Omaha: 6012 U.S. Post Office, Omaha, Nebraska 68101.
Philadelphia: Custom House, Philadelphia, Pennsylvania 19106.
Pittsburgh: 564 Forbes Avenue, Pittsburgh, Pennsylvania 15219.
Portland: 628 Pittock Block, Portland, Oregon 97205.
Rock Island: Clark Tower Building, Rock Island, Illinois 61202.
Sacramento: P.O. Box 1739, Sacramento, California 95808.
St. Louis: 906 Oliver Street, St. Louis, Missouri 63102.
St. Paul: 180 East Kellog Boulevard, St. Paul, Minnesota 55101.
San Francisco: 180 New Montgomery Street, San Francisco, California 94105.
Savannah: P.O. Box 889, Savannah, Georgia 31402.
Seattle: 1519 South Alaskan Way, S., Seattle, Washington 98134.
Tulsa: P.O. Box 61, Tulsa, Oklahoma 74102.
Vicksburg: P.O. Box 60, Vicksburg, Mississippi 39181.
Walla Walla: City–County Airport No. 62, Walla Walla, Washington 99632.
Waltham: 424 Trapelo Road, Waltham, Massachusetts 02154.
Wilmington: P.O. Box 1890, Wilmington, North Carolina 28402.

PROVINCIAL AND STATE GEOLOGY AND MAP AGENCIES

ALABAMA

Geological Survey
University of Alabama
Tuscaloosa, Alabama 35401

ALASKA

Department of Natural Resources
3001 Porcupine Drive
Anchorage, Alaska 99504

ALBERTA

Surveys Branch
Mapping Office
Department of Highways and Transport
97th Avenue and 106th Street
Edmonton, Alberta   T5K 2B8

ARKANSAS

Geological Commission
3819 West Roosevelt Road
Little Rock, Arkansas   72204

BRITISH COLUMBIA

Ministry of the Environment
Map and Photo Sales
Map Production Division
Lands Service
Parliament Buildings
Victoria, British Columbia   V8V 2M3

CALIFORNIA

Division of Mines and Geology
Department of Conservation
1416 Ninth Street
Sacramento, California   95814

COLORADO

Geological Survey
Department of Natural Resources
1845 Sherman
Denver, Colorado   80203

CONNECTICUT

Department of Environmental Protection
165 Capitol Avenue
Hartford, Connecticut   06115

DELAWARE

Geological Survey
University of Delaware
Newark, Delaware   19711

FLORIDA

Bureau of Geology
Department of Natural Resources
Gunter Building
Tallahassee, Florida   32304

GEORGIA

Earth and Water Division
Department of Natural Resources
19 Hunter Street, S.W.
Atlanta, Georgia   30334

HAWAII

Water and Land Development Division
Department of Land and Natural Resources
State Office Building
Honolulu, Hawaii   96813

IDAHO

Bureau of Mines and Geology
Department of Lands
University of Idaho
Moscow, Idaho   83843

ILLINOIS

State Geological Survey
139 Natural Resources Building
Urbana, Illinois   61801

INDIANA

Department of Natural Resources
Indiana University
Bloomington, Indiana   47401

IOWA

Geological Survey
16 West Jefferson Street
Iowa City, Iowa   52240

KANSAS

Geological Survey
University of Kansas
Lawrence, Kansas 66044

KENTUCKY

Geological Survey
University of Kentucky
Lexington, Kentucky 40506

LOUISIANA

Department of Conservation
Louisiana State University
Geology Building
Baton Rouge, Louisiana 70804

MAINE

Bureau of Geology
Department of Conservation
308 State House
Augusta, Maine 04330

MANITOBA

Surveys, Mapping, and Lands Branch
1007 Century Street
Winnipeg, Manitoba R3H OW4

MARYLAND

Geological Survey
Johns Hopkins University
Baltimore, Maryland 21218

MICHIGAN

Geological Survey Division
Department of Natural Resources
Stevens T. Mason Building
Lansing, Michigan 48926

MINNESOTA

Waters, Soils, and Minerals Division
Department of Natural Resources
Centennial Building
St. Paul, Minnesota 55155

MISSISSIPPI

Geological Survey
2525 North West Street
Jackson, Mississippi 39205

MISSOURI

Division of Research and Technical
Information
Department of Natural Resources
P.O. Box 250
Rolla, Missouri 65401

NEBRASKA

Conservation and Survey Division
University of Nebraska
Lincoln, Nebraska 68509

NEW BRUNSWICK

Department of Natural Resources
575 Centennial Building
Fredericton, New Brunswick E3B 5H1

NEW HAMPSHIRE

University of New Hampshire
Durham, New Hampshire 03824

NEW JERSEY

Bureau of Geology
Department of Environmental
Protection
John Fitch Plaza
Trenton, New Jersey 08625

NEW MEXICO

State Geologist
Office of the Governor
Santa Fe, New Mexico   87503

NORTH CAROLINA

Division of Resource Planning and
Evaluation
Department of Natural and Economic
Resources
112 West Lane Street
Raleigh, North Carolina   27603

NORTH DAKOTA

University of North Dakota
Geology Department
University Station
Grand Forks, North Dakota   58201

NOVA SCOTIA

Government Book Store
1683 Barrington Street
Halifax, Nova Scotia   B3J 1Z9

OHIO

Geological Survey
Department of Natural Resources
Fountain Square
Columbus, Ohio   43224

OKLAHOMA

Geological Survey
University of Oklahoma
Norman, Oklahoma   73069

ONTARIO

Surveys and Mapping Branch
Ministry of Natural Resources
Whitney Block, Room 2609
Queen's Park
Toronto, Ontario   M7A 1X1

OREGON

Department of Geology and Mineral
Industries
1069 State Office Building
Portland, Oregon   97201

PENNSYLVANIA

Bureau of Topographic and Geologic
Survey
Department of Environmental Resources
Towne House Apartments
Harrisburg, Pennsylvania   17101

PRINCE EDWARD ISLAND

Land Use Planning
P.O. Box 1660
Summerside, Prince Edward Island
C1N 2V5

QUEBEC

Department of Natural Resources
1620 boulevard de l'Entente
Quebec, Province of Quebec
G1S 4N6

SASKATCHEWAN

Lands and Surveys
Department of Tourism and Renewable
Resources
2340 Albert Street
Regina, Saskatchewan   S4P 2V7

SOUTH CAROLINA

Geological Division
Development Board
Harbison Forest Road
Columbia, South Carolina   29210

SOUTH DAKOTA

Geological Surveys
Department of Natural Resources
Development
University of South Dakota
Vermillion, South Dakota 57069

TENNESSEE

Department of Conservation
State Office Building
Nashville, Tennessee 37219

UTAH

Geological and Mineral Survey
University of Utah
Geological Survey Building
Salt Lake City, Utah 84112

VERMONT

Department of Water Resources
5 Court Street
Montpelier, Vermont 05602

VIRGINIA

Division of Mineral Resources
Department of Conservation and Economic
Development
Alderman and McCormick Roads
Charlottesville, Virginia 22903

WASHINGTON

Division of Geological and Earth
Resources
Department of Natural Resources
Public Lands Building
Olympia, Washington 98504

WEST VIRGINIA

Geology Department
West Virginia University
Morgantown, West Virginia 26505

WISCONSIN

Geological and Natural History
Survey
University of Wisconsin
Madison, Wisconsin 53702

WYOMING

Geological Survey
P.O. Box 3008, University Station
Laramie, Wyoming 82070

PROVINCIAL AND STATE HIGHWAY AGENCIES

ALABAMA

Highway Department
11 South Union Street
Montgomery, Alabama 36104

ALASKA

Department of Highways
P.O. Box 1467
Juneau, Alaska 99801

ALBERTA

Motor Transport Branch
Department of Highways and Transport
97th Avenue and 106th Street
Edmonton, Alberta T5K 2B9

ARIZONA

Department of Transportation
State Capitol
Phoenix, Arizona 85007

ARKANSAS

Highway Department
9500 New Benton Highway
Little Rock, Arkansas 72203

BRITISH COLUMBIA

Department of Highways
Parliament Buildings
Victoria, British Columbia V8V 2M3

CALIFORNIA

Division of Highways
Department of Transportation
1120 N Street
Sacramento, California 95814

COLORADO

Department of Highways
4201 East Arkansas Avenue
Denver, Colorado 80222

CONNECTICUT

Department of Transportation
24 Wolcott Hill Road
Wethersfield, Connecticut 06109

DELAWARE

Division of Highways
Department of Highways and Transportation
P.O. Box 778
Dover, Delaware 19901

FLORIDA

Division of Road Operations
Department of Transportation
Burns Building
Tallahassee, Florida 32304

GEORGIA

Department of Transportation
2 Capitol Square
Atlanta, Georgia 30334

HAWAII

Highways Division
Department of Transportation
869 Punchbowl Street
Honolulu, Hawaii 96813

IDAHO

Division of Highways
Department of Transportation
3311 West State Street
Boise, Idaho 83720

ILLINOIS

Division of Highways
Department of Transportation
2300 South Dirksen Parkway
Springfield, Illinois 62706

INDIANA

Highway Commission
1101 State Office Building
Indianapolis, Indiana 46204

IOWA

Highway Division
Department of Transportation
Administration Offices
Ames, Iowa 50010

KANSAS

Department of Transportation
State Office Building
Topeka, Kansas   66612

KENTUCKY

Department of Transportation
State Office Building
Frankfort, Kentucky   40601

LOUISIANA

Department of Highways
1201 Capitol Access Road
Baton Rouge, Louisiana   70804

MAINE

Department of Transportation
State House
Augusta, Maine   04330

MANITOBA

Department of Highways
1075 Portage Avenue
Winnipeg, Manitoba   R3G OS1

MARYLAND

Highway Administration
Department of Transportation
P.O. Box 717
Baltimore, Maryland   21203

MASSACHUSETTS

Department of Public Works
100 Nashua Street
Boston, Massachusetts   02114

MICHIGAN

Department of State Highways and
Transportation
Highways Building
Lansing, Michigan   48913

MINNESOTA

Department of Highways
Highways Building
St. Paul, Minnesota   55155

MISSISSIPPI

Highway Department
1004 Woolfolk Building
Jackson, Mississippi   39205

MISSOURI

Highway Department
State Highway Building
Jefferson City, Missouri   65101

MONTANA

Department of Highways
6th and Roberts Streets
Helena, Montana   59601

NEBRASKA

Department of Roads
P.O. Box 94759
Lincoln, Nebraska   68509

NEVADA

Department of Highways
Highway Building
Carson City, Nevada   89701

Map Sources

NEW BRUNSWICK

Department of Highways
Centennial Building
Fredericton, New Brunswick E3E 5H1

NEWFOUNDLAND

Department of Transportation and
Communication
Confederation Building
St. John's, Newfoundland A1C 5T7

NEW HAMPSHIRE

Department of Public Works and Highways
85 Loudon Road
Concord, New Hampshire 03301

NEW JERSEY

Department of Transportation
1035 Parkway Avenue
Trenton, New Jersey 08618

NEW MEXICO

Highway Department
1120 Cerillos Road
Santa Fe, New Mexico 87501

NEW YORK

Design and Construction Division
Department of Transportation
Campus Building 5
Albany, New York 12226

NORTH CAROLINA

Highway Department
Department of Transportation and
Highway Safety
Highway Building
Raleigh, North Carolina 27611

NORTH DAKOTA

Highway Department
Highway Building
Bismarck, North Dakota 58501

NOVA SCOTIA

Department of Highways
Provincial Building
Hollis Street
Halifax, Nova Scotia B4J 2N2

OHIO

Department of Transportation
25 South Front Street
Columbus, Ohio 43215

OKLAHOMA

Department of Highways
2101 North Lincoln Boulevard
Oklahoma City, Oklahoma 73105

ONTARIO

Ministry of Transportation and
Communications
1201 Wilson Avenue
Downsview, Ontario M3M 1J8

OREGON

Highway Division
Department of Transportation
140 Highway Building
Salem, Oregon 97310

PENNSYLVANIA

Highway Administration
Department of Transportation
1200 Transportation and Safety Building
Harrisburg, Pennsylvania 17120

PRINCE EDWARD ISLAND

Department of Industry and Commerce
P.O. Box 2000
Charlottetown, Prince Edward Island
C1A 7N8

QUEBEC

Transport Commission
La Fayette Building
585 Charest Boulevard, E.
Quebec, Province of Quebec
G1K 3J2

RHODE ISLAND

Division of Roads and Bridges
Department of Transportation
State Office Building
Providence, Rhode Island   02903

SASKATCHEWAN

Department of Highways and
    Transportation
Legislative Building
Regina, Saskatchewan   S4S OB3

SOUTH CAROLINA

Highway Department
1100 Senate Street
Columbia, South Carolina   29201

SOUTH DAKOTA

Division of Highways
Department of Transportation
Transportation Building
Pierre, South Dakota   57501

TENNESSEE

Department of Transportation
802 Highway Building
Nashville, Tennessee   37219

TEXAS

Highway Department
Brazos and 11th Streets
Austin, Texas   78701

UTAH

Department of Transportation
State Office Building
Salt Lake City, Utah   84114

VERMONT

Department of Highways
133 State Street
Montpelier, Vermont   05602

VIRGINIA

Department of Highways
1401 East Broad Street
Richmond, Virginia   23219

WASHINGTON

Department of Highways
Highway Administration Building
Olympia, Washington   98504

WEST VIRGINIA

Department of Highways
State Office Building 5
Charleston, West Virginia   25305

WISCONSIN

Department of Transportation
4802 Sheboygan Avenue
Madison, Wisconsin   53702

WYOMING

Highway Department
Highway Department Building
Cheyenne, Wyoming   82001

Chapter 21

LIBRARIES, SPECIAL COLLECTIONS, AND MUSEUMS

Adirondack Museum and Library
Blue Mountain Lake, New York   12812

> This museum, operated by the Adirondack Historical Association
> contains a comprehensive collection of small boats as well as
> canoes and an "Adirondack Guideboat." The library of 8,000
> volumes is open to researchers by prior arrangement. The mu-
> seum is open to the public.

Canada Department of Energy, Mines, and Resources
Geological Survey of Canada Library
601 Booth Street
Ottawa, Ontario   K1A OE8

> The library has 150,000 titles and a staff of fifteen. Subject
> interests include earth science, physical geography, and maps.

Canada Department of Energy, Mines, and Resources
Surveys and Mapping Branch
615 Booth Street, Room 136
Ottawa, Ontario   K1A OE9

> This library has 17,000 volumes with subject interests in geodesy,
> photogammetry, Canadian history and geography, cartography,
> legal surveys, and international boundary.

Canada Department of Indian Affairs and Northern Development
Departmental Library
Laurier Avenue, W., Room 822
Ottawa, Ontario   K1A OH4

> The library contains 82,000 volumes. Among the collection in-
> terests are: conservation of natural resources, economic develop-
> ment of the North, national parks, Indians, Eskimos, parks, and
> recreation.

Friends of the Wilderness Library
3515 East Fourth Street
Duluth, Minnesota 55804

> The Friends of the Wilderness maintain a library of 400 volumes on the Boundary Waters Canoe Area (BWCA). The group is dedicated to the preservation of the BWCA.

Hudson's Bay Company Archives
Beaver House
Great Trinity Lane
London EC 4 England

> The Hudson's Bay Record Society maintains historical records of the company's business activities between 1668 and 1870. This archival stock may be used on site by qualified investigators.

Kandalore International Museum of Canoes and Kayaks
Camp Kandalore
Minden, Ontario KOM 2KO

> Kandalore is a newer, relatively unknown, specialized museum where canoes and kayaks are the featured items of display. The museum is located at Camp Kandalore on Lake Kebakwa, a few miles north of Minden, Ontario. The director is Kirk A.W. Wipper, of the School of Physical and Health Education at the University of Toronto. The collection is composed of over 120 working, pleasure, and racing craft, assembled primarily through donations. Included is a birch-bark freighter, Indian dugouts from the northwest coast and the southeastern United States, and many noncommercial antique craft. The museum is free of charge and open from May through October.

Library of Congress
General Reference and Bibliography Division
Washington, D.C. 20540

> This is a central division in the world's largest library with extensive general and specialized collections. Materials are available to the general public for in-library use, and to qualified researchers through interlibrary loan.

Library of Congress
Geography and Map Division
845 South Pickett Street
Alexandria, Virginia 22304

> The "Pickett Street Annex" contains one of the largest cartographic collections in the world. It houses 3,500,000 maps; 38,000 atlases; and 400 globes.

Marine Museum of Upper Canada
Exhibition Park
Toronto, Ontario

>The museum's displays depict the exploration of central Canada
>and navigation on the inland waterways of the St. Lawrence
>River and Great Lakes Basin.

National Library of Canada
395 Wellington Street
Ottawa, Ontario   K1A ON4

>This library houses 800,000 books and thousands of maps, charts,
>and art prints. As the national library, it acts as a clearing-
>house for information about all Canadian libraries.

National Recreation and Park Association Library
1601 North Kent Street
Arlington, Virginia   22209

>This 4,000-volume library has a collection specializing in
>conservation. The general acquisitional thrust is toward mate-
>rials on group recreational pursuits.

New York State Historical Association Library
American Canoe Association Historical Collection
Lake Road
Cooperstown, New York   13326

>This library has most of the yearbooks of the American Canoe
>Association (ACA) from 1887 to 1968. Within the Library
>Special Collections are 327 ACA photographs, accompanied by
>two boxes of magazine articles, programs, pennants, and scrap-
>books.

Public Archives of Canada Library
395 Wellington Street
Ottawa, Ontario   K1A ON3

>Among the special interests of the archives are Canadian art and
>pictures, geography, history, and Nordic exploration. Depart-
>mental libraries include: Picture Division, Machine Readable
>Archives, National Film Archives, Public Records Division,
>National Map Collection, and National Photography Collection.

San Jose State University Library
Fred Imhof Sports Collection
250 Fourth Street
San Jose, California   95192

The university library maintains the special sports collection of Fred Imhof. All references to a particular sport are shelved together. Authorized scholars may request permission to consult the collection.

Saskatchewan Provincial Library
1352 Winnipeg Street
Regina, Saskatchewan   S4R 1J9

The library has a general stock of 160,000 books and a bibliographical interest in the literature of canoeing, evidenced by the publication of two bibliographies: CANOEING: A BIBLIOGRAPHY and CANOES AND CANOEING: A BIBLIOGRAPHY (see chapter 1).

U.S. Department of the Interior
Natural Resources Library
18th and C Streets, N.W.
Washington, D.C.   20240

This 850,000-volume library has strong subject collections in conservation and development of natural resources, including: scientific engineering, legal and social aspects of mining and minerals, oil, gas, land reclamation, hydroelectric and related activities, fish and wildlife management, land management, outdoor recreation, and preservation of scenic and historic sites.

ADDENDUM

The following books were published subsequent to the completion of the manuscript for the main portion of WILDERNESS WATERWAYS. The publication dates of 1977 and 1978 predominate, although there are several earlier works included which were not verified prior to manuscript deadlines. All books cited below were published in either Canada or the United States.

Abbey, Rita Deanin. RIVERTRIP. Flagstaff, Ariz.: Northland Press, 1976.

Anderson, Dorothy H.; Leatherberry, Earl C.; and Lime, David W., comps. AN ANNOTATED BIBLIOGRAPHY ON RIVER RECREATION. United States Department of Agriculture, Forest Service. General Technical Report, NC-41. St. Paul, Minn.: North Central Forest Experiment Station, 1978.

Beymer, Robert. THE BOUNDARY WATERS CANOE AREA. Edited by Thomas Winnett. Berkeley, Calif.: Wilderness Press, 1978.

Blacklock, Les. MEET MY PSYCHIATRIST. Bloomington, Minn.: Voyageur Press, 1977.

Blaustein, John, and Abbey, Edward. THE HIDDEN CANYON: A RIVER JOURNEY. New York: Viking Press, 1977.

BOATING, CANOEING IN MICHIGAN. Saginaw, Mich.: Oakleaf Publishing, 1972.

Breining, Greg, and Watson, Linda. A GATHERING OF WATERS: A GUIDE TO MINNESOTA'S RIVERS. St. Paul: Minnesota Department of Natural Resources, Division of Parks and Recreation, Rivers Section, 1977.

Bridge, Raymond. THE COMPLETE CANOEIST'S GUIDE. New York: Scribner, 1978.

_____. THE COMPLETE GUIDE TO KAYAKING. New York: Scribner, 1978.

Brosius, Jack, and LeRoy, David. BUILDING AND REPAIRING CANOES AND KAYAKS. Chicago: Contemporary Books, 1978.

Carrey, John, and Conley, Jim Cort. RIVER OF NO RETURN. Cambridge, Idaho: Backeddy Books, 1978.

Conley, Jim Cort, and Carrey, John. THE MIDDLE FORK AND THE SHEEP-EATER WAR. Cambridge, Idaho: Backeddy Books, 1977.

Detels, Pamela, and Harris, Janet. SHORT CANOE TRIPS IN CONNECTICUT. Chester, Conn.: Pequot Press, 1977.

Evans, G. Heberton III. CANOE CAMPING. Cranbury, N.J.: A.S. Barnes, 1977.

Fisher, Ron. STILL WATERS, WHITE WATERS: EXPLORING AMERICA'S RIVERS AND LAKES. Washington, D.C.: National Geographic Society, 1977.

Foshee, John H. YOU, TOO, CAN CANOE: THE COMPLETE BOOK OF RIVER CANOEING. Huntsville, Ala.: Strode Publishers, 1977.

Gordon, I. Herbert. THE CANOE BOOK. New York: McGraw-Hill, 1978.

Graves, John. GOODBYE TO A RIVER: A NARRATIVE. Lincoln: University of Nebraska Press, 1977.

Hillerman, Tony, and Reynolds, Robert. RIO GRANDE. Portland, Oreg.: Graphic Arts Center Publishing, 1975.

Hubbard, Lucius Lee. WOODS AND LAKES OF MAINE: A TRIP FROM MOOSEHEAD LAKE TO NEW BRUNSWICK IN A BIRCH BARK CANOE, TO WHICH ARE ADDED SOME INDIAN PLACENAMES AND THEIR MEANINGS. Somersworth: New Hampshire Publishing, 1971.

Johnson, Joann M. CANOE CAMPING. Physical Education Activities Series. Dubuque, Iowa: William C. Brown, 1978.

Kaufmann, Paul. PADDLING THE GATE. Santa Monica, Calif.: Mara Books, 1978.

McGuire, Thomas. NINETY-NINE DAYS ON THE YUKON: AN ACCOUNT OF WHAT WAS SEEN AND HEARD IN THE COMPANY OF CHARLES A. WOLF, GENTLEMAN CANOEIST. Anchorage: Alaska Northwest, 1977.

Olson, Sigurd. REFLECTIONS FROM THE NORTH COUNTRY. New York: Alfred A. Knopf, 1976.

Parnes, Robert. CANOEING THE JERSEY PINE BARRENS. New York: Eastwoods Press, 1977.

Roth, Bernhard A. THE COMPLETE BEGINNER'S GUIDE TO CANOEING. New York: Doubleday, 1977.

Schafer, Ann. CANOEING WESTERN WATERWAYS: THE COASTAL STATES. New York: Harper and Row Publishers, 1978.

_____. CANOEING WESTERN WATERWAYS: THE MOUNTAIN STATES. New York: Harper and Row Publishers, 1978.

Skinner, Rulon Dean. BASIC CANOEING TECHNIQUES. Provo, Utah: Brigham Young University Press, 1975.

Sloan, A. Tony. BLACKFLIES AND WHITEWATER. Toronto: McClelland and Stewart, 1977.

Smith, Clyde H. THE ADIRONDACKS. New York: Viking Press, 1976.

Snow, Edward Rowe. THE ROMANCE OF CASCO BAY. New York: Dodd, Mead, 1975.

Stearns, William, and Stearns, Fern Crossland, eds. THE CANOEIST'S CATALOG. Camden, Maine: International Marine Publishing, 1978.

Tejada-Flores, Lito. WILDWATER: THE SIERRA CLUB GUIDE TO KAYAKING AND WHITEWATER BOATING. San Francisco: Sierra Club Books, 1978.

Teller, Walter Magnes, ed. ON THE RIVER: A VARIETY OF CANOE AND SMALL BOAT VOYAGES. New Brunswick, N.J.: Rutgers University Press, 1976.

Theriault, Alain. CANOTAGE ET CANOT-CAMPING. Montréal: Éditions du Jour, 1974.

Van Tamelen, John P. CANADA BY CANOE: HUDSON'S HOPE, BRITISH COLUMBIA TO MONTREAL, QUEBEC, 5200 MILES BY CANOE. Hudson's Hope, B.C.: Alaska Highway News, 1972.

Williamson, Bob, and Defalco, Ralph, eds. ADVENTURE BOOKSHELF: CANOEING AND RIVER TOURING BIBLIOGRAPHY. Bayside, N.Y.: Adventure Bookshelf, 1977.

Wood, Peter. RUNNING THE RIVERS OF NORTH AMERICA. Barre, Mass.: Barre Publishers, 1978.

Wright, Richard, and Wright, Rochelle. CANOE ROUTES: BRITISH COLUMBIA. Seattle: Mountaineers, 1977.

_____. CANOE ROUTES: YUKON TERRITORY. Seattle: Mountaineers, 1977.

GENERAL INDEX

This index is an integrated author, title, and subject listing and is alphabet-
ized letter by letter. Editors and compilers are also included. Titles of full
length books (and other media from chapters 10 and 11) are shown in capital
letters. Short titles are used except in instances where one short title dupli-
cates another. Underlined numbers following names and titles refer to main
entries. The addendum (pages 291-94) is indexed using the designation: add.
Key concepts and topics of general interest are emphasized in the subject portion. Waterways guidebooks, descriptions, and guide maps are analyzed in a
separate index immediately following this general index. Not indexed are the
brochures, sketchmaps, and other ephemera listed in chapter 12, and the various directories comprising chapters 13 through 21.

General Index

General Index

W

INDEX TO WATERWAYS GUIDEBOOKS, DESCRIPTIONS, AND GUIDE MAPS

This index is a listing of all waterways mentioned in the main bibliographical chapters of this text (chapters 1-10). Also indexed are the names of geographical areas in which waterways occur, including provinces, states, national parks, canyons, and mountain ranges. Historical aspects of waterways may be found through the general index. Alphabetization is letter by letter.